Praise for Four Weathercocks

"Let's consider wind a force as internal as it is external, that there is a spiritual wind as surely as there is an elemental one. Thinking so might be prerequisite to hearing Cassandra Cleghorn's granular, singular, creaturely music and the world to which it gives score. 'Please fill / this dreamspent mouth,' she asks, agitating not only that boundary line between the unconscious and the outer world, but attuning us to that aspect of language certain poets find themselves so deeply attuned to and tuned by — Ancient Greek's *middle voice*, Keats's sense of *diligent indolence*. In *Four Weathercocks*, Cleghorn works poem by poem with the instrument of the body to unfold songs at once active and passive. Just as the weathercock must move to record a force not its own, so this poet records how 'the sensing spills into / the sensed,' and we trust her, for she is one for whom 'winds blow through me winds blow / through me I can do nothing' — nothing, that is, save turn the way it blows. And then we get this most important of poetic gifts: we know from which way the weather is coming, and to what direction it will go."

— Dan Beachy-Quick

"Throughout Cassandra Cleghorn's debut collection, 'the sensing spills into the sensed,' and sense is always half a step behind direct apprehension. Cleghorn flings herself into her poems as Hopkins did, with an abandon trued by the 'muscle memory' that comes of mastering her craft. Myth, memory, and close observations of the natural world where sap flows 'unsentimental' are continually subsumed into each other. Daphne pries bark from an oak to cloak her skin, 'an organ of agitation.' A stringed instrument maker, perhaps the unsettling father figure who reappears several times in the collection, instructs her to play until 'sound moves through' an instrument whose provenance is 'amber washes: / dragon blood, saffron,' generations of sweat where now her own 'palm / homes.' And sound does move through, dazzlingly, its source the cave 'where we lodge our griefs,' the poet's chest 'a resonator.'"

— Lee Sharkey

Applied Science Review™

Oceanography

Applied Science Review™

Oceanography

William Corso, PhD
Assistant Professor of Marine Science
Stockton State College
Pomona, New Jersey

Paul S. Joyce, PhD
Staff Scientist
Sea Education Association
Woods Hole, Massachusetts

Springhouse Corporation
Springhouse, Pennsylvania

Staff

EXECUTIVE DIRECTOR, EDITORIAL
Stanley Loeb

SENIOR PUBLISHER, TRADE AND TEXTBOOKS
Minnie B. Rose, RN, BSN, MEd

ART DIRECTOR
John Hubbard

ACQUISITIONS EDITOR
Maryann Foley

EDITORS
Diane Labus, David Moreau, Neal Fandek

COPY EDITORS
Diane M. Armento, Pamela Wingrod

DESIGNERS
Stephanie Peters (associate art director),
Matie Patterson (senior designer)

ILLUSTRATORS
Jackie Facciolo, Jean Gardner, Judy
Newhouse, Amy Smith, Stellarvisions

MANUFACTURING
Deborah Meiris (director), Anna Brindisi,
Kate Davis, T.A. Landis

EDITORIAL ASSISTANTS
Caroline Lemoine, Louise Quinn, Betsy K.
Snyder

Cover: *Landscape of the ocean.* Scott Thorn
Barrows.

Library of Congress Cataloging-in-Publication Data
Corso, William.
  Oceanography / William Corso, Paul S. Joyce
    p. cm. — (Applied science review)
  1. Oceanography I. Joyce, Paul S. II. Title. III. Series.
GC11.2.C67 1995
551.46—dc20   94-16317
ISBN 0-87434-608-8   CIP

Contents

Advisory Board

Leonard V. Crowley, MD
   Pathologist
   Riverside Medical Center
   Minneapolis;
   Visiting Professor
   College of St. Catherine, St. Mary's
      Campus
   Minneapolis;
   Adjunct Professor
   Lakewood Community College
   White Bear Lake, Minn.;
   Clinical Assistant Professor of Laboratory
      Medicine and Pathology
   University of Minnesota Medical School
   Minneapolis

David Garrison, PhD
   Associate Professor of Physical Therapy
   College of Allied Health
   University of Oklahoma Health Sciences
      Center
   Oklahoma City

Charlotte A. Johnston, PhD, RRA
   Chairman, Department of Health
      Information Management
   School of Allied Health Sciences
   Medical College of Georgia
   Augusta

Mary Jean Rutherford, MEd, MT(ASCP)SC
   Program Director
   Medical Technology and Medical
      Technicians—AS Programs;
   Assistant Professor in Medical Technology
   Arkansas State University
   College of Nursing and Health Professions
   State University

Jay W. Wilborn, CLS, MEd
   Director, MLT-AD Program
   Garland County Community College
   Hot Springs, Ark.

Kenneth Zwolski, RN, MS, MA, EdD
   Associate Professor
   College of New Rochelle
   School of Nursing
   New Rochelle, N.Y.

Reviewers

Mimi Bres, PhD
   Assistant Professor of Biology
   Philadelphia College of Pharmacy and
      Science

Susan M. Henrichs, PhD
   Associate Professor of Marine Science
   University of Alaska
   Institute of Marine Science
   Fairbanks

Acknowledgments

Our thanks to family and friends for their support while writing this book. We also thank our colleagues at Sea Education Association and Stockton State College and the many students we have worked with for their help in developing this book.

Preface

This book is one in a series designed to help students learn and study scientific concepts and essential information covered in core science subjects. Each book offers a comprehensive overview of a scientific subject as taught at the college or university level and features numerous illustrations and charts to enhance learning and studying. Each chapter includes a list of objectives, a detailed outline covering a course topic, and assorted study activities. A glossary appears at the end of each book; terms that appear in the glossary are highlighted throughout the book in boldface italic type.

Oceanography provides conceptual and factual information on the various topics covered in most introductory oceanography courses and textbooks and focuses on helping students to understand:
- the geologic structure of oceans
- the dynamic theory of plate tectonics
- the composition and distribution of marine sediments
- global processes that affect the ocean
- tidal forces
- wind-driven and thermohaline circulations
- the chemistry of seawater
- the importance of primary production in the sea
- the distinguishing characteristics of major marine organisms
- the nature of mesopelagic and bathypelagic life.

1

Overview of the Science of Oceanography

Objectives

After studying this chapter, the reader should be able to:
- Describe the science of oceanography.
- List and explain the four major subdisciplines of oceanography.
- Describe various methods and techniques that marine scientists use to study the ocean.
- Relate the study of the ocean to past, present, and future uses of the ocean.

I. Subdisciplines of Oceanography

A. General information

1. The science of oceanography is the study of the ocean, which covers 70.8% of the earth's surface and contains nearly 1.4 billion cubic kilometers of salt water
2. Oceanography is a multidisciplinary science because the ocean is a complex system of geological, physical, chemical, and biological phenomena
3. The technology used to study the ocean has become increasingly complex since the 1940s, and oceanographers typically concentrate on one of four subdisciplines: geological and geophysical oceanography, physical oceanography, chemical oceanography, and biological oceanography
4. An oceanographer also may contribute to ancillary fields, such as marine law, marine policy and management, marine pollution remediation, and ocean engineering
5. Oceanographers also help explore and develop marine resources, such as oil, fish, and energy

B. Geological and geophysical oceanography

1. Geological and geophysical oceanography is the study of the shape and structure of ocean basins, basin formation and evolution, and the accumulation of sediments in the basins
2. The earth consists of a series of layers — the crust, mantle, outer core, and inner core — which is differentiated by their composition and density
3. Ocean basins occur in the earth's outermost layer, the crust
4. The formation and evolution of ocean basins are explained by the *plate tectonic paradigm,* which was first espoused in the early 1960s

      a. The paradigm states that the crust and outermost part of the mantle form a rigid layer called the *lithosphere* that "floats" on top of a denser part of the upper mantle called the *asthenosphere*

      b. The lithosphere is broken up into a series of plates that move across the earth's surface

      c. The paradigm also explains how geological processes affect the entire earth

  5. Over the course of geologic time, ocean basins change shape, become filled with sediment, and, in response to plate tectonic processes, may become part of continents or diminish in size

C. Physical oceanography

  1. Physical oceanography is the study of ocean currents, air-sea interactions, waves, tides, and global water circulation

      a. Ocean currents, air-sea interactions, waves, and global water circulation are controlled by energy that originated as solar radiation

      b. Tides are controlled primarily by the rotations of and gravitational interactions among Earth, the moon, and the sun

  2. Because Earth rotates on its axis, all freely moving objects (including water and air) undergo an apparent deflection; this is called the *Coriolis effect*

  3. Like the layers of the earth, the waters of the oceans are layered as a result of their density differences

  4. Global water circulation is the product of two types of circulation

      a. *Wind-driven circulation* is caused by complex interactions among air-sea motions, the Coriolis effect, and gravity

      b. *Thermohaline circulation* is caused by density differences among water masses (that is, volumes of water with identifiable physical and chemical characteristics)

D. Chemical oceanography

  1. Chemical oceanography is the study of seawater and water chemistry

  2. Studying the chemistry of water is vital to chemical oceanography because it predicts how water will react to ions; an atom or molecule that has lost an electron is a positively charged ion, or *cation,* and one that has gained an electron is a negatively charged ion, or *anion*

      a. Water chemistry is influenced greatly by the structure of the water molecule

      b. The water molecule is distinctive among naturally occurring molecules of similar size and composition

         (1) It is dipolar, and has one positively charged pole and one negatively charged pole

         (2) It can form *hydrogen bonds* — relatively weak bonds between the positively charged hydrogen ion of one water molecule and the negatively charged oxygen ion of another water molecule

  3. The chemistry of seawater depends on the properties of water and the solutes dissolved in the water

      a. The chemical composition of seawater is characterized by four types of matter: dissolved inorganics, dissolved organics, dissolved gases, and solid matter

      b. Most sea salts are composed of 11 particular ions and compounds: chloride, sodium, sulfate, magnesium, calcium, potassium, bicarbonate, bromide, boric acid, strontium, and fluoride

c. The composition of sea salts has remained nearly constant for hundreds of millions of years; this is called the *steady state* or *kinetic principle*

d. The relative proportions of these salts also have remained nearly constant; this is known as **Forchhammer's principle of constant proportions** or **Marcet's principle of constant proportions**

4. Water and sea salts are transported via one of two major cycles

    a. The *hydrologic cycle* is the movement of water among the earth's various reservoirs (oceans, lakes and rivers, glaciers, atmosphere, and groundwater) via evaporation, precipitation, river flow, groundwater flow, and *transpiration* (the release of water vapor into the atmosphere by plants)

    b. The *biogeochemical cycle* is the movement of water and sea salts among ocean basins, continents, and deeper layers of the earth via geological processes (such as volcanism), biological processes (such as bacterial decomposition of organic matter), and chemical processes (such as chemical precipitation)

E. Biological oceanography

1. Biological oceanography is the study of marine organisms, their interactions with each other and their environment, and the controls on their distribution within the ocean

2. Marine plants and animals are classified according to many different characteristics

    a. One common classification is based on mobility

        (1) **Plankton** are organisms that cannot move freely against a current

        (2) **Nekton** are organisms that move freely against a current

    b. Other classifications rely on differences in marine environments, including depth gradients, land-to-sea gradients, and latitudinal gradients

3. The marine realm differs significantly from the terrestrial realm

    a. The marine realm has a greater medium density because water is denser than air

    b. It has a different light field

    c. Many marine organisms move horizontally and vertically in seawater, in contrast to the horizontal motions that are characteristic of terrestrial organisms

4. The transfer of energy and food resources within the marine environment is described by food webs or food chains

    a. Primary producers (such as plants) use energy to make organic matter

        (1) Primary production is driven by two forms of energy: solar radiation and chemical reactions

        (2) Solar radiation occurs near the surface of the ocean; chemical reactions typically occur on the deep-sea floor or within the water column

    b. Herbivores (plant eaters) then consume the plants

    c. Carnivores (animal eaters) then consume the herbivores

    d. Microbes then break down dead organic matter, thus recycling essential nutrients

II. History of Oceanography

A. General information
1. From the time of ancient Egypt and Greece to the mid 1800s, most oceanographic studies focused on charting and navigating the ocean
2. Modern oceanography begins with the HMS *Challenger,* a British research vessel that circumnavigated the globe from 1872 to 1876
3. Because the ocean can be difficult to study and examine — due to its constant motion, storms, saltwater corrosion, and limitations in establishing precise locations in the ocean itself — oceanography is strongly linked to technology
   a. The expense of technology has helped shape oceanographic research
   b. The costs of some types of research are extremely high; a vessel can cost more than $10,000 per day and a cruise can last several weeks
4. Many aspects of oceanography are still in their infancy, compared to other physical and biological sciences
   a. The theory of **sea-floor spreading,** which explains how an ocean basin grows, is only about 30 years old
   b. Hydrothermal vents and their role in geochemical cycles have been investigated only for the past 20 years

B. The Pre–HMS *Challenger* period
1. The earliest surviving oceanographic documents are Egyptian charts of rivers and coastlines that date back to approximately 3,800 B.C.
2. The term *okeanos* (the ocean-river that flowed past Gibraltar) was coined by the Greeks in approximately 900 B.C.; this word probably is the root of "ocean"
3. Ancient Greeks, notably Herodotus (circa 450 B.C.), Pytheas (circa 325 B.C.), and Ptolemy (circa 150 A.D.), also compiled charts of their local and regional coastlines
4. Charts made from sticks demonstrate that South Pacific cultures also possessed fundamental knowledge about navigating the Pacific Ocean
5. The oceans continued to be explored and studied by medieval Europeans; for example, the English monk Bede published *De Temporum Ratione,* a treatise that discussed the lunar origin of tides, in the 8th century
6. Interest in the ocean revived during the Renaissance; during the latter part of the 15th century, for example, Leonardo da Vinci noted the presence of marine fossils (skeletons of marine organisms preserved in rock) in the mountains of Italy, and suggested that the sea level had once been higher
7. Oceanography advanced significantly during the 16th through 19th centuries
   a. In 1515, Peter Martyr proposed an origin for the Gulf Stream
   b. In 1609, Hugo Grotius published *Mare Liberum,* the "law of the sea"
   c. In 1674, Robert Boyle proposed theories explaining temperature, salinity, and pressure changes with depth
   d. In 1725, Luigi Marsigli published *Histoire Physique de La Mer,* the "science of the sea"
   e. Alexander Marcet and Johann Forchhammer published studies that indicated the relative proportions of sea salts did not vary throughout the world's ocean basins in the 19th century
   f. In 1835, Gaspard Coriolis discussed how Earth's rotation influences an object's horizontal motion

g. In 1847, Hans Oersted identified phytoplankton (single-celled plants) and their role in marine ecology

h. In 1854, Edward Forbes proposed that no life existed below 600 m in the ocean (the azoic zone); however, subsequent expeditions have proven him wrong

C. Expeditionary period

1. Beginning in 1872 and continuing through the early part of the 20th century, a series of international expeditions collected data from the world's oceans

   a. Between 1872 and 1876, the HMS *Challenger,* with a crew of 243 and scientific party of 6, traversed more than 127,000 km across all ocean basins (except the Arctic Ocean)

      (1) The *Challenger* crew took observations at 362 sites

         (a) These observations included meteorological data, water depths, water samples, sediment samples from the sea floor, and surface current speeds and directions

         (b) The crew also sampled animal and plant life by towing nets and dredging the sea floor

      (2) So much information was gathered by the HMS *Challenger* that it took 15 years (from 1880 to 1895) to publish 50 volumes

   b. From 1877 to 1880, prominent American scientist Alexander Agassiz sampled 355 stations aboard the USS *Blake,* an American vessel

   c. From 1893 to 1895, the Norwegian explorer Fridtjof Nansen, aboard the *Fram,* explored the Arctic Ocean

      (1) He established circulation patterns in the Arctic Ocean

      (2) His observations of iceberg motion also led to a fundamental concept of physical oceanography called **Ekman transport**

      (3) He devised a water-sampling bottle that was used widely until the 1960s

   d. From 1925 to 1927, the German ship *Meteor* surveyed the Atlantic Ocean, using acoustic techniques for the first time

2. Also during the late 19th and early 20th centuries, several preeminent private and public oceanographic institutions were established

   a. In 1888, the Marine Biological Laboratory in Woods Hole, Massachusetts, was founded

   b. In 1906, the Musée Oceanographique in Monaco was founded

   c. In 1912, the Scripps Institution of Oceanography in La Jolla, California, was founded

D. The post-World War II period

1. Technology developed during World War II has been applied to oceanographic research

   a. Antisubmarine warfare techniques (for example, magnetic and acoustic surveys) were used to study the shapes, depth (the science of bathymetry), sediment, crust, and organism motions (diel, or daily, vertical migrations) of oceans

   b. Amphibious assaults led to better wave and tidal predictions

2. Between the 1950s and 1980s, several important programs of international scope were undertaken

a. These included the International Geophysical Year (1957-58), the International Indian Ocean Expedition (1959-65), and the International Decade of Ocean Exploration (1970s)

b. The International Decade of Ocean Exploration spawned several important programs: the Geochemical Ocean Sections Program, the Mid-Ocean Dynamics Experiment, the French-American Mid-Ocean Undersea Study, and the Deep-Sea Drilling Project (replaced in 1985 with the Ocean Drilling Program)

3. In 1970, the U.S. government established the National Oceanic and Atmospheric Administration (NOAA) in the Department of Commerce; NOAA is one of the principal federal agencies that coordinates and sponsors oceanographic research

4. In 1978, *SEASAT,* the first satellite dedicated exclusively to oceanographic research, was launched

5. During the 1980s and early 1990s, oceanographic research has incorporated increasingly sophisticated technologies from other fields, including space and atmospheric sciences, isotope chemistry, electronics, computer science, robotics, global positioning systems, acoustic tomography, and remote sensing, on a global scale

III. Techniques Used to Study Oceanography

A. General information

1. The oceanographic surface research vessel continues to be the most important platform for deploying oceanographic instruments

2. Research submersibles, remote-controlled vehicles, and satellites also play important roles in oceanographic research, and are becoming more important and commonplace

3. The role of computers in oceanographic research has changed as computer technology has become more advanced

a. Computers once were used to manage and reduce large data sets

b. Now, complex phenomena are modelled using powerful computers and sophisticated mathematics

4. Advanced electronics also enhance oceanographic research by contributing to global positioning systems

a. The location of a sample station once was determined by celestial navigation, shore-based electronic navigational systems, or relatively limited satellite systems

b. Today, a series of Earth-orbiting satellites provide much greater accuracy and precision in determining positions at sea

B. Geological oceanography

1. Dredges and submersibles are used to collect hard rock samples

2. A sediment grab, like the clam-shell grabs used in land excavations, collect surface sediments

3. Gravity-driven cores or drilling apparatuses recover sediments and rocks beneath the sea floor

4. Acoustic techniques, such as *seismic reflection* or *refraction,* measure the thickness and structure of oceanic crust and overlying sediments

5. Changes in oceanic crust can be inferred by measuring differences in gravity
6. Magnetic measurements can determine the relative ages of oceanic rocks and sediments
7. Heat probes measure the amount of heat emanating from the sea floor
8. Acoustic tomography can delineate changes in sound velocities, which are related to differences in the composition, density, and thermal properties of the earth's layers
9. A satellite with a radar altimeter can determine sea-floor topography by measuring extremely small differences in sea-surface elevations
10. The ages of rocks and sediment can be determined using fossils (biostratigraphy and paleontology) or radioactive isotopes (radiometric dating)

C. Physical oceanography

1. Water movement (currents) can be measured at a fixed point as water flows past an instrument (this is the *Eulerian method*), or it can be measured by tracing the movement of a float within the moving water (this is the *Lagrangian method*)
2. Satellites equipped with different types of sensors (such as infrared radiometers and radar) can measure sea-surface temperatures, sea state, surface and internal waves, and wind speed and direction
3. A bathythermograph (BT) measures temperature changes with depth; BTs date from the 1940s
   a. Early BTs recorded temperatures by etching a glass slide in a reusable instrument
   b. Modern BTs are single-use instruments (expendable BTs, or XBTs) that record temperatures electronically
4. The density stratification of the ocean originally was determined by taking water samples from selected depths and then measuring each sample's temperature and salinity; density was then calculated from these data
5. Since the 1970s, a conductivity-temperature-depth (CTD) sensor has been used to measure seawater densities
   a. A CTD measures temperature and conductivity (which is then converted to salinity values) as a function of depth (actually pressure)
   b. Density is calculated using these data
6. The density and temperature of a particular water mass can be ascertained across great distances using acoustic techniques, such as tomography; this technique is used to determine if the average temperatures of the world's oceans have risen as a result of global warming

D. Chemical oceanography

1. Seawater chlorinity — and its subsequent salinity — was measured by a method called the *Knudsen titration* between the late 1800s and 1960s
2. Since the 1960s, salinity has been routinely determined by measuring the electrical conductivity of seawater; the conductivity is proportional to the amount of dissolved ions in water
3. Specific sea salts and dissolved gases can be measured using various techniques, including the Winkler titration (measures dissolved oxygen content), a dissolved oxygen probe (measures changes in electrical properties associated with oxygen concentration), and colorimetry (changes in color or color intensity associated with certain chemical reagents and reactions)

E. Biological oceanography

1. Towing a net is the classic method for collecting plants and animals from the ocean
2. Problems associated with net towing include plants' and animals' avoidance of the net, inadvertent destruction of fragile organisms, and opening and closing of the net at selected depth intervals
3. Today, a series of nets are towed using a conducting cable; an electrical signal opens and closes individual nets at predetermined depths
4. Samples of seawater also can be trapped in a container at predetermined depths to collect tiny or extremely fragile organisms, or a water sample can be pumped into a filtration apparatus on the ship
5. Traps are deployed to collect *benthic,* or bottom-dwelling, organisms
6. Acoustic methods have been used since World War II to identify organism distribution patterns
7. Observations from submersibles, fixed cameras, video recorders, and remote-controlled vehicles have contributed to our understanding of how certain marine organisms live

IV. Marine Resources and Laws

A. General information

1. Oceanography's focus has changed over time
   a. Initially, the science of oceanography was driven by a practical need to better understand currents, the shapes of ocean basins, and the location of specific resources (particularly fish)
   b. During the expeditionary period, research focused less on applied science and more on exploratory science
   c. Today, research once again is focusing on the location of resources (such as fish, minerals, natural gas, and oil) because of dwindling global supplies
2. Marine research is becoming increasingly difficult
   a. The expense of technology, which can be prohibitive, mandates that private, public, and international groups collaborate; the establishment of such consortia can take years
   b. Governments increasingly are limiting access to their coastal waters, claiming large parts of the oceans as territorial seas for economic, military, and security reasons
3. In this book, human use of the ocean is classified as one of two broad categories: resources (nonbiogenic resources, biogenic resources, and energy) and applications (transportation, communications, military use, and waste disposal)

B. Nonbiogenic resources

1. Seawater itself is an important resource
   a. It can be transformed into freshwater by desalination
   b. Many of the dissolved substances can be economically recovered (for example, sodium chloride, magnesium, and bromine)
2. The extraction of more valuable substances from seawater (such as gold) currently is not feasible because these substances are present in seawater only in minute concentrations; enormous volumes of seawater would need to be processed to recover appreciable amounts

3. Numerous minerals — including sand, limestone, and phosphorite — can be mined from the sea floor
   a. Most of these resources are relatively close to land, along the continental shelf (that is, the relatively shallow area adjacent to land)
   b. They are among the most valuable and commercially exploited resources
4. Below the sea floor, the principal resources are hydrocarbons (oil and natural gas); most of these resources also occur along the continental shelf
5. There are numerous resources in the deep sea; however, most of these have not been exploited because of the great depths at which they exist (thousands of meters)
   a. Manganese nodules are perhaps the best known deep-sea resource; they are rich in iron, manganese, and a variety of other commercially important metals (such as copper, nickel, and cobalt)
   b. Recently discovered hydrothermal vents have sulfur-rich deposits and are used as models to locate sulfur deposits on land
   c. Hydrothermal circulation has resulted in accumulations of metal-rich sediments in the central parts of some ocean basins, such as the Red Sea; these also are used as analogues for land deposits

C. Biogenic resources

1. Different types of fish are caught in different environments; for example, pelagic fish are found in the water column, while demersal fish are found near or on the sea floor
2. Fishing techniques vary, depending on the type of fish pursued; purse-seine nets, long lines, and drift nets are used for pelagic fish, otter or beam trawls for demersal fish, and traps for benthic dwellers
3. Approximately 75% of the world's fisheries are in coastal and continental shelf waters
4. Technological advances have helped fishermen locate and catch more fish; however, increases in both the catches and number of fishermen have resulted in the expenditure of more effort to catch the same amount of fish as their predecessors
5. Worldwide fisheries, although renewable, have declined over the last century as a result of overfishing and pollution
6. Because many species are caught in the high seas where no nation claims jurisdiction, controversy rages among nations regarding controls on fishing (for example, what species can be caught, how big an individual fish must be, appropriate fishing techniques, and the size of the nets used)
7. Fish farming (aquaculture and mariculture) has been an important industry in some parts of the world, such as China, for centuries, and has become more popular in North America and elsewhere since the 1960s
8. Mariculture is an important technique used in raising certain mollusks and crustaceans (including clams, mussels, oysters, lobsters, and shrimps)

D. Energy from the sea

1. Water motion — the tides, waves, and currents — is the principal source of marine energy
   a. Tidal power is the most easily harnessed form of water motion
      (1) More than 20 sites throughout the world have a tidal range in excess of 5 m, the range necessary for tidal power to be economically feasible

(2) Two large tidally driven hydroelectric power plants presently are in operation, one in France and one in Russia

b. Energy derived from waves and currents has been harnessed only on a relatively small scale because of problems with costs, the environment, and the maintenance of equipment

2. Another marine energy source taps thermal gradients

a. A thermal gradient of approximately 20° C over 1,000 m deep occurs in broad bands around the equator

b. This gradient can be used to evaporate and condense a fluid (such as ammonia) that, in turn, drives the turbine of an electrical generator; this is called Ocean Thermal Energy Conversion, or OTEC

c. OTEC dates back to the 1880s; however, it has several limitations constraining its commercial use

(1) Large volumes of warm and cold seawater must be continuously pumped through the system

(2) The overall efficiency of the system is relatively low compared to other power plants

(3) Corrosion and marine organisms can foul the system's plumbing

E. Use of ocean space

1. Although transportation technologies have advanced significantly over the past 1,000 years, shipping still is the most economical way to transport such bulk commodities as grains, coal, iron ore, and petroleum

2. Submarine cables continue to be an important part of worldwide communication networks

a. A fiber-optic telephone cable was laid across the northern Atlantic Ocean in the early 1990s

b. Older submarine communication cables are being converted to marine acoustic research

3. Because the ocean can acoustically mask its deeper layers, nations have used the deep ocean as a place to hide important military assets, such as nuclear submarines

4. Perhaps the most common use of ocean space is as a dump site

a. Although the oceans were once considered a bottomless sink, problems associated with continuous dumping have alerted nations to the limitations of this practice

b. Ironically, dumping continues in coastal waters and continental shelves

(1) These areas traditionally have been considered feasible dump sites because they are nearby, thus reducing transportation costs

(2) These areas are the least suited to accept anthropogenic wastes because they have the highest concentrations of marine organisms

F. Marine law

1. The oceans traditionally have been considered a common resource or a resource claimed by an individual state

a. Commonality dates back to the Holy Roman Empire and initially was called *res communis*

b. Sovereignty dates back to medieval times and was called *res nullis*

2. During the 13th century, the city-state of Venice was one of the first states to claim sovereignty over its adjacent coastal waters, declaring these waters as its territorial sea
   a. Venice considered its territorial sea part of the Venetian state, subject to the same laws governing its land
   b. Beyond the Venetian territorial sea lay the high sea, which is part of the ocean open to all
3. In 1609, Dutch lawyer Hugo Grotius further defined the concepts of territorial and high seas in his treatise, *Mare Liberum*
4. Between the 17th and 20th centuries, the territorial sea was defined as the approximate distance that a cannon could fire offshore (about three nautical miles)
5. The high sea was beyond the territorial sea, and no nation had a sovereign claim to it; all ships could freely travel there
6. The first attempt to develop an international Law of the Sea was initiated by the League of Nations in the early 20th century, as technology made more of the ocean accessible
7. Several international conferences on the Law of the Sea were convened between 1924 and 1958, while individual states invoked unilateral measures (notably, 200-nautical-mile exclusive fishing or economic zones)
8. The first United Nations Law of the Sea Conference in 1958 adopted four conventions based primarily on existing and customary laws; the conventions dealt with the issues concerning territorial seas, high seas, fishing, and continental shelves
9. Two additional U.N. Law of the Sea Conferences have been convened; one in 1960 and the other from 1973 to 1982
10. The result of the third U.N. Law of the Sea Conference was the United Nations Convention of the Law of the Sea (UNCLOS), which was issued in 1983
    a. UNCLOS was adopted by a vote of 130 to 4
    b. The United States, Turkey, Venezuela, and Israel voted against the convention
    c. The United States voted against the convention primarily because of its treatment of high-sea resources
    d. In response to UNCLOS, the United States unilaterally claimed sovereignty rights and jurisdiction over all marine resources within a 200-nautical-mile zone (called the U.S. Exclusive Economic Zone)
    e. As of early 1994, 60 countries have ratified the convention, which is expected to become international law later in 1994

Study Activities

1. List the major objectives and purposes of oceanography's four subdisciplines.
2. Make a table that lists the techniques (both historical and modern) used in the four subdisciplines of oceanography.
3. Describe the major events that have influenced the development of the science of oceanography.
4. List the various resources of the ocean.
5. Describe the historical development of the Law of the Sea.

2

Geologic Structure of the Oceans

Objectives

After studying this chapter, the reader should be able to:
- Identify the characteristics of the earth's principal layers.
- Differentiate between oceanic and continental crust.
- Explain why ocean basins are deep.
- Describe the main physiographic provinces of the ocean.

I. Structure of the Earth

A. General information
1. The structure of the ocean reflects larger geological phenomena and processes that are at work in the entire earth, not just the oceans
2. Earth-orbiting satellites have shown that, although traditionally pictured as a sphere, the earth is an oblate spheroid, meaning that it bulges at the equator and is flattened at the poles
3. This shape reflects the difference between the equatorial and polar radii (6,378 and 6,357 km, respectively); this influences gravity on the earth's surface
4. The earth consists of a series of layers that are differentiated by changes in density, temperature, pressure, composition, and phase
   a. The major layers of the earth are the inner core, outer core, mantle, and crust
   b. The crust is subdivided into continental and oceanic crust (see *Characteristics of the Major Layers of the Earth,* page 13)
5. Very little direct information has been gathered about the deep interior of the earth
   a. The deepest well ever drilled is about 10 km deep (a minor fraction of the earth's average 6,370-km radius)
   b. Material from most volcanic eruptions originates in the upper 50 km of the earth
6. Our knowledge of the earth's interior comes from three sources: seismology, meteorites, and models
   a. Seismology is the study of the sound that is transmitted through the earth; the sound typically is generated by earthquakes
      (1) Seismological studies date back to the late 19th century
      (2) Sound transmission is defined by the acoustic properties of rocks and sediments

Characteristics of the Major Layers of the Earth

The earth has three primary layers: the core, the mantle, and the crust. The core and the crust are further subdivided. The chart below provides data about these layers.

Layer	Average thickness (km)	Average density (g/cm³)	Average temper-ature (° C)	Average P wave velocity (km/sec)	Average compo-sition	Percentage of earth's mass	Percentage of earth's volume
Core							
Inner core	1,220	17.0	6,660	11.0	Iron-nickel solid mixture	31.5%	16.0%
Outer core	2,250	11.8	5,000	9.2	Iron-nickel-sulfur liquid mixture		
Mantle	2,900	4.5	2,500	10.5	Iron and magnesium silicates	68.1%	83.0%
Crust							
Continental crust	35	2.8	500	6.5	Aluminum silicates	0.4%	1.0%
Oceanic crust	10 (includ-ing water)	3.0	500	4.5	Magnesium silicates		

(3) Different layers of the earth have different acoustic properties, so sound waves, or seismic waves, are reflected and refracted (bent) at boundaries between layers

(4) The movement of a seismic wave through a layer of earth depends on the type of wave, the layer's density, and other elastic properties of the layer

(5) Two primary types of seismic waves exist: a *P wave* or *primary wave* and an *S wave* or *secondary wave*

(6) In a P wave, acoustic energy is transmitted via wave motions that are parallel to the overall direction of the wave
   (a) P waves also are referred to as compressional waves
   (b) P waves can travel through solids and liquids

(7) In an S wave, acoustic energy is transmitted via wave motions perpendicular to the overall direction of the wave
   (a) S waves also are referred to as shear waves
   (b) S waves can travel only through solids because liquids cannot transmit S waves

(8) Because S waves do not travel completely through the earth, scientists believe that the outer core is liquid (see *Characteristics of the Major Layers of the Earth,* page 13)

(9) In 1909, Andrya Mohorovicic first noted an abrupt change in the velocity of seismic waves from about 7 km/sec above a depth of about 50 km to about 8 km/sec below 50 km
   (a) This boundary, known as the *Mohorovicic discontinuity* or simply Moho, is the depth at which Mohorovicic noted the velocity change in seismic wave transmission
   (b) The Moho is considered the base of the crust

(c) The depth of the Moho varies from about 30 to 50 km (below the continents) to approximately 5 to 10 km (below ocean basins)

(10) By 1914, all of the major layers of the earth had been established through seismology

(11) After 1914, several other seismic discontinuities have been identified, including the fact that seismic velocity increases at a depth of about 670 km; geophysicists are debating the geological significance of this discontinuity

b. The study of meteorites also has strengthened our knowledge of the composition of the earth's layers

(1) Geologists believe that a specific type of meteorite (chondrite) represents the original material of the solar system, from which the earth and all other planetary bodies were formed

(2) By comparing the composition of chondrites to rocks found in the earth's crust, geologists can predict the composition of the deeper layers

(a) The percentages of certain elements are different in chondrite meteorites than in the rocks found in the earth's crust

(b) For example, the atomic abundance of nickel (relative to 1×10^6 atoms of silicon) in chondrite meteorites is 4.0×10^4, whereas the atomic abundance of nickel in the earth's crust is only 130; this suggests that the earth's crust has been depleted of nickel and that additional nickel must therefore exist in a deeper layer (see *Characteristics of the Major Layers of Earth,* page 13)

(c) Because nickel is extremely dense, geologists assume that nickel is concentrated in the core

(d) Throughout the earth's 4.5-billion-year history, material has been segregated into layers based on differences in density; for example, the least dense material is at the surface, the most dense deeper down

c. Advances in technology have permitted scientists to imitate physical conditions in the earth's interior in extremely small models

(1) Diamond-anvil cells and lasers duplicate pressures and temperatures

(2) These models suggest how elements and compounds are formed and evolve in the deep earth

B. Layers of the earth

1. The earth formed as various materials accreted, or came together, as a result of gravitational attraction

2. Geologists believe that the earth's core formed while the earth was accreting, or soon after the earth's initial formation (within hundreds of millions of years)

a. The core comprises approximately 16% of the earth's volume but 31.5% of its mass because it consists of very dense iron and nickel

b. The core has two parts: a solid inner and a liquid outer core

c. *Convection* (circulation driven by heat differences: warm, less dense material rises and cools, while denser material sinks) in the outer core may generate the earth's magnetic field

(1) Convection probably results from heat generated by radioactive decay, heat transfer between the inner and outer cores, and chemical reactions

Continental vs. Oceanic Crust

The earth's continental crust is characterized by a mosaic of rocks that do not form a coherent series of layers on a global scale. Conversely, oceanic crust is found throughout the world's ocean basins and consists of a systematic series of three layers. The illustration below contrasts the structural differences between crustal types.

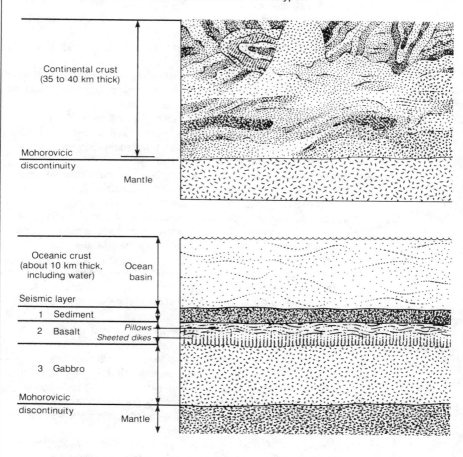

(2) The magnetic field probably is caused by *dynamo action*, the generation of an electrical current and a magnetic field by the motion of an electrically conductive fluid

3. The mantle is the earth's largest layer, in terms of mass and volume
   a. Several significant forces occur within the mantle
      (1) Convection within the mantle probably drives plate movements along the surface of the earth; this is part of the plate tectonic paradigm
      (2) Two hypotheses concerning convection in the mantle currently are being debated
         (a) Convection may occur throughout the entire mantle
         (b) Convection may be confined to certain layers within the mantle

    b. *Igneous rocks,* especially the *basalt* and gabbros that form oceanic crust,
      originate in the mantle
4. The crust is earth's smallest layer, in terms of volume and mass
    a. The crust also is the best-known layer because of its accessibility; geologists
      have used boreholes to obtain numerous samples and seismic techniques
      to obtain imaging studies of the crust
    b. The crust can be subdivided into two types based on composition, density,
      age, and thickness: *continental* and *oceanic*
      (1) Continental crust has a relatively low density compared to oceanic
         crust
         (a) The composition of continental crust indicates that it is the result of
            a series of temperature and pressure changes over time that has
            produced silicon- and aluminum-rich rocks
         (b) Continental crust may be up to billions of years old
         (c) The oldest continental crust typically exists in the center of a conti-
            nent, with progressively younger material extending toward sur-
            rounding ocean basins
         (d) Continental crust is structurally complex; mountain-building proc-
            esses, volcanism, sedimentation, and metamorphism have cre-
            ated mosaics of different rock compositions and ages
      (2) Oceanic crust has an average density greater than that of continental
         crust because it consists of denser substances; for example, magne-
         sium is plentiful in oceanic crust whereas lightweight aluminum is
         plentiful in continental crust
         (a) Oceanic crust is formed by volcanism that brings upper mantle ma-
            terial to the earth's surface, where it undergoes *chemical frac-
            tionation* (separation by crystallization, distillation, and other
            processes)
         (b) Oceanic crust generally is older the farther away it is from the cen-
            tral parts of an ocean
         (c) Oceanic crust is less than approximately 200 million years old
         (d) Scientists have developed a three-layered model for oceanic crust
            based on drilling, dredging, geophysical surveying techniques,
            and field studies of displaced pieces of oceanic crust called
            ophiolites (for details, see *Continental vs. Oceanic Crust,* page
            15)
         (e) Scientists established this three-layer oceanic crust model by not-
            ing differences in seismic wave velocities among the layers
         (f) Layer 1, the top layer, is composed of sediments or *sedimentary
            rocks* and may be up to 10 km thick
         (g) Older crust adjacent to continents typically has a thicker Layer 1
            compared to the central parts of oceans
         (h) Layer 2 is composed of basalt, which is further subdivided into two
            sublayers according to how the basalt accumulated
         (i) *Pillow basalt* (which resembles a stacked pile of pillows in a cross
            section) is formed by overlapping lava flows
         (j) *Sheeted dikes* are formed from lava that rose from the upper man-
            tle in vertical pipes and cooled into basalt before leaving the
            pipes

(k) Layer 3 consists of material that is left in a magma chamber after lava has been ejected via submarine volcanism

(l) This layer is characterized by gabbro

5. The relative elevations of continental and oceanic crusts vary according to composition, density, and structural differences

    a. A *hypsometric curve,* a figure which shows the percentages of a planet's surface at specific elevations above and below a benchmark (for example, the sea floor on earth), illustrates these differences

    b. The earth's hypsometric curve indicates that the mean elevation of continents is 840 m above sea level and that the ocean's mean depth is 3,800 m below sea level

    c. Continental crust forms as various geological processes (for example, volcanism and mountain-building processes) accrete material onto a central body

    d. Oceanic crust forms as a result of one geological process, called **sea-floor spreading;** in this process, material from the mantle is expelled via volcanism and constantly creates new oceanic crust at an ocean's center

    (1) Because the genesis of oceanic crust is associated with only one geological process, igneous rock comprising the crust has not been depleted of denser elements (such as iron and magnesium)

    (2) Consequently, oceanic basalts have a greater average density than the granites that form continents

C. Isostasy

1. *Isostasy* is responsible for deep oceans and high mountains

2. Isostasy is a balance of earth's layers; a rigid outer layer of the earth floats on a denser, more plastic layer

    a. The rigid outer layer is called the lithosphere, and it includes the crust and uppermost mantle (approximately the upper 100 km of the earth)

    b. The lithosphere is generally defined by temperature or elastic parameters; these parameters influence the elastic properties and hence the buoyancy of the lithosphere

    c. The asthenosphere is the denser, more plastic layer, and it generally extends from 100 km to about 700 km

3. While surveying the Himalayas during the late 19th century, English explorers John Pratt and George Airy proposed separate hypotheses to explain how the lithosphere floats on the asthenosphere

    a. Pratt proposed that the density of the lithosphere changed laterally, with the densest material floating lower than less dense material; thus, dense oceanic crust would float lower than less dense continental crust

    b. Airy proposed that the lithosphere had a laterally uniform density, with differences in the thickness of the lithosphere resulting in different buoyancies (for example, thicker continental crust [about 40 km thick] floats higher than thinner oceanic crust [about 5 km thick])

4. Because both the densities and thicknesses of oceanic and continental crust vary laterally, a combination of the two hypotheses explains why oceans are deep and mountains high

II. Continental Margins

A. General information

1. Continental margins (which include shelves, slopes, and rises) are important to terrestrial and marine life
   a. Continental margins are closest to land and are used by humans for transportation, resources (minerals, hydrocarbons, and fish), and waste disposal
   b. Continental margins account for a small part of the total area of the world's oceans (about 21%) but account for about 99% of the total fish production
   c. Their economic and political importance is emphasized by most coastal nations' declarations of a 200-nautical-mile exclusive economic zone
2. The physiographic characteristics (size, shape, and depth) of continental margins are associated with their relationships to plate tectonics
   a. Continental margins along plate boundaries that are tectonically active (meaning that they have earthquakes) tend to be narrow and steeply sloping
   b. Continental margins along plate boundaries that are tectonically inactive tend to be broad and gently sloping
3. Although continental margins are considered part of an ocean basin, most continental margins overlie continental crust or altered continental crust (called *transitional crust*)

B. Continental shelves

1. Continental shelves border land
   a. Shelves can be either broad (100 to 200 km) or narrow (less than 1 km), depending on how they were formed and their plate tectonic setting
      (1) Along continental margins that have little or no seismic activity, sediment can accumulate over long geologic periods and create broad continental shelves
      (2) Alternatively, narrow shelves form where earthquakes or other geological processes (such as faulting) consistently disturb sediment deposition and sediment may not accumulate
   b. All shelves are shallow (less than 200 m deep) and relatively flat (less than 1° gradient)
2. A common geological definition of a shelf is that part of the sea floor that extends from the shoreline to the *shelf break* (a dramatic change in slope); shelf breaks generally occur in 130 to 200 m of water
3. Shelves are frequently defined by other criteria (for example, a specific distance offshore) because of their economic and political importance
4. The sea floor of a continental shelf may include hills and depressions, reflecting water currents that redistribute shelf sediment
5. The physiography of a shelf also reflects changes in the sea level
   a. During the course of geologic time, the sea level has risen or fallen hundreds of meters; during the past 20,000 years, for example, the sea level along the U.S. Atlantic coast has risen about 100 m
   b. Three major phenomena cause sea-level changes
      (1) *Glaciation* is the formation of glaciers
         (a) When glaciers form, the sea level drops
         (b) When glaciers melt, the sea level rises

(2) *Isostatic adjustments* between land and an adjacent ocean basin cause the sea level to fluctuate

(3) The sea level also changes when the volume of the world's ocean basins changes; for example, the altered shape of an ocean basin may result from plate tectonics

6. Sediments accumulate differently on shelves
    a. The coarsest material commonly is deposited near the shore because it settles from the water column more readily than finer-grained sediment
    b. Shelves in middle latitudes, however, typically have coarse sediment near the present shelf break
        (1) These sediments were transported to the sea via rivers when the sea level was lower
        (2) These coarse sands are called *relict sediments*

C. Continental slopes

1. The continental slope lies seaward of the shelf break
    a. It typically extends between 200 and 4,000 m below sea level
    b. Slopes vary from less than 1° to nearly 90°, depending on the amount and type of material forming the slope
2. Three major types of formations characterize continental slopes
    a. Thick wedges of unconsolidated sediment, which have accumulated along the edges of a continent, taper seaward
    b. Faults or other geologic processes expose cliffs of sedimentary rock
    c. Certain types of sedimentary rocks (for example, vertical accumulations of coral reef limestone) form steeply sloped precipices
3. Deep, V-shaped depressions often incise continental slopes; these submarine canyons commonly extend downslope from the shelf break
    a. A variety of gravity flows transport sediment into these submarine canyons
    b. *Turbidity currents* — which are caused by density contrasts between seawater and a slurry of sediment — are the most common form of sediment transport in submarine canyons
4. Because slopes form the transition between the relatively shallow and deep parts of ocean basins, they are studied by physical, chemical, and biological oceanographers
    a. Physical oceanographers study slopes because slopes influence the vertical movement of water
    b. Chemical oceanographers study slopes because slopes influence the distribution of nutrients dissolved in seawater
    c. Biological oceanographers study slopes because a locally induced *upwelling* of water (a rising, cold, nutrient-rich current) results in high rates of productivity

D. Continental rises

1. Continental rises are gently sloping (less than 0.5°), broad (hundreds to thousands of kilometers) regions at the base of continental slopes
2. A continental rise consists of sediments forming a wedge-shaped accumulation
3. The thickness of a rise varies between 1 and 10 km, depending on its tectonic setting, rate of sediment accumulation, and rate of sediment erosion
4. Continental rises generally are found only along tectonically inactive continental margins

Physiographic Characteristics of the Main Ocean Basins

Ocean basins are characterized by various sea-floor settings. The table below lists the relative percentages of physiographic characteristics found in the world ocean and the principal ocean basins.

CHARACTERISTIC	WORLD OCEAN	ATLANTIC	PACIFIC	INDIAN
Ocean area (1×10^6 km^2)	361	107	180	74
Percentage of continental margin (including shelf, slope, and rise)	20.6	27.9	15.8	14.8
Percentage of deep-sea floor	41.9	38.1	42.9	38.1
Percentage of seamounts and aseismic ridges	3.1	2.1	2.5	5.4
Percentage of midocean ridges	32.7	31.2	35.9	30.2
Percentage of trenches	1.7	0.7	2.9	0.3

5. Deep-sea currents can sweep parallel to a continental margin and move sediments along the base of the margin; currents can erode a rise in one area and thicken another, a process characteristic of the U.S. Atlantic coast

III. Deep-Sea Floors

A. General information
1. Deep-sea floors may extend from 2,000 to 11,035 m
2. Deep-sea floors typically are covered with fine-grained sediments (clay-sized) that originate from landmasses and are transported into oceans primarily by wind
3. The shape, depth, and structure of deep-sea floors are controlled by the processes associated with ocean basin development (such as sea-floor spreading and isostasy)
4. Five major physiographic provinces exist in ocean basins: abyssal plains and hills, seamounts and guyots, oceanic plateaus, trenches, and oceanic ridges (for details about characteristics, see *Physiographic Characteristics of the Main Ocean Basins*)

B. Abyssal plains and hills
1. Abyssal plains are broad (hundreds to thousands of kilometers wide), flat (less than 0.05°) areas seaward of continental rises
2. Slow accumulation of muds in an ocean basin form abyssal plains; these muds are deposited by settling of a water column or by turbidity currents
3. Sediment thicknesses vary in abyssal plains, depending on the age of the oceanic crust; they generally are thicker over older oceanic crust
4. Seismic activity and gravitational instability are nearly nonexistent in abyssal plains
   a. They are therefore considered geologically stable and will likely remain unchanged for millions of years

      b. Consequently, abyssal plains are regarded as potential dump sites for harmful anthropogenic waste, such as radioactive waste
5. Abyssal hills are scattered throughout abyssal plains in all ocean basins
      a. Abyssal hills are relatively low, extending about 1 km above the surrounding sea floor
      b. Abyssal hills are small, measuring tens of kilometers wide
      c. They commonly are extinct submarine volcanoes covered by a veneer of sediment
      d. New abyssal hills have been discovered recently as a result of advances in bathymetric profiling

C. Seamounts and guyots
1. Seamounts and guyots are similar to abyssal hills; they also are extinct volcanoes, but extend more than 1 km above the surrounding sea floor
2. Seamounts and guyots generally are found in clusters or chains
3. Seamounts have a conical cross section
4. Guyots are flat-topped seamounts that result from erosion caused by wave action near the surface of the sea
5. A deep guyot, therefore, suggests that sea level has risen or fallen
      a. No geologic evidence indicating that the sea level has fluctuated thousands of meters exists
      b. Many guyots and other deep-sea features are so far below sea level because the sea floor constantly is sinking
      c. *Subsidence* refers to the phenomena of ocean basins and their contents gradually sinking as more sediments are loaded onto oceanic crust and the densities of oceanic rocks (basalt and gabbros) increase because of cooling

D. Oceanic plateaus
1. Oceanic plateaus extend hundreds to thousands of square kilometers, rising more than 1 km above the surrounding sea floor
2. The foundations of plateaus are both continental and oceanic
      a. Microcontinents are plateaus that include rocks typically found in continental crust
      b. Other oceanic plateaus have volcanic foundations
3. Plateaus are especially prominent in the western Pacific Ocean, but occur in all ocean basins
4. Calcium carbonate sediment readily accumulates on top of plateaus because the tops of plateaus are relatively shallow; the deep waters of the world's oceans are chemically corrosive to calcium carbonate sediment, and this mineral cannot accumulate below certain depths
      a. Calcium carbonate sediment can reveal information about ocean temperatures and depths during the geologic past
      b. These data provide scientists with a tool to assess the evolution of an ocean basin and how marine phenomena will react to temperature changes in the future (for example, global warming)

E. Trenches
1. Deep-sea trenches are V-shaped depressions that have steep slopes (10° to 45°) and extend to thousands of kilometers

2. Some trenches have flat floors because they are being filled with sediments; these trenches typically are near a continent
3. Trenches form arcs because of the rules of spherical geometry
4. Trenches are among the most seismically active provinces of an ocean basin
    a. The plate tectonic paradigm explains this seismic activity
    b. When two tectonic plates collide, one may slide beneath the other; this is called **subduction**
5. Trenches generally are associated with volcanoes
    a. Some volcanoes form long chains of islands called **island arcs** (for example, the islands of Japan)
    b. They also can form mountain chains on land (for example, the western part of Central America)
6. Trenches occur in all ocean basins, but primarily occur around the rim of the Pacific Ocean; this area of the Pacific, with its trenches and their associated seismicity and volcanism, is called the *ring of fire*
7. The seismicity associated with trenches can cause **tsunamis** (catastrophic tidal waves)

F. Oceanic ridges
1. Oceanic ridges make up nearly one-third of the world's oceans
2. They form the longest mountain chain on the globe; it is more than 60,000 km long
3. Oceanic ridges are classified as seismically active or aseismic, according to their seismicity
    a. Seismically active ridges generally occur in the central parts of ocean basins; these ridges are called *midocean ridges (MORs)*
    b. Aseismic ridges can be found in any part of a particular ocean basin and typically extend away from an MOR
    c. Both types of ridges extend 1 to 3 km above the surrounding sea floor and are formed by submarine volcanism
4. MORs are an integral part of the plate tectonic paradigm
    a. Their role in ocean basin evolution was not established fully until the 1960s, although their existence has been known since the 1800s
    b. MORs are the sites of sea-floor spreading
5. MORs typically reach within 2 to 3 km of the sea surface
6. Their crests have central valleys called *axial* or *median rift valleys*
    a. Rift valleys are V-shaped, have steep slopes, and are up to 2 km deep
    b. Rift valleys are the principal sites of submarine volcanism along MORs
7. Little or no sediment covers MORs because their surrounding oceanic crust is relatively young (several million years)
8. MORs are elevated because the crust is heated by submarine volcanism
    a. Hot rocks are less dense than cooler rocks and thus float above cooler rocks
    b. The basalts become denser and subside as they cool and age
9. The increase in depth away from MORs and toward continents has been correlated with the age of oceanic crust (older = deeper) and heat flow (cooler = deeper)
10. Submersible expeditions along rift valleys have identified hydrothermal circulation on the sea floor
    a. Only a few hydrothermal fields have thus far been identified because it is difficult, technologically demanding, and expensive to locate them; they are

relatively small (less than 1 km² in area) and are located in very rugged submarine mountain terrain
  b. Scientists assume that many more hydrothermal fields occur along MORs
  c. Exotic fauna (black smoker communities) have been found near these fields
11. Some parts of a ridge can spread faster than an adjacent ridge because the rates of submarine volcanism and sea-floor spreading are not consistent along the length of a MOR
  a. The ridge then becomes offset by *transform faults,* faults that are perpendicular to the MOR
  b. Transform faults segment the 60,000-km-long mountain chain
  c. Transform faults are aseismic away from MORs, but still form fracture zones that extend hundreds to thousands of kilometers away from the ridges
  d. Transform faults and fracture zones provide passages for water masses flowing along the sea floor
12. Many aseismic ridges are thought to have formed as a result of volcanism occurring along a transform fault–fracture zone
13. Chains of closely spaced seamounts, guyots, or abyssal hills also can form aseismic ridges
14. Like MORs, aseismic ridges also influence deep water mass movements

Study Activities

1. Draw a cross section of the earth and label all its major layers. List the particular characteristics (such as composition and seismic velocity) for each layer, and explain their importance.
2. Compare and contrast the structures of oceanic and continental crusts; explain their differences.
3. Sketch a depth profile from Cape Cod, Massachusetts, to Lisbon, Portugal, and identify all of the major physiographic provinces; explain their oceanographic significance and origin.

3

Plate Tectonics

Objectives

After studying this chapter, the reader should be able to:
- Define the plate tectonic paradigm and its elements.
- Describe the importance of the plate tectonic paradigm to oceanography.
- Explain how the physiographic and structural elements of ocean basins are formed.
- Explain the geological evolution of an ocean basin.

I. The Plate Tectonic Paradigm

A. General information

1. The **plate tectonic paradigm** is a model that unites several concepts, including sea-floor spreading, continental drift, and tectonics (mountain-building processes)
2. Scientists use the paradigm to explain the workings of geological processes throughout the earth
3. The paradigm is important to oceanography because it describes the formation and evolution of ocean basins, placing ocean-basin development in a global context
4. Although the plate tectonic paradigm is a fundamental part of modern earth science (much like Darwin's theory of evolution for biology), it is a relatively young concept compared with the essential elements of other basic sciences
5. Scientists developed the basic tenets of the paradigm during 1965 to 1968
   a. In 1965, J. Tuzo Wilson identified the major network of plate boundaries
   b. In 1968, W. Jason Morgan definitively stated the paradigm as follows: the earth's lithosphere is divided into a series of plates that move across the earth's surface
6. However, individual elements of the plate tectonic paradigm were recognized well before the 1960s; for example, the idea of continental drift can be traced back to the writings of Antonio Snider (1858) and Alfred Wegener (1915)
7. Sea-floor spreading, the keystone of the plate tectonic paradigm, was not established until improved technology (derived primarily from World War II defense efforts) permitted scientists to study the geology and geophysics of ocean basins
8. Many geological phenomena (mountain building, formation of midocean ridges, faults, earthquakes, and folding) occur along plate boundaries as a result of interactions between plates

9. Most plate boundaries have been identified using seismological evidence (earthquakes)
10. Geologists believe that the processes associated with the plate tectonic paradigm have occurred throughout geologic time
11. However, little evidence exists that these processes were active billions of years ago because the rock record older than 600 million years is incomplete
12. The plate tectonic paradigm, like most models in natural sciences, is based on several concepts
    a. New lithosphere is generated by sea-floor spreading along midocean ridges (MORs)
    b. Lithosphere sinks back into the deep earth at subduction zones
    c. The earth's surface area has not changed over time; therefore, the global rate of lithosphere generation equals the rate of lithosphere destruction
    d. Individual plates are perfectly rigid and transmit stress across great distances
    e. Plate motions are driven by convective processes within the deep earth
13. Although the plate tectonic paradigm is a powerful model, it does not explain all of the observed geological and geophysical phenomena on earth; for example, the model predicts that deformation within the lithosphere occurs in relatively narrow belts (tens to hundreds of kilometers), but continental deformation occurs in zones thousands of kilometers wide
14. Scientists continue to refine the plate tectonic paradigm as new technology becomes available; for example, satellites can measure relative plate motion more accurately than ever before

B. The lithosphere and the asthenosphere
1. The relationship between the lithosphere and the asthenosphere is a fundamental element of the plate tectonic paradigm
2. In 1926, Beno Gutenberg identified the asthenosphere using seismological evidence; he noted low seismic wave velocities and high seismic wave attenuation at a depth of about 100 km
3. The lithosphere and the asthenosphere are defined according to the mechanical properties of earth, and they are distinct from the earth's layers, which are characterized according to their composition
4. The boundary between the lithosphere and the base of the asthenosphere is difficult to identify
    a. The lithosphere and the asthenosphere are differentiated based on their mechanical characteristics (rigid versus plastic material)
       (1) These mechanical characteristics are dependent on temperature, pressure, density, and composition
       (2) Generally, the base of the lithosphere is defined by an abrupt change in temperature (a sharp gradient in *isotherms* [lines of constant temperature]) and a low seismic velocity zone
       (3) The base of the lithosphere varies from about 70 km (below ocean basins) to an average of 100 km (below continents)
       (4) The importance of this boundary extends beyond the mechanical characteristics that separate the lithosphere and the asthenosphere
          (a) Many scientists consider the base of the lithosphere an important boundary that affects heat transfer within the earth because of its dramatic temperature change

(b) Heat can be transferred via convection below the lithosphere, whereas heat is transferred by conduction in the lithosphere
   b. The base of the asthenosphere is more ambiguous than that of the lithosphere
      (1) It begins at a depth of about 350 km, based on recorded pressure changes; at 350 km, the pressure is great enough that material no longer behaves plastically
      (2) Alternatively, some geologists believe that it begins at about 670 km because that is the deepest depth at which earthquakes have been detected

C. Tectonic plates

1. In 1968, Morgan first identified the major tectonic plates (see *Major Tectonic Plates,* page 28)
2. Because plates are segments of lithosphere and not the crust, an individual plate can include both oceanic and continental crust
3. Plate size varies; for example, the Cocos plate is smaller than the Pacific plate
4. Likewise, the age of crustal rocks within plates varies; for example, the North American plate consists of new oceanic crust and continental crust that is 3 billion years old
5. The thickness of plates also varies (from tens to hundreds of kilometers)

D. Plate boundaries

1. Plate boundaries have been identified primarily by seismicity
   a. Stress builds up when blocks of rigid lithosphere attempt to move past each other because sections of the plates stick to each other as a result of friction
   b. When that stress is released, an earthquake occurs
2. Three different types of plate boundaries exist (for illustrations, see *Types of Plate Boundaries,* page 30)
   a. A **divergent plate boundary** separates two plates that are moving away from each other
      (1) As the plates move away, magma (typically in the form of lava) from the asthenosphere rises and forms new lithosphere along the axis of divergence
      (2) MORs are the edifices formed by this rising magma
   b. A **convergent plate boundary** occurs when two plates come together; it can be characterized by a subduction zone (one plate going below another) or mountain building (colliding plates piling upward)
      (1) A subduction zone generally forms when one plate is denser than the other; for example, when a plate with dense oceanic crust collides with another plate with less dense continental crust, the oceanic plate typically is subducted below the continental plate
      (2) A mountain chain generally forms when both plates have similar crustal types (such as two plates containing continental crust)
   c. A **transform plate boundary** occurs when two plates slide past each other; this type of boundary commonly is characterized by a transform or strike-slip fault

E. Plate motions
  1. Plate motions can be relative or absolute
     a. Relative plate motions can be described using *Euler's fixed point theorem*
        (1) This theorem states that as one plate moves relative to another on the surface of the earth, that plate's motion is depicted as a rotation about an appropriate axis (rotation axis) that passes through the center of the earth
        (2) The points where the rotation axis intersects the earth's surface are called poles of rotation
     b. Absolute plate motions can be determined by locating intraplate volcanoes
        (1) Scientists believe that many of these volcanoes, called **hot spots,** originate beneath the moving lithosphere
        (2) The feeder vents for these hot spots come from deep within the mantle and are fixed relative to the lithosphere
  2. Plates move at varying speeds
     a. Plates moving away from divergent plate boundaries travel at about 1 to 10 cm/year
     b. Because it is exceptionally difficult to gauge how fast a plate is being subducted, the rates at which plates converge are not well established; scientists believe that they equal the rate of sea-floor spreading on a global scale
     c. Rates of plate motions along transform plate boundaries range from 1 to 15 cm/year

F. Forces driving plate motions
  1. Although the forces driving plate motions are well known by scientists, they are poorly understood
  2. Thermal convection in the asthenosphere is generated by radioactive decay in the mantle
  3. Convection cells presumably drag the overlying lithospheric plates across the earth's surface as a result of the friction between the convection currents and the bases of the plates
  4. Scientists have not yet established a convincing relationship between convection currents and plate motions, although convection currents widely are accepted as the principal generating force
  5. Moreover, the depth at which convection occurs and to what extent it occurs continues to be debated by scientists
     a. Some scientists believe that convection cells are confined to the upper 670 km of the earth's surface
     b. Others contend that the cells extend from the base of the lithosphere (100 km) to the base of the mantle (2,900 km)
  6. Two alternatives have been proposed to explain plate motions
     a. One posits that plates move because they are being pushed by the formation of new lithosphere at spreading centers
     b. The other posits that plates move because they are being pulled by sinking lithosphere at subduction zones

Major Tectonic Plates

Based on the plate tectonic paradigm, geologists have identified a series of rigid plates that form a mosaic across the earth's surface. The illustration shows the location and boundaries of these plates as well as significant sea-floor features

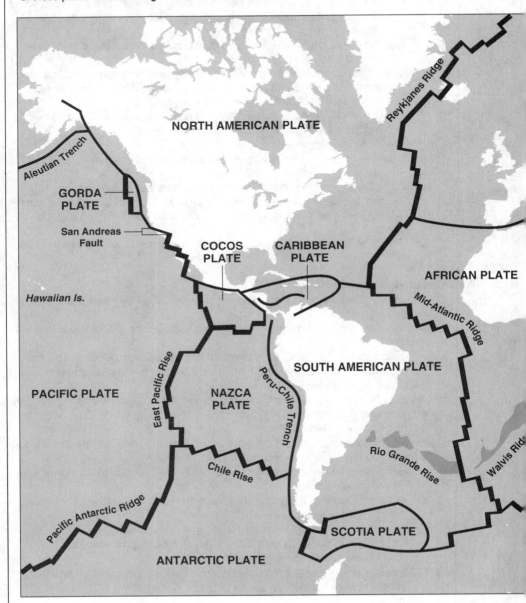

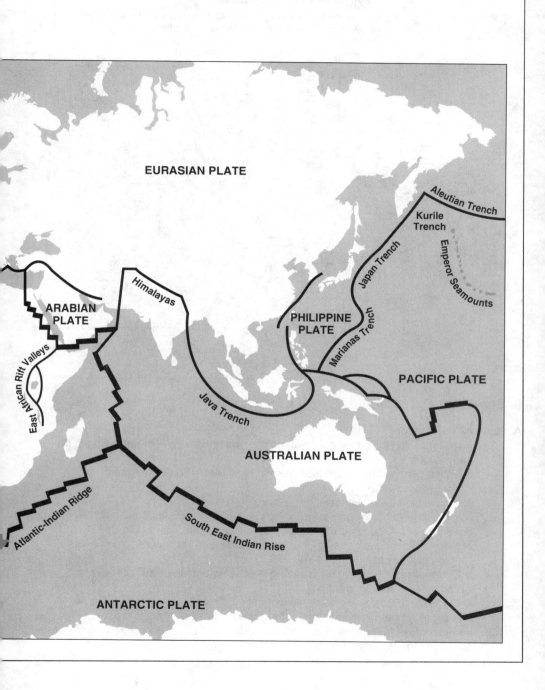

Types of Plate Boundaries

The three major types of plate boundaries — divergent, convergent, and transform — are shown in the illustration below. Asterisks indicate the location of earthquakes.

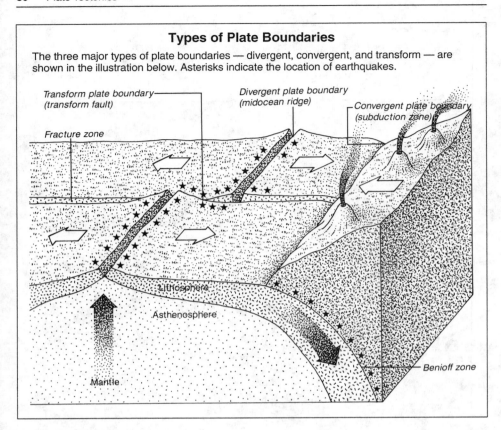

II. Sea-Floor Spreading

A. General information

1. Harry Hess and Robert Dietz originated the concept of sea-floor spreading in the early 1960s
   a. These two men proposed that oceanic crust is formed by submarine volcanism along MORs
   b. Hess called his hypothesis "geo-poetry"
2. Their hypothesis has been confirmed by the dating of rocks that make up the oceanic crust — ocean crust is older the farther away it is from MORs
   a. Scientists first used a relative time scale based on the magnetic properties of oceanic crust
   b. During the 1960s and 1970s, the ages of sediments in Layer 1 of oceanic crust were determined
   c. Since the 1980s, scientists have used absolute dating methods (using isotopes) to determine the age of basalts in Layer 2 of oceanic crust
3. The rates of sea-floor spreading have been calculated by relating the ages of oceanic crust to their distance from MORs

    a. MORs can be grouped into two general categories based on sea-floor
       spreading rates
       (1) *Slow-spreading ridges* move approximately 1 to 2 cm/year; one example
          is the mid-Atlantic ridge
       (2) *Fast-spreading ridges* move approximately 10 cm/year; an example is
          the East Pacific rise
    b. Because the width of an MOR is proportional to its spreading rate, the crest
      of a fast-spreading ridge is broader than that of a slow-spreading ridge
    c. A connection between the spreading rates and the presence of rift valleys
      also exists; slow-spreading ridges tend to have rift valleys within them,
      whereas fast-spreading ridges generally do not
    d. Sea-floor spreading also accounts for other physiographic features of ocean
      basins
       (1) The crust near an MOR is warmer and less dense than older and cooler
          crust farther away from the ridge because hot volcanic material is
          brought to the earth's surface at MORs
       (2) Consequently, MORs rise thousands of meters above surrounding
          abyssal plains
       (3) As aging oceanic crust cools and becomes denser, it moves away from
          the ridge (via continued sea-floor spreading) and subsides
4. The rate of sea-floor spreading generally is not constant parallel to the ridge axis;
   thus, the ridge becomes segmented with transform faults connecting ridge seg-
   ments
5. Because sea-floor spreading is a dynamic geological process, two features char-
   acterize most MORs
    a. Seismologists have discovered that earthquakes are common along MORs
    b. Oceanographers have discovered that seawater, flowing through cracks in
      young oceanic crust, becomes heated and recirculates through the crust
      into the ocean
       (1) This process is called **hydrothermal circulation**
       (2) Hydrothermal circulation establishes an environment in which the chemi-
          cal alteration and precipitation of minerals occur
6. Sea-floor spreading generates new oceanic crust, which moves away from an
   MOR as if it were on a conveyor belt
7. A **passive margin** occurs where oceanic crust abuts continental crust on the
   same plate and little or no seismic activity occurs
8. An **active margin** occurs where one plate meets another and there is a high level
   of seismicity; this type of margin typically is associated with a subduction zone

B. Rock magnetism

1. The earth's magnetic field is *dipolar,* meaning that it has both a positive pole and
   a negative pole
2. The magnetic field is generated by convection within the outer core
3. Magnetic minerals (for example, magnetite, which consists of iron and oxygen)
   will be affected by the earth's magnetic field during formation
4. One of the primary effects of the earth's magnetic field on magnetic minerals is
   the orientation of mineral crystals parallel to the prevailing field
    a. Analogies include a needle on a compass aligning itself with the earth's field
      and iron filings aligning themselves with a field generated by a nearby
      magnet

b. Magnetic minerals in basalts align themselves with the earth's magnetic field

c. *Thermoremnant magnetization* is the preservation of the magnetic orientation in the rock after the magnetic minerals cool below their *Curie temperature* (which is dependent on the mineral's chemical composition)

5. The alignment of magnetic minerals in oceanic crust affects the local magnetic field

   a. For example, if all of the minerals are aligned in the same direction as the earth's present field, the measured local field will be strong

   b. Conversely, if they are aligned in the opposite direction to today's field, the local field will be weak because the opposing fields partially cancel each other out

6. Scientists can model a local magnetic field, assuming there are no additions or subtractions (as a result of magnetic mineral alignments)

   a. The differences between the models and the observed values are called **magnetic anomalies**

   b. Scientists have been able to measure magnetic anomalies associated with oceanic crust since the 1950s

7. The earth's magnetic field periodically has changed direction over geologic time

   a. The poles have switched from north to south

   b. The current consensus is that this phenomenon is related to convective processes within the earth

8. The change in direction of the earth's magnetic field is recorded in the magnetic minerals in oceanic crust

   a. When the field was oriented the way it is today, magnetic mineral crystals pointed north

   b. When the field was reversed, the magnetic crystals pointed south

9. Scientists discovered that the anomalies — which are generated by oceanic crust magnetic mineral alignments and pole reversals — form stripe patterns that alternate between positive and negative fields, parallel MORs, and generally are symmetrical about an MOR

10. These stripe patterns were used as data to support the sea-floor spreading hypothesis

    a. New oceanic crust separates the preexisting crust as it forms an MOR

    b. This process forms symmetrical bands of similarly aged and magnetized crust on either side of the ridge

C. Deep-sea drilling

1. The relatively rapid evolution and acceptance of the plate tectonic paradigm is, in large part, based upon deep-sea drilling

   a. Project Mohole, the first major drilling project, was an unsuccessful attempt to drill down to the Mohorovicic discontinuity

   b. Project Mohole led to the establishment of the Joint Oceanographic Institutions Deep Earth Sampling (JOIDES) program in 1965

2. The JOIDES program evolved into the Deep-Sea Drilling Project (DSDP) in 1968; during 1968 to 1985, approximately 1,000 boreholes were drilled in the Atlantic, Pacific, and Indian Ocean basins

   a. The DSDP program documented the age of oceanic crust and confirmed the theory of sea-floor spreading by showing that oceanic crust moves away from MORs

   b. It confirmed that isostasy plays a major role in controlling ocean basin depths

 c. The DSDP program also delineated marine sediment patterns on a global scale, detailed many of the controls on sedimentation, and provided scientists with sedimentary records of past climatic and ecological phenomena
 3. In 1985, the DSDP program was succeeded by the Ocean Drilling Program (ODP)
  a. ODP continues to drill in all major ocean basins
  b. It also drills in regions DSDP could not reach, such as subpolar areas
  c. The ODP's most important accomplishment may be the continuous recovery of more than 1 km of oceanic crust (including Layers 1 and 2) from a borehole near the Galapagos Islands in the eastern Pacific Ocean

III. Volcanoes and Earthquakes

A. General information
 1. Most volcanic activity and earthquakes can be explained by the plate tectonic paradigm
 2. Generally, earthquakes are generated by plate interactions; thus, their locations reflect plate boundaries
 3. However, some volcanic activity and earthquakes do not occur at plate boundaries
  a. These events are called *intraplate phenomena* because they occur within the central parts of plates
  b. The number and frequency of intraplate phenomena are lower than those along plate boundaries

B. Volcanoes and plate boundaries
 1. Volcanoes that occur in subduction zones produce two types of geological features
  a. They can produce an island arc when subduction occurs between two oceanic crust plates
  b. They also create a mountain chain, when a plate with oceanic crust is subducted beneath a plate with continental crust
 2. The chemical composition of lava originating from subduction zone volcanoes differs from that of lava expelled at MOR volcanoes because lava generated at a subduction zone is remelted material (this lava forms as a subducted plate melts)
 3. The volcanoes associated with MORs are not as large as those along subduction zones; sea-floor spreading is constantly creating new oceanic crust and moving the volcanic edifices away from the ridge

C. Hot spots
 1. Intraplate volcanoes are rare (approximately 20 major ones have been identified); however, they are an important element of the plate tectonic paradigm
 2. Scientists believe the origins of these volcanoes are *mantle plumes* (narrow columns of hot mantle rock that rise and spread out radially), based on the chemical composition of lava from these volcanoes
 3. This type of volcano is called a hot spot
  a. A volcano forms as a plate moves over a fixed mantle plume
  b. One volcano will become extinct as the plate continues to move (it no longer is over the mantle plume) and another volcano will form (hence the age progression of volcanoes)

4. Hot spot research during the past several years suggests that some hot spots are caused by volcanoes with shallow origins and distinctive lava (resulting from geochemical processes) rather than mantle plumes; however, this hypothesis is controversial and continues to be debated among marine geologists and geophysicists

5. Hot spots are important for several reasons
   a. Hot spots provide a fixed frame of reference for tracing absolute plate motion
   b. Hot spots serve as a conduit for heat transport from deep within the mantle
   c. Volcanic structures created by hot spots form many prominent topographic features (for example, the Hawaiian Islands and the Emperor Seamount Chain)
   d. The ridges that are formed when a hot spot occurs on an MOR also can significantly control deep-sea circulation patterns

D. Earthquakes

1. An earthquake is characterized by three factors: epicenter, focus, and magnitude
   a. The *epicenter* defines the earthquake's location on the earth's surface; it is directly above its focus
   b. The *focus* defines the earthquake's origin of seismic wave emanation in the earth's interior
   c. The *magnitude* defines its force, calculated from the measured amplitude of a seismic wave and the distance between the seismograph and the epicenter

2. Scientists classify earthquakes according to their focal depth, which varies from 1 to 700 km
   a. Shallow-focus earthquakes, the most common type, occur at a depth of less than 100 km
   b. Intermediate-focus earthquakes occur at a depth of 100 to 300 km and are the second most common type of earthquake
   c. Deep-focus earthquakes occur at a depth of 300 to 700 km; these are relatively rare and generally lie along convergent plate boundaries

3. In 1954, Hugo Benioff noted the existence of zones of earthquake foci that dipped from the surface of oceanic trenches to several hundred kilometers downward to the earth; these zones are called **Benioff zones**

4. The average slope of foci was 45°, and slopes varied from about 10° to 90°

5. The existence of Benioff zones can be explained by subduction since the development of the plate tectonic paradigm
   a. In subduction, a plate descends into the asthenosphere
   b. As it does so, stresses that build up between the downward and overriding movement of plates are released as earthquakes

6. About 80% of the total earthquake energy currently being released throughout the earth is associated with earthquakes in Benioff zones around the Pacific ring of fire

7. Scientists use Benioff zones to estimate plate thicknesses, the types of processes associated with subduction, and the mechanical characteristics of subducting plates

IV. Subduction

A. General information

1. Subduction zones are characterized by a series of physiographic and geologic features
   a. Deep-sea trenches, the deepest parts of the world's oceans, are the surface expression of a downward plate
   b. An *accretionary wedge* is a wedgelike shape of marine sediment (Layer 1) that is scraped off by the subduction of an oceanic plate
   c. An island arc or volcanic mountain chain may develop behind the accretionary wedge, depending on the types of plates that are converging
   d. A *back-arc basin* is a basin with active sea-floor spreading that develops landward from an island arc; such a basin is rare
2. Seismic activity frequently does not extend along the entire length of the subduction zone
   a. *Seismic gaps* (regions with no earthquakes) occur along many convergent plate boundaries
   b. The cause of these gaps is uncertain; possible explanations include subduction of geologic structures and lateral changes in the mechanical properties of the lithosphere

B. Island arcs and back-arc basins

1. Island arcs and back-arc basins are intriguing physiographic features because they reflect divergent geological processes occurring side by side
   a. Island arcs result from volcanism associated with plate convergence
   b. Back-arc basins result from the divergent process of sea-floor spreading
2. Scientists have two hypotheses to explain why these two processes occur adjacent to each other
   a. As a plate subducts, the overriding plate moves toward the subduction zone
      (1) This motion cracks the overriding plate
      (2) New lava flows into these cracks and creates a mini-ocean basin
   b. Alternatively, the descending plate alters heat flow
      (1) Additional convection cells then form
      (2) These cells induce sea-floor spreading landward of the deep-sea trench

V. The Wilson Cycle

A. General information

1. In 1968, J. Tuzo Wilson proposed the *Wilson Cycle,* a model of ocean basin evolution that incorporated elements of the plate tectonic paradigm
2. The Wilson Cycle depicts four main stages of basin evolution: continental fragmentation, rift valley formation, basin maturation, and basin closing (see *Ocean Basin Evolution: The Wilson Cycle,* page 36)
3. Ocean basins throughout the world are at different stages of development; the Wilson Cycle demonstrates where each basin fits into an overall evolutionary model
4. The inclusion of continental geological phenomena with ocean basin evolution is one of the most significant aspects of the cycle

Ocean Basin Evolution: The Wilson Cycle

The evolutionary sequence of ocean basin development is named after J. Tuzo Wilson. It consists of four primary stages. The illustrations below show the principal elements of the Wilson cycle.

Continental fragmentation

A continent warms and begins stretching because of heat flow from the mantle; horsts and grabens form.

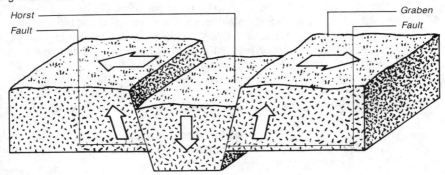

Young ocean basin

Continued heating causes crustal cracks to deepen; magma rises to the surface, lava flows, the fragmented continent separates, and a midocean ridge forms.

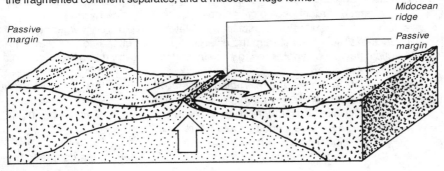

Basin maturation

The ocean basin continues widening over time as a result of sea-floor spreading; subduction begins.

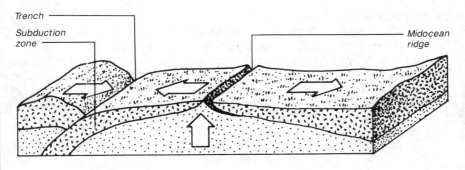

Ocean Basin Evolution: The Wilson Cycle *(continued)*

Basin closing

When subduction exceeds sea-floor spreading, the ocean basin begins to shrink; as shrinking continues, opposite continents begin moving toward each other, ultimately resulting in tectonic plate collision, deformed sediments, and mountain formation.

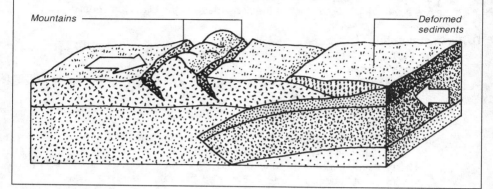

    a. The Wilson Cycle explains how continental fragmentation results in two matching coastlines (an important element of continental drift)
    b. It also explains how mountains and continents form from ocean basins

B. Continental fragmentation

1. The first stage of ocean basin development is characterized by the warming and initial stretching of a continent
2. Heat rising from the mantle warms the base of a lithospheric plate containing continental crust
3. The hot mantle material creates a swelling beneath the warming plate (because of low densities and isostasy), and the plate deforms in response to this warming
4. Because the plate is still somewhat rigid, it buckles and cracks
    a. The resultant geological structures are called horsts and grabens
    b. *Horsts* are the elevated fragments of continental crust, and *grabens* are the depressed regions of crust in between the horsts
    c. Both are bounded by faults

C. Rift valley formation

1. With continued heating from below, the cracks in the continental crust deepen; eventually, hot mantle material rises all the way through a crack
2. A rift valley forms in the graben where this lava begins to flow
3. As the lava continues to rise, it forces the fragments of continental crust away from each other
4. A rift valley generally does not develop in the exact center of a preexisting continent; frequently, rifting splits a continent asymmetrically
5. Seawater then invades the region and a new ocean basin is formed
6. Sometimes, a rift valley forms, and the rising flow of magma is stopped
    a. Rifting then ceases at that valley

b. The process can start at another graben where magma has broken through the crust; this phenomenon is called *ridge jumping*
7. If the connection between a young ocean basin and an adjacent ocean basin becomes closed (as a result of a ridge jump, for example), the seawater in the young basin can become isolated and eventually evaporate
8. Ridge jumping may have resulted in the deposit of massive salt accumulations that are several kilometers thick in the subsurface of the U.S. Gulf coast

D. Basin maturation
1. Sea-floor spreading continues once a rift valley has developed, and it can go on for millions of years
2. As oceanic crust forms and moves away from the rift valley, it becomes cooler and denser, and then subsides
3. The deepening ocean basin creates a depression that becomes filled with sediment
   a. Material eroded from adjoining continents accumulates along the edges of the basin and forms continental margins
   b. The remains of marine organisms and fine debris, which is transported by wind, simultaneously settle in the deep, central parts of the basin
4. The oceanic crust along the edges of the basin may subside more rapidly than earlier because of the sediment load
5. Subduction may occur when the oceanic crust has aged sufficiently and it is extremely dense; it also may be caused by the density contrast between converging plates, changes in sea-floor spreading rates, or convection cells

E. Basin closing
1. The plate tectonic paradigm assumes that the rates of sea-floor spreading equal the rates of subduction throughout the earth
2. For an individual ocean basin, these two rates generally are not equivalent
3. If the subduction rate of oceanic crust exceeds the rate of sea-floor spreading, an ocean basin will gradually shrink (as in the Pacific Ocean basin)
4. Eventually, the spreading center itself will be subducted and the basin will be completely closed
5. As the last traces of an ocean basin are subducted, the adjacent continents, which may have been a single landmass before sea-floor spreading began, come back together
   a. The continental collision creates mountains
   b. Remnants of the ocean basin may be incorporated into those mountains

---

Study Activities

1. Describe the elements of the plate tectonic paradigm.
2. Develop arguments for and against the plate tectonic paradigm.
3. Explain the role that mantle convection plays in the distribution of plate boundaries, volcanoes, hot spots, and back-arc basins.
4. Identify a modern ocean basin that represents each stage of the Wilson Cycle; explain your choices.

4

Marine Sediments

Objectives

After studying this chapter, the reader should be able to:
- Identify the major types and origins of marine sediments.
- Describe the principal transport pathways of marine sediments.
- Recognize the distribution and controls of marine sediment patterns throughout the world's oceans.

I. Types of Sediments

A. General information
1. Marine sediments, particles that have accumulated in ocean basins, comprise Layer 1 of the oceanic crust
2. Marine sediments form sublayers within Layer 1; these are segregated according to composition, shape, density, grain size, age, and mode of deposition
3. Marine sediments can be classified according to origin (for example, biogenous or nonbiogenous), grain size, or the mechanisms that created or transported them
4. Marine sediments generally are categorized according to origin
   a. **Lithogenous sediments** are derived from the mechanical and chemical erosion of existing rock, which can be **igneous, metamorphic,** or **sedimentary** rock
   b. **Biogenous sediments** are the remains of plants and animals; these sediments commonly consist of microscopic shells, which marine geologists call *tests*
   c. **Authigenous sediments** are chemical precipitates (solids that result from the chemical reactions of substances dissolved in seawater); they also are called **hydrogenous sediments**
   d. **Cosmogenous sediments** are particles that have fallen into the water from outer space
5. Lithogenous sediments, the principal component of continental margins, are the second most abundant type of sediment found in ocean basins
   a. Lithogenous sediments also are found in the deep sea, where they are called deep-sea, red, brown, or pelagic clays
   b. These clays blanket the abyssal plains
6. Biogenous sediments, the primary type of sediments, form major reservoirs of important elements (such as carbon)

7. Authigenous sediments are the third most abundant type, and some consist of economically important substances (for example, manganese nodules contain iron, manganese, nickel, cobalt, copper, zinc, and lead)
8. Cosmogenous sediments are rare — they make up less than 1% of the total volume of marine sediments — but provide evidence of meteorite impacts

B. Lithogenous sediments

1. Lithogenous sediments principally are derived from the erosion of continental rocks but also are derived from the erosion of submarine rocks
2. Lithogenous sediments that originate from continental rocks are called ***terrigenous sediments*** or terrigenous clastic sediments
3. Lithogenous sediments vary from boulder-sized to clay-sized particles
4. The distribution of lithogenous sediments is affected significantly by their grain size
   a. Larger particles tend to be transported via water movement (rivers and ocean currents) and are deposited near continents
   b. Finer material is transported via wind and accumulates in the deep ocean
5. The type and chemical characteristics of continental rocks also influence lithogenous sedimentation
   a. Some minerals are more readily eroded by chemical processes (for example, feldspar)
   b. Others are resistant to chemical processes and are broken down only by mechanical processes (for example, quartz)

C. Biogenous sediments

1. Biogenous sediments vary in size from the skeletal remains of whales to tests
2. Most tests consist of calcium carbonate ($CaCO_3$) or silicon dioxide (SiO_2)
3. Biogenous sediments generally are subdivided into two groups based on their chemical composition
   a. *Siliceous oozes* consist of more than 30% silicon dioxide tests
      (1) Siliceous ooze, which generally is found in the deepest parts of ocean basins and polar regions, constitutes approximately 15% of all deep-sea sediments (see *Distribution of Deep-Sea Sediments,* page 41)
      (2) It consists of diatoms and radiolaria, the two principal ***plankton*** groups that have siliceous tests
      (3) These tests are made of opal, an amorphous (meaning that it has no crystalline structure) form of silicon dioxide
   b. *Calcareous oozes* consist of more than 30% calcium carbonate tests
      (1) Calcareous ooze is more abundant than siliceous ooze
      (2) Calcareous ooze consists primarily of foraminifera ***(zooplankton),*** pteropods (zooplankton), and coccolithophores ***(phytoplankton)*** tests
4. Ecological factors that influence phytoplankton and zooplankton growth also affect biogenous sedimentation because the sediments are skeletal remains
5. For example, high input of nutrients and physical processes that mix nutrients throughout the water column will result in high rates of biogenous sedimentation
6. The ***carbonate compensation depth (CCD)*** is the depth at which less than 20% of the total number of calcareous tests found in surface water are preserved
   a. The CCD is a boundary between seawater saturated with calcium carbonate above it and the undersaturated water below it
   b. No calcareous ooze accumulates below the CCD

Distribution of Deep-Sea Sediments

The chart below provides a breakdown of the primary inorganic (clay) and organic (ooze) sediment deposits in ocean basins.

SEDIMENT TYPE	WORLD OCEAN	ATLANTIC OCEAN	PACIFIC OCEAN	INDIAN OCEAN
Deep-sea (red) clay	38%	26%	49%	25%
Calcareous sediment				
• Foramniferal ooze	47%	65%	36%	54%
• Pteropod ooze	0.5%	2%	0.01%	—
Siliceous sediment				
• Diatomic ooze	12%	7%	10%	20%
• Radiolarian ooze	3%	—	5%	0.5%

    c. The depth of the CCD varies from ocean basin to ocean basin and has changed over geological time

7. Coral reefs are another type of carbonate sediment
    a. Coral reef material is deposited on continental shelves in equatorial latitudes
    b. Reefs are cemented accumulations of calcareous skeletal debris that form wave-resistant, topographic highs

D. Authigenous sediments
1. Authigenous sediments tend to form in specific areas in ocean basins and are not carried far away from their origin (for example, around hydrothermal vents and on abyssal plains)
2. Authigenous sediments accumulate at extremely slow rates of millimeters per millions of years, in contrast with meters per millions of years for lithogenous and biogenous sediments
3. There are four major types of authigenous sediments
    a. Ferromanganese deposits, the most widely known type of authigenous sediment, occur as nodules and crusts
      (1) Manganese nodules were first discovered during the HMS *Challenger* expedition
      (2) A nodule consists of layers of manganese and iron oxides around a nucleus, typically a piece of bone, tooth, or sand grain
      (3) Nodules also contain minor quantities of other elements, such as cobalt, nickel, copper, and chromium
      (4) Nodules therefore are a potentially important deep-sea mining resource
      (5) Ferromanganese crusts form over rocks exposed along the sea floor; they commonly are found along continental margins, whereas nodules are found on abyssal plains
    b. Phosphorite deposits also form as nodules or crusts
      (1) Phosphorite deposits commonly form along continental margins
      (2) Phosphorite deposits consist of P_2O_5, an important ingredient of fertilizers
      (3) Unlike manganese nodules, phosphorite deposits can be mined readily because of their proximity to land and of their shallow depth
    c. Metal sulfide deposits form around hydrothermal vents and other submarine volcanic fumaroles (holes)

(1) Like other authigenous sediments, they also consist of economically important minerals (such as copper)

(2) Unlike other authigenous sediments, these deposits are not mined directly; rather, they are studied to interpret how metal deposits form

d. *Evaporite* sediments are formed when seawater evaporates, thereby leaving several types of salts

(1) Sodium chloride, or table salt, is the most common type of salt; others include gypsum, anhydrite, and calcium carbonate

(2) Today, evaporites form in shallow coastal areas

(3) In the geologic past, thick accumulations of evaporites formed when water evaporated from small, restricted ocean basins like the Mediterranean Sea

(4) Like other authigenous sediments, evaporites are economically important; salt is a major export commodity of many tropical countries

E. Cosmogenous sediments

1. In the early 20th century, John Murray first recognized cosmogenous material (cosmic dust) in marine sediments originally collected during the *Challenger* expedition

2. Cosmogenous material consists of small spherules (hundreds of microns $[1 \times 10^{-6}$ m] in diameter) of iron, iron-rich, and silicate minerals

3. Iron spherules are readily recognizable; silicate spherules are difficult to distinguish from lithogenous sediment

4. Spherules commonly are shaped like a tear drop; this shape reflects rapid cooling and solidification

5. A *tektite* is a spherule that forms when a meteorite collides with continental rock, thereby creating material that is ejected into the atmosphere, which then falls back into the ocean

6. Rates of lithogenous and biogenous sedimentation are much greater than cosmogenous sedimentation, even though tons of cosmogenous material accumulate on the earth's surface each year; thus, spherules are mixed with and diluted by these other sediments

7. Tektites occur more frequently in some ocean basins (such as the Indian Ocean); scientists have interpreted these higher concentrations as evidence of local major meteorite impacts

II. Sediment Distribution Patterns

A. General information

1. Sediment distribution patterns in the world's oceans are characterized by several distinctive trends

a. Polar latitudes typically have lithogenous sediment, which has been transported via glaciation; this is known as glacial sediment

b. Siliceous ooze dominates subpolar regions because the combination of physical, chemical, and biological oceanographic phenomena result in high primary production (that is, the formation of marine plant life) in these areas

c. Siliceous ooze also dominates equatorial and coastal areas because of high productivity in these regions

d. Calcareous ooze blankets the sea floor above the CCD

e. Deep-sea clays dominate in abyssal plains

2. Calcareous ooze occurs at less than 5,000 m in the Atlantic and Indian Ocean basins but at less than 4,000 m in the Pacific Ocean

3. The distribution of calcareous ooze follows the trends of MORs; because ridges rise above the CCD, ooze accumulates on ridge crests (much like snow accumulating on mountaintops)

B. Continental margin sediments

1. Deposits of sediments on continental margins generally vary according to latitude

   a. Glacial sediments accumulate in polar latitudes

   b. Terrigenous sediments accumulate in the middle latitudes

   c. Biogenous sediments accumulate in equatorial latitudes

2. These generalizations may vary if a margin has an atypical oceanographic setting; for example, terrigenous and not biogenous sediments have accumulated along the Brazilian shelf because of the outflow of the Amazon River

3. Coarse sands near shore become mud at the shelf break of many continental shelves because of lateral gradients in wave energy and physiography that affect waves (but this too may vary because of sea-level fluctuations, productivity, river outflow, and shelf physiography)

4. The main movement of lithogenous sediment at continental margins is away from land (perpendicular to the margin); material deposited on shelves by rivers and nearshore processes (for example, waves and tidal currents) typically move downslope

5. Deep-sea currents also can transport sediments parallel to the bases of continental margins

C. Deep-sea (pelagic) sediments

1. Sediments found in deep ocean basins are principally oozes and deep-sea clay

2. Oozes occur in regions with high primary production in the surface water

3. Clays accumulate everywhere, but are diluted in regions with high rates of biogenous sedimentation

4. Manganese nodules are patchily distributed in the Pacific and Atlantic Oceans, rarely in the Indian Ocean

III. Controls on Sediment Distribution Patterns

A. General information

1. Controls of sediment distribution patterns depend on several factors

   a. Distance from land influences the type and grain size of lithogenous sediments

   b. Water depth regulates the distribution of calcareous ooze

   c. Water depth also affects physical processes, such as waves, that transport biogenous and lithogenous sediments

   d. Availability of light and nutrients affects primary production, which affects the distribution of phytoplankton and zooplankton and biogenous sedimentation

   e. Geochemical reactions influence authigenous sediment accumulation rates

      f. Particle settling rates affect the length of time that particles are suspended in seawater
         (1) Settling rates range from less than 0.001 mm/second for clay-sized particles to more than 1.0 cm/second for sand- and larger-sized particles
         (2) The duration of suspension also affects the rates of chemical reactions that occur between particles and seawater
  2. A sample of marine sediment from any ocean basin is likely to include all types of marine sediments; however, certain sediments will be more abundant than others because of controls
  3. Three factors have the greatest impact on the distribution of deep-sea clays: wind, location, and interactions between climate and continental rocks
    a. Clays can travel farther offshore than any other type of marine sediment because they are the most readily wind-transported particle as a result of their smaller size
    b. Clays do not occur as often near the shore because they are diluted by coarser grains
    c. Interactions between climate and continental rocks affect distribution of deep-sea clays
        (1) Kaolinite is the principal type of clay found in equatorial latitudes; it is generated readily from continental rock in warm and wet climatic conditions
        (2) Chlorite is most abundant in the middle polar latitudes; it is destroyed by chemical processes in subtropical and tropical latitudes
        (3) Illite is ubiquitous in the world's ocean basins because it is more chemically stable than any other clay mineral
        (4) Montmorillonite generally is associated with volcanic rock because it is a byproduct of volcanic rock erosion
  4. Several oceanographic phenomena interact to control the distribution of calcareous ooze
    a. More calcareous ooze is deposited in the Atlantic Ocean than in the Pacific Ocean because Pacific water has more dissolved carbon dioxide in it, making it more corrosive to calcium carbonate
    b. Biogeochemical processes account for this difference in water chemistry between the Atlantic and Pacific Oceans; water becomes enriched with carbon dioxide as it moves from the Atlantic into the Pacific
    c. The relationship between depth and the CCD partly reflects the fact that the Atlantic is a younger ocean basin than the Pacific; thus, Atlantic oceanic crust is shallower, on average, than Pacific oceanic crust

B. Gravitational processes
  1. Terrigenous sediments are transported from land to continental shelves via rivers, wave action along shelves, wind, and tidal currents
  2. The declivity of continental slopes results in the movement of terrigenous sediments from shelves to abyssal plains via gravity-driven processes
  3. Four general types of gravity-driven flows have been identified
    a. ***Turbidity currents,*** powerful flows associated with submarine canyons, are distinguished by their turbulence
        (1) Turbidity currents begin at the shelf break and can extend to an MOR
        (2) They have two major parts: a head (the most turbulent and powerful part) and a tail (less energetic and less turbulent than the head)

(a) The speed of the head depends primarily on the density difference between seawater and suspended sediments

(b) The speed of the tail depends on the slope's angle

(3) Turbidity currents also act as powerful eroding agents, scouring the sea floor from the shelf to the abyssal plain

(4) Turbidity currents produce a characteristic series of graded (that is, segregated according to size) layers called *turbidites*

b. *Fluidized sediment flows* are characterized by an upward motion of suspended particles and are less turbulent than turbidity currents

c. *Grain flows* are characterized by direct grain-grain interactions

d. *Debris flows* are characterized by particles suspended in mud

4. In addition to these gravity flows, coherent masses of sediment may be transported down continental slopes (on land); this is called *slump*

IV. Stratigraphy

A. General information

1. *Stratigraphy* is the analysis of sedimentary layers, including the types of sediments present, their age, mode of deposition, and geographic extent

2. Marine geologists study these layers via sediment samples and seismic profiling

3. Using stratigraphy, marine geologists can ascertain past depositional conditions (such as paleodepths, temperatures, energy regimes, and biogeochemical conditions) and develop a chronological sequence of events that correspond to the sedimentary filling of an ocean basin

4. Stratigraphy of ocean basins has documented two patterns of sediment accumulation: lateral and vertical changes in sediments caused by plate tectonics (called plate stratigraphy) and sea-level changes

B. Plate stratigraphy

1. Borehole samples from the Atlantic, Pacific, and Indian Oceans show a general, two-layered sequence of marine sediments within Layer 1

   a. The deeper layer consists of calcium carbonate (limestone)

   b. The shallower layer consists of deep-sea clay

2. Both types of sedimentary sublayers occur away from MORs; however, only the calcium carbonate layer occurs along MORs

3. Marine geologists interpret the sequence of sediments as evidence of sea-floor spreading

   a. When oceanic crust forms at an MOR, the warm crust is buoyant and rises above the CCD

   b. Thus, the first type of marine sediment to accumulate on top of Layer 2 is calcareous ooze

   c. The crust ages, cools, and subsides below the CCD as the oceanic crust moves away from the spreading center

   d. The ooze solidifies into limestone

   e. The limestone is covered by deep-sea clay once the sea floor is below the CCD; the limestone is sufficiently lithified (cemented into rock) to resist dissolution below the CCD

4. An alternative explanation for this sequence of sediments is vertical movement of the CCD
   a. Evidence from borehole samples suggests that the CCD has migrated vertically
   b. However, scientists do not think that CCD migration alone accounts for these two sedimentary layers found in all the world's ocean basins

C. Sea-level changes
1. The deposition of coarse- to fine-sized grains of sediment along shore to the shelf break does not occur on many continental shelves in the middle to polar latitudes; however, coarse sand exists near the shore and along the shelf break
2. Marine geologists interpret this phenomenon as evidence of changes in sea level
   a. During the geologic past, sea level was lower than it currently is (water was transported from ocean basins to glaciers)
   b. Nearshore areas developed where shelf breaks now exist, and coarse sands were deposited in these areas
   c. Because the sea level has risen (as a result of glaciers having melted and water having gone back into ocean basins), these sands have yet to be buried by finer material
3. The coarse sands found along continental shelf breaks are called *relict sands*

Study Activities

1. List the major characteristics of the four principal types of marine sediment.
2. Contrast the controls on the deposition of lithogenous and biogenous sediments.
3. Pick three areas where you think authigenous sediments are formed; explain your choices.
4. Sketch the types and thicknesses of sediments found on the sea floor, moving from an MOR south of the equator to an abyssal plain north of the equator.

5

Global Processes

Objectives

After studying this chapter, the reader should be able to:
- Explain the Coriolis effect and its importance to oceanography.
- Describe Earth's heat budget.
- Characterize the ways energy is transferred between the atmosphere and the ocean.
- Describe the characteristics of light and sound in the ocean.

I. Physical Processes

A. General information
1. Physical oceanographic phenomena are driven primarily by heat and gravity
2. Oceanographers evaluate these forms of energy on a global scale because solar radiation striking the earth varies with latitude, gravitational attractions exist between Earth and objects on its surface, and attractions occur between Earth and other bodies in the solar system
   a. Atmospheric pressure gradients develop as a result of the latitudinal variability in solar energy
      (1) These gradients generate global wind patterns
      (2) The winds, in turn, initiate waves and currents
   b. The *hydrosphere* (the layer of water surrounding the earth) is deformed by gravitational attractions
      (1) The resultant bulges and depressions in the hydrosphere influence tides
      (2) The hydrosphere also is deformed because Earth rotates on an axis
3. Earth's rotation influences the motions of all freely moving objects; this is called the ***Coriolis effect***

B. The Coriolis effect
1. The Coriolis effect is an apparent change in direction of any freely moving object over the surface of the earth; it is named after Gaspard Gustave de Coriolis, a French mathematician who first quantified its physical cause in 1835
   a. In the northern hemisphere, the apparent change is to the right of an object's trajectory
   b. In the southern hemisphere, it is to the left
2. All freely moving objects are influenced by the Coriolis effect; examples include moving water (currents), moving air (winds), and moving projectiles (missiles and airplanes)

3. Although the Coriolis effect influences every moving object, it is not always apparent
   a. An object must travel tens to thousands of kilometers for the effect to be readily observed
   b. Other factors, such as friction, have a greater effect on an object's motion
4. The Coriolis effect is an apparent deflection because of the frame of reference used to track moving objects
   a. Objects in motion are tracked from points on Earth's surface
   b. While an object is moving relative to Earth, Earth also is spinning underneath the freely moving object, causing an apparent deflection
   c. When viewed from a fixed point in space, no deflection would be evident
5. The mathematical expression of the Coriolis effect is relatively simple and illustrates the controls on the effect; it is written as $2\Omega \sin\theta\ (v)$, where Ω is the earth's rotational velocity in degrees per unit time, v is the linear velocity of the object, and θ is the latitude in degrees
   a. Because $\sin 0° = 0$, any object moving east or west along the equator (0°) will not experience the Coriolis effect; east-west motion along the equator is the only global motion that is not subject to the Coriolis effect
   b. The magnitude of the Coriolis effect depends on the speed of the moving object — the faster the object moves, the greater the effect
   c. This expression also indicates that the Coriolis effect becomes greater toward the poles
      (1) As θ approaches the 90° latitude north or south of the equator, $\sin\theta$ approaches 1
      (2) Thus, the tendency to deflect to the right increases north of the equator and the tendency to deflect to the left increases south of the equator
6. The Coriolis effect has important practical and oceanographic consequences
   a. For example, airline pilots must compensate for the effect in order to stay on course
   b. Parcels of air moving through the atmosphere also undergo the Coriolis effect; thus, global winds do not move only from high-pressure to low-pressure regions
   c. Currents and parcels of water moving through ocean basins are deflected according to latitude; the closer the current or parcel of water is to the pole, the more it is deflected

II. Heat Budget

A. General information

1. Scientists have developed a budget (a balance of inputs and outputs) of heat on Earth to evaluate atmospheric and oceanographic processes
2. The inclination of Earth's axis (23.5°) and seasonal variations associated with its rotation about the sun result in significant latitudinal variations in the amount of solar radiation received
   a. For example, during the vernal and autumnal equinoxes (the first day of spring and fall, respectively), the solar radiation that strikes Earth at 60°N is only 50% of what strikes Earth at the equator
   b. More heat is gained between 30° N and 30° S latitudes than between 50° N to 90° N or 50° S to 90° S because of this latitudinal variability

3. Global wind patterns and ocean currents transport excess heat from the tropics toward the poles, thereby moderating Earth's climate
4. Heat can be categorized in two ways
   a. *Latent heat,* heat lost or gained by a system at a constant temperature, cannot be measured with a thermometer
   b. *Sensible heat,* heat lost or gained by a system that is reflected in the system's temperature, can be measured with a thermometer

B. Inputs and outputs

1. The earth's surface has two heat inputs or sources — solar radiation and radioactivity originating within the earth's interior (see *Global Heat Budget,* page 50)
2. A comparison of these two sources confirms that heat at the earth's surface comes primarily from solar radiation
   a. The rate at which solar radiation is received and reradiated by the earth is approximately 4×10^2 Watts/m^2
   b. As radioactive isotopes decay within the earth, heat is generated and transported through the earth's layers to the surface; the average internal heat flow is about 8×10^{-2} Watts/m2
3. The earth has many heat outputs (in contrast to the two heat inputs)
   a. Approximately 6% of incoming solar radiation is *backscattered* (scattered in a direction opposite to the incoming radiation) by water droplets, ice, or other particles in the atmosphere
   b. Approximately 20% of incoming solar radiation is reflected by clouds
   c. Approximately 4% of incoming solar radiation is reflected by water and land surfaces
      (1) A surface's ability to reflect incoming solar radiation is quantified by its *albedo,* the ratio of reflected light to incident radiation on a surface or body
         (a) For example, snow has a high albedo because it is very reflective
         (b) A dark rock has a very low albedo
      (2) Earth's albedo has changed over time; for example, the amount of ice covering the globe has decreased dramatically during the past 20,000 years
4. Approximately 51% of incoming solar radiation reaches ocean and land surfaces and is absorbed
   a. The earth heats up as a result of this absorption and internally derived radioactive heat
   b. It reradiates energy back into space, generating additional outputs
   c. Energy reradiated by the earth is slightly different than incoming solar radiation
      (1) Solar radiation primarily is in the visible part of the electromagnetic spectrum (between 0.4 and 0.7 μm in wavelength)
      (2) Earth reradiation is in the infrared part of the spectrum (0.7 to 100 μm)
   d. Some atmospheric gases, such as carbon dioxide, are transparent to the visible part of the spectrum, allowing incoming solar radiation to readily pass through
      (1) These gases are opaque to reradiated, longer-wavelength energy
      (2) These gases trap the long-wavelength energy in the atmosphere, causing the atmosphere to heat up
      (3) This is known as the *greenhouse effect*

Global Heat Budget

The earth has a global heat budget, meaning that it has heat input and outputs. The table below lists these inputs and outputs.

INPUTS	OUTPUTS
• Solar radiation (primary heat source) • Radioactivity within the Earth (negligble)	• Backscatter by air • Reflected by clouds • Reflected by Earth's surface • Eradiated by Earth • Emissions by clouds, water vapor, and other gases (such as carbon dioxide)

III. Air-Sea Interactions

A. General information

1. Because the atmosphere and the ocean are in constant contact and exchange fluids and gases, they can be considered one system when discussing global climate
2. However, several fundamental physical differences exist between the ocean and the atmosphere
   a. Because water is denser than air, the ocean surface tends to be more stable than the atmosphere
   b. For example, a plume of hot air can rise hundreds to thousands of meters into the atmosphere, mixing with surrounding air and forming a thunder-head (or anvil cumulonimbus cloud), whereas that same plume of hot air will not penetrate the ocean to any significant depth
   c. Because the mass of the ocean is approximately 270 times that of the atmos-phere, 10 square meters of seawater has the same weight per unit area (pressure) as the entire atmosphere at the earth's surface
   d. *Hydrostatic pressure* (that is, the pressure generated by the column of water in the ocean) increases by 1 *atmosphere* (a unit of pressure equivalent to the pressure of air at sea level) with every 10 m of depth; 1 atmosphere is approximately equal to 14.7 psi
   e. The ocean has a much greater heat capacity than the atmosphere; thus, the ocean has a moderating influence on climate and weather patterns
   f. Light is more readily absorbed and scattered by the ocean than the atmos-phere; this greatly affects biological processes in the ocean
   g. Sound travels faster in the ocean than in the atmosphere
   h. Both the ocean and atmosphere are stratified (layered) according to density
      (1) The ocean is least dense at the sea surface and becomes denser as depth increases
      (2) The atmosphere is densest where the air and sea meet and becomes less dense as altitude increases
3. Many of these characteristics reflect differences in the chemistry of water and air (see Chapter 10, Seawater Chemistry, for details about the chemical properties of water and seawater)
4. The most easily seen interactions between the ocean and atmosphere are waves
   a. Although waves also are one of the least understood air-sea interactions, sci-entists have developed a consensus about this interaction over the past several centuries

    b. An instability in the sea surface develops as wind travels across the surface of the ocean

    c. Wind velocity and pressure constantly change; this atmospheric instability generates a *capillary wave* at the sea surface

    d. Capillary waves evolve into other types of surface waves, conditions permitting (see Chapter 6, Waves)

5. The ocean absorbs solar radiation that has passed through the atmosphere, thereby increasing sea-surface temperatures

    a. The ocean typically becomes thermally stratified (that is, layered by temperature)

    b. A warm water layer generally forms between about 50 and 200 m

        (1) Because seawater density is controlled partly by temperature, the warm surface water forms a low-density layer

        (2) Marine scientists call this layer the *surface layer* or *warm-water layer*

    c. The *thermocline* is a zone in the ocean where temperatures change dramatically

        (1) A permanent thermocline exists between the warm-water layer and cooler, deeper water layers

            (a) The permanent thermocline in all oceans occurs between 200 and 1,500 m

            (b) This thermocline effectively separates the world's oceans into two distinct layers, which are important to vertical movements of seawater, seawater chemistry, and primary production

        (2) *Seasonal thermoclines,* thermoclines that form nearer the sea surface during the warm summer months in ocean basins in the middle latitudes, can extend between 50 and 100 m

6. Solar radiation also affects salinity

    a. Salinity also controls the density of seawater

    b. As relatively warm, dry air moves across the sea surface, water evaporates and the salinity of the remaining seawater increases in these regions

    c. The resultant warm, salty surface water may be denser than deeper, cooler, less salty water

    d. If so, the saltier and warmer surface water then sinks, moving water vertically

    e. This action is a type of *convection,* a process that involves circular movement via density differences or gravity

7. Air-sea interactions are not limited to the atmosphere interacting with the ocean; the ocean also plays a major role in controlling atmospheric phenomena

    a. Because of the ocean's larger heat capacity, heat stored in warm surface water can be transferred to cooler, drier air overlying the sea surface, thereby influencing weather patterns

    b. Monsoons are an example of seasonal wind shifts caused by ocean-atmosphere interactions

        (1) During the summer, air overlying an ocean basin is relatively cool (compared with air over an adjacent landmass) and saturated with water vapor

        (2) Air over an adjacent land mass will warm and rise because of its lower density

        (3) The moisture-rich air over the ocean then moves landward to replace the rising air over land

(4) The moisture-rich ocean air then generates monsoon rains over the land-mass

(5) During the winter, this cycle is reversed

c. Land and sea breezes, commonly observed along shorelines, are caused by processes similar to those that generate monsoons

(1) During the day, the ocean absorbs more heat than the adjacent landmass

(2) At night, the warm water heats the overlying air, which then rises

(3) Cooler air over land moves seaward to replace the rising warm ocean air, giving rise to a nighttime land breeze

(4) The cycle is reversed during the day

B. Global wind patterns

1. The latitudinal variability in solar radiation causes uneven heating of the atmosphere and the earth's surface

    a. Latitudinal belts of warm and cool air develop

    b. The motion of these air masses in a particular area can be described as a *convection cell*

    c. Because warm air is less dense than cool air, warm air rises to the top of the atmosphere, while cool air sinks to the earth's surface

    d. Cool air flows along the surface toward regions where air is heating and rising

2. In 1735, English meteorologist George Hadley researched this type of air circulation in the tropics

    a. Today, these tropical convection cells that extend north and south of the equator are called *Hadley cells*

    b. Hadley cells consist of warm air that rises near the equator, spreading north and south along the top of the atmosphere as they cool

    c. Cool air eventually sinks to the surface at about 30° latitude north and south of the equator

    d. At the surface, the air flows back toward the equator to replace the warm, rising air there

3. Two other atmospheric convection cells occur: *Ferrel cells* in the middle latitudes and *polar cells* in polar regions

4. Uneven heating of ocean and land surfaces also creates *Walker cells,* convection cells that extend from east to west

5. All these convection cells control atmospheric pressure

    a. High-pressure systems are associated with regions of sinking cool air

    b. Low-pressure systems are associated with regions of rising warm air

6. These cells also influence the saturation of the atmosphere

    a. When cool air sinks, it is relatively dry because its water content has decreased (caused by precipitation that occurred when that air mass rose)

    b. When warm air rises, its water content decreases via precipitation

7. Convection cells and the pressure systems associated with them control global climate and heat transport

    a. Air moving from high- to low-pressure systems defines wind patterns; remember that wind also is affected by the Coriolis effect

    (1) In the northern hemisphere, for example, air moving from the sinking arm of a Hadley cell at about 30° N to the equator is deflected to the right of its southward trajectory (in this case, west is to the right of a southward moving air mass)

        (2) These winds, which travel in a southwesterly direction, are called Trade Winds because sailing ships relied on them to travel between Europe and North America

    b. Within high- and low-pressure systems, air movement is primarily vertical

        (1) Therefore, no strong winds blow along the equator (a major low-pressure region) and 30° N and S latitudes (high-pressure regions)

        (2) Mariners called these calm areas the doldrums and the horse latitudes, respectively

    c. High-pressure zones typically force weather systems to move along their edges; for example, hurricanes in the North Atlantic are deflected by the high-pressure zone at about 30° N

    d. Heat is transported from the equator toward the poles primarily via evaporation and condensation of water (latent heat transport)

        (1) These processes occur in air masses moving within the convection cells

        (2) Global heat transfer is not accomplished primarily by a warm air mass moving toward a region that is cool

        (3) Heat that evaporates water near the equator is released when water vapor condenses as it moves north or south of the equator

C. The Southern Oscillation, El Niño, and La Niña

  1. The Southern Oscillation, El Niño, and La Niña are atmosphere-ocean phenomena that occur in the Pacific Ocean basin

    a. The Southern Oscillation is a change in air flow between low- and high-pressure systems

        (1) Typically, a high-pressure cell exists over the eastern Pacific and a low-pressure cell over the western Pacific; these cells generate westward winds

        (2) During an oscillation, the low-pressure system expands while the high-pressure system shrinks

        (3) Western winds then diminish greatly or even reverse their direction because the pressure gradient between high- and low-pressure systems no longer exists

    b. El Niño is an oceanographic phenomenon in which a relatively warm, nutrient-poor current flows south and east along the western coast of South America; its name is derived from the Spanish word for the Christ child because it generally occurs around Christmastime

        (1) Prevailing westerly winds typically push surface water away from the western coast of South America

        (2) This water is replaced by deeper, cooler, nutrient-rich water that rises from the depths of the ocean in a process called **upwelling**

        (3) During El Niño, upwelling diminishes

    c. La Niña is a cold, nutrient-rich current that flows north and west along the western coast of South America

        (1) La Niña is caused by intense westerly winds that generate strong coastal upwelling

        (2) In functional terms, La Niña is the opposite of El Niño

  2. The Southern Oscillation, El Niño, and La Niña occur approximately once every 3 to 7 years

  3. Based on observations and computer simulations, scientists believe that La Niña precedes the Southern Oscillation, which in turn triggers El Niño

4. These phenomena have global and local importance
    a. The Southern Oscillation influences weather patterns throughout the Pacific Ocean and as far away as India and Africa
    b. El Niño shuts down a prolific fishery along the Peruvian coast

IV. Light in the Ocean

A. General information
1. Light is a form of electromagnetic radiation
    a. Visible light has wavelengths between 0.4 μm (for violet light) and 0.7 μm (for red light)
    b. Light behaves like a stream of particles as well as a wave
    c. The wavelike characteristics of light are important in oceanography because seawater reflects, refracts, absorbs, and scatters wave energy
2. How much light initially penetrates the sea surface depends on the surface's texture and the angle at which the light strikes the surface
    a. Light from directly overhead is reflected to a lesser extent than light coming in at an angle (for example, near the horizon)
    b. Waves generally increase the amount of light reflected off the sea surface; thus, they increase the sea surface's albedo

B. Vertical controls on light
1. Light is readily absorbed by seawater because of its chemical and physical properties (for details, see Chapter 10, Seawater Chemistry); approximately 60% of the light striking the surface is absorbed within the first meter, 80% within the top 10 meters
2. Light's electromagnetic energy is converted to heat when it is absorbed by water molecules; thus, light helps warm the surface layer
3. Light is selectively absorbed according to its wavelength
    a. Long wavelengths (such as red, orange and yellow) are absorbed most readily
    b. Short wavelengths (such as green and blue) are absorbed less quickly
    c. Because the red and yellow wavelengths are absorbed before the blue and green ones, ocean water that is clear and does not have any plants, animals, or suspended sediments looks blue
4. Light is scattered by water molecules and other particles suspended in seawater; for example, seawater filled with microscopic plants looks green primarily because of the plants' green pigment
5. A *downwelling* field (a downward directed field of light) results from this combination of absorption and scattering; this field strongly influences organisms that live within the upper 1,000 m
6. Light penetrates water to different depths
    a. In clear water, light can penetrate to a depth of about 200 m
    b. In coastal waters with many suspended particles, light can penetrate only several meters
7. Marine scientists refer to two zones within the ocean on the basis of light penetration
    a. The *euphotic* or photic zone is the well-lit part of the ocean

(1) The base of this zone is the depth at which only 1% of the light at the surface is visible

(2) This zone can extend to a depth of 100 to 200 m in the open ocean and less than 10 m in coastal waters

b. The *aphotic zone* lies below the euphotic zone

(1) It has very little visible light

(2) Most of the world ocean lies within this zone

(3) Darkness plays a major role in biological activity at depths of more than 200 m

C. Latitudinal variability of light

1. The availability and penetration of light varies with latitude because solar radiation strikes the surface of the earth unevenly

   a. At the equator, light is available 12 hours per day, has the greatest intensity, and produces more heat

   b. At the poles, low-intensity light is available continuously for 6 months, followed by 6 months of darkness

2. Available light and associated heat affect the thermal stratification of the ocean; for example, a deep, permanent thermocline exists year-round in the tropics

   a. Although light is most plentiful in the tropics, the thermocline restricts vertical water movements

   b. Deep, nutrient-rich water cannot rise to the euphotic zone

   c. Thus, in the open ocean, marine plants have enough light but insufficient food to proliferate

V. Sound in the Ocean

A. General information

1. Sound is a vibration transmitted through an elastic medium, such as seawater

2. Like light, sound waves are absorbed and scattered within the ocean

   a. Higher frequencies have shorter wavelengths and are absorbed more readily than lower frequencies, which have longer wavelengths

   b. The sea surface, sea floor, bubbles, suspended particles, organisms, ships, and submarines scatter and reflect sound; this is a basic principle used in acoustic fish-finding instruments and more sophisticated sonar devices

3. Sound travels through the ocean more efficiently than light

   a. Sound travels faster in seawater than in air (1,500 m/second compared to 330 m/second)

   b. This increased velocity of sound has led many marine animals to develop acoustic sensory organs to communicate, navigate, and sense predators or prey

4. The speed of sound in the ocean increases with increases in temperature, salinity, and hydrostatic pressure

B. Sound fixing and ranging (SOFAR) channel

1. Temperature and pressure primarily control sound transmission through the water column

2. High temperatures cause relatively fast sound velocities at the surface

3. Temperatures and sound velocity decrease dramatically at the thermocline, which is centered about 1,000 m deep in the open ocean; an increase in hydrostatic pressure cannot offset the decrease in sound velocity caused by temperature
4. Sound velocity increases as hydrostatic pressure increases below the thermocline
5. The combined effects of temperature and pressure result in a zone centered around the thermocline that has the lowest sound velocities in the ocean; this zone is called the *SOFAR* channel or zone (from *sound* *f*ixing *and* *r*anging)
    a. Sound waves emitted in this low-velocity zone are trapped within it; sound is refracted in this channel because of the velocity contrasts above and below it
    b. Sound can propagate thousands of kilometers within the SOFAR channel because sound waves are confined to the channel and do not lose energy by spreading out
    c. Marine animals (for example, whales) and humans in submarines use the sofar channel as a viaduct to transmit information

Study Activities

1. Explain why the Coriolis effect causes an apparent rightward deflection in the northern hemisphere and an apparent leftward deflection in the southern hemisphere.
2. Evaluate how each element of the global heat budget has been affected by anthropogenic carbon dioxide that enhances the greenhouse effect and induces global warming.
3. Describe how the atmosphere and the ocean interact with each other and the results of this interaction.
4. Outline an experiment in which oceanographers could use sound to study global warming (because sound transmission in the ocean is dependent on ocean temperature).

6

Waves

Objectives

After studying this chapter, the reader should be able to:
• Describe the characteristics of a wave.
• List types of waves.
• Define wave shoaling, interference, dispersion, and refraction.
• Describe the effects that waves have in different oceanographic settings.

I. Wave Types

A. General information
1. A wave is a disturbance transmitted along an interface between two media or within a medium
2. All types of ocean waves can be described by defining specific characteristics of the disturbance (see *Wave Characteristics,* page 58)
   a. *Wave height* is the vertical distance between the apex of a wave's crest and the zenith of its trough
   b. *Wave amplitude* is the vertical distance between the highest or lowest part of the wave and a horizontal reference level (for example, an ocean surface that has no waves); wave amplitude equals one-half the wave height
   c. *Wavelength* is the horizontal distance between two equivalent points on consecutive waves (such as between one wave crest and another wave crest)
   d. *Wave steepness* is the ratio of wave height to wavelength
   e. *Wave period* is the time it takes for a wave to pass a fixed point
      (1) Wave period remains constant while other characteristics can change (for example, wavelength typically shortens as a wave approaches shore)
      (2) Wave period is used to classify waves because of its constancy
   f. *Wave frequency* is the number of waves that occur per unit of time; it equals 1/period
   g. *Wave phase* is a wave's position with respect to a fixed reference point
   h. *Wave speed* equals wavelength divided by wave period; physical oceanographers use the term *celerity* rather than *speed* because there is no net particle movement in the direction of wave propagation
3. Ocean waves also are classified according to several other parameters

Wave Characteristics

The illustration below shows the basic elements of a wave. These terms can be used to describe other types of waves as well as waves on the sea surface.

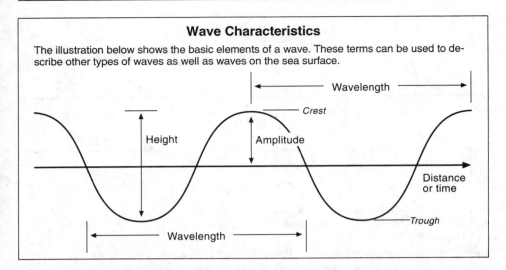

a. One such parameter may be the source of energy that triggers the disturbance (that caused the wave); for example, wind generates waves at the sea surface, and gravitational attractions generate tidal waves
b. Another is the force that stops the disturbance; for example, gravity
c. Another classification involved is the manner in which the disturbance transmits energy
  (1) A **progressive wave** transmits energy away from the area of initial disturbance
    (a) Energy is transmitted via oscillatory motions of water
    (b) Oscillatory motion is greatest at the sea surface and diminishes as depth increases
    (c) Motion becomes negligible at a depth equal to about one-half the wavelength; this depth is called the *wave base*
  (2) A **standing wave** moves water vertically and horizontally around a fixed point, called a *node*
4. Most ocean waves can be mathematically modeled using the sine function

B. Progressive waves
1. Progressive waves are the most common type of waves
2. These waves can be further categorized by their period
  a. *Chop* or *sea waves* have periods of 1 to 10 seconds and develop in areas directly affected by wind
  b. *Swells* have periods greater than 10 seconds and develop away from areas of direct air-sea interactions
3. The development of progressive waves is controlled by wind velocity, wind duration, the sea-surface area directly affected by wind (called *fetch*), and the original state of the sea surface
  a. Wind generates capillary waves as it blows across a smooth sea surface
  b. Capillary waves roughen the sea surface, causing air to flow unevenly over the surface
  c. Uneven air flow generates small zones of high and low pressure that amplify wave height and length

d. Capillary waves evolve into gravity waves (waves that are restored by gravity)
4. Waves transfer energy but not significant amounts of water away from the fetch
5. The orbital motions associated with progressive waves are not closed completely, but form corkscrew-like patterns that cause very small horizontal motions of particles
    a. This process is called *wave mass transport*
    b. Although wave mass transport is not important in the open ocean, it influences nearshore phenomena
6. Another classification of progressive waves involves the water depth–to–wavelength ratio
    a. For **shallow-water waves,** this ratio is less than 0.05
        (1) The orbital motions of these waves are compressed into ovals
        (2) Their celerity equals 3.13 $\sqrt{\text{water depth}}$
    b. For **intermediate waves,** this ratio ranges from 0.05 to 0.5
        (1) The orbital motions of these waves are complex; they vary between oval and circular
        (2) Their celerity also is complicated, depending on both water depth and wavelength
    c. For **deep-water waves,** this ratio is greater than 0.5
        (1) Their orbital motions are circular
        (2) Their celerity equals 1.25 $\sqrt{\text{wavelength}}$
7. Not all shallow-water waves occur near the shore; a wave with a very long wavelength, when compared to water depth, can occur in deep water

C. Tsunamis
1. **Tsunamis** are a particularly destructive type of shallow-water progressive waves; their wave crests can reach tens of meters high and flood coastal regions
2. Although tsunamis sometimes are called tidal waves, they are not related to tides or tide-producing forces but are generated by submarine volcanic eruptions, submarine gravity flows, or earthquakes
3. In the open ocean, tsunamis have low wave heights (less than 1 m), long wavelengths (hundreds of kilometers), and long periods (several hours)
4. Tsunamis are classified as shallow-water waves because the ratio of water depth to wavelength is extremely small
    a. For example, the average depth of the ocean (3.8 km) divided by a typical tsunami wavelength of 100 km equals .038; remember that a wave with a ratio below .05 is a shallow-water wave
    b. Therefore, the celerity of a tsunami is controlled by water depth; it typically ranges from 500 to 700 km/hour
5. Because tsunamis have such small wave heights in the deep ocean, they pose no threat and are barely detectable to ships at sea
6. As a tsunami approaches land, its wave height increases dramatically; this results from shoaling effects
7. Because a wave's energy is proportional to its height, tsunamis can release tremendous amounts of energy and water, thereby flooding areas far inshore
8. Tsunamis are common in the Pacific Ocean basin because of the *ring of fire;* an international network of seismographs throughout the basin now monitors seismic activity that can trigger a tsunami

D. Internal waves
1. *Internal waves* are progressive waves that occur along water density boundaries
2. Typically, internal waves are characterized by long wavelengths and periods
3. The celerity of an internal wave is determined by the density contrast between the layers, gravity, and the overlying layer's thickness
4. Most internal waves travel at relatively slow speeds because density contrasts are relatively small
5. Internal waves are noteworthy for several reasons
   a. They help mix layers within the ocean
   b. They can cause abrupt vertical displacements of water

E. Standing waves
1. Because standing waves oscillate around a node, they do not transfer energy away from a disturbance
2. Water moves horizontally at the node; no vertical motion occurs
3. Points on the wave with maximum vertical motion and no horizontal motion are called *antinodes*
4. A standing wave with a node and antinodes can be created in a cup; the center of the cup is the node, and antinodes will form along the wall of the cup
5. True tidal waves oscillate around a node and have standing wave characteristics
6. Winds also can generate standing waves
   a. If a wind consistently blows in one direction across a basin, water will be pushed to one end of the basin
   b. As the water piles up, gravity sloshes the water back toward the other side of the basin
   c. This type of standing wave is called a *seiche*
7. Standing waves occur in partially or completely enclosed basins, such as bays, harbors, and lakes; they raise the surface of the water at one side of the basin and lower it at the other side of the basin
8. A standing wave with an oscillation period similar to a basin's natural period — this is called *resonance* — can be extremely dangerous to structures and vessels in a basin because the standing wave may become amplified

II. Wave Phenomena

A. General information
1. Once generated, all types of ocean waves conform to the basic laws of wave theory listed below
   a. They are reflected by boundaries
   b. They interfere with each other constructively (when one trough coincides with another trough or a crest coincides with another crest) or destructively (when a trough coincides with a crest)
   c. They diffract (bend around an obstacle) and refract (bend because of changes in celerity)
   d. They separate themselves according to wavelength and period; this process is called *wave dispersion*
2. Wave dispersion and refraction probably are the most important of these phenomena because they influence wave transmission from the fetch and wave impact at shorelines

B. Wave dispersion
1. Variations in wind speed, duration, and direction generate waves of different periods and wavelengths within the fetch
   a. In the open ocean, these waves are deep-water waves and their celerity is controlled by their wavelengths; thus, they move away from the fetch at different speeds
   b. Waves with similar periods, wavelengths, and celerities will form a group of waves that can interfere with each other
2. The process by which waves sort themselves is called wave dispersion
3. Swells form as a result of wave dispersion and interference

C. Wave refraction
1. Deep-water waves can evolve into shallow-water waves as the waves interact with the sea floor
   a. Waves interact with the bottom when water depth is approximately one-half the wavelength
   b. Thus, swells with 100- to 200-m wavelengths will change into shallow-water waves in water that is 50 to 100 m deep
2. The deeper the water, the faster a shallow-water wave travels
3. Because waves typically approach a shoreline at an angle, part of a wave can be in shallow water and closer to shore while another part of it will be in deeper water and farther offshore
4. The part of the wave that is in shallower water will travel more slowly than the part in deeper water, and the wave will bend or refract

III. Wave Effects

A. General information
1. The transfer of energy by waves affects all physiographic settings in the ocean
2. Capillary waves, for instance, have transitory and localized effects on roughening the sea surface, changing albedo, mixing thin layers of water at the sea surface, and influencing nutrient and plankton distribution
3. At the opposite end of the spectrum, tidal waves are long-term phenomena with extremely far-reaching consequences (see Chapter 7, Tides)

B. Wave effects near the shore
1. Wave refraction tends to erode headlands more quickly than other parts of coastlines
2. Seasonal differences in winds create different wave patterns
   a. For example, strong winter winds generate powerful wave trains that erode beaches and redeposit the material in bars, which are offshore and parallel to the coastline
   b. During the summer, sediments are transported continuously shoreward because of wave mass transport; because the waves are not very energetic (as a result of less powerful winds), little or no material is eroded
   c. Thus, beaches generally are wide and gently dipping in the summer and narrow and steep in the winter
3. Because water depth controls wave height, one wave line can have higher and lower wave heights as depth changes along the shore

a. The different wave heights cause water to flow in the lower regions; this process is called *wave setup*

b. *Rip currents* are currents that flow perpendicular to the shoreline and are caused by water moving downslope (away from the beach) as a result of wave setup

4. Progressive waves undergo changes as water depth changes

a. Decreasing wave celerity, decreasing wavelength, increasing wave height, and increasing wave steepness (caused by increase in wave height and decrease in wavelength) characterize *shoaling waves,* waves that move into shallower water

b. When a shoaling wave's height exceeds about 0.143 of its wavelength, it becomes unstable and will collapse, or break; breaking waves are classified into three types

(1) Surging breakers, which do not actually break, move up the beach evenly

(2) Spilling breakers continuously cascade down the face of the wave

(3) Plunging breakers roll forward, creating the curl favored by surfers

c. Depth changes also can trap the energy of progressive waves

(1) A wave approaching shore will be refracted

(2) The wave may then reflect from the shoreline before it breaks

(3) As the wave moves offshore, it is refracted once again, and turns back toward the shore

(4) These types of waves are called *edge waves* and occur parallel to a shoreline

(5) Edge waves influence the physiography of the shoreline and help generate rip currents

C. Wave effects on continental margins

1. Progressive, internal, or tidal waves can have the most impact on a specific shelf, depending on the shelf's geographic setting (for example, orientation to prevailing wind patterns)

2. Because most continental margins are less than 200 m deep, most progressive waves are transformed from deep-water to intermediate and shallow-water waves over continental shelves

3. These intermediate and shallow-water waves erode and deposit sediment along continental shelves

a. Wave trains are refracted by lateral changes in depth, such as submarine canyons, as they approach a shelf break

b. Wave refraction contributes to shelf erosion and sedimentation

c. The oscillatory motion of progressive waves tends to mix waters vertically over continental shelves

(1) This mixing results in poor water stratification

(2) Nutrients constantly are mixed throughout the water column; thus, primary production rates generally are relatively high on shelves

4. Tidal and internal waves also mix water vertically over continental shelves

D. Wave effects in the open ocean

1. In the open ocean, the oscillatory motions of progressive waves thoroughly mix the upper 100 to 200 m of water; as a result, this layer of water is called the mixed layer

2. The lack of stratification in the mixed layer causes nutrients to be evenly distributed throughout the layer
3. Combined with light availability and penetration, this mixing influences primary production
4. Capillary waves and swells alter the albedo of the sea surface; the more irregular the surface, the higher its albedo
5. Internal waves also influence the sea surface's albedo by deforming deeper stratification
   a. The thermocline rises and falls as a wave passes by
   b. The sea surface above a wave's crest will be rougher than the surface above an adjacent trough
   c. This roughness changes the albedo; thus, internal waves can be detected by satellites monitoring the reflectiveness of the sea surface

Study Activities

1. Draw a wave and identify all its characteristics.
2. Contrast shallow-water and deep-water waves.
3. Describe the differences between progressive and standing waves.
4. Describe wave effects in the open ocean, on a continental margin, and near the shore.

7

Tides

Objectives

After studying this chapter, the reader should be able to:
• Describe the basic elements of a tidal wave.
• Explain the differences between the equilibrium and dynamic theories of tide genera-
tion.
• Characterize different types of tides.
• Relate tidal currents to the passage of a tidal wave.

I. Tidal Theories

A. General information
1. **Tides,** the regular rise and fall of sea level during a day, are caused by waves with
   extremely long wavelengths (thousands of kilometers) and long periods (12.4
   or 24.8 hours)
2. Tidal waves are considered shallow-water waves, because the ratio of the average
   ocean depth (3.8 km) to the wavelength is less than 0.05
3. Because of the importance of tides in coastal oceanography, some characteristics
   of tidal waves are referred to differently than those of other waves
   a. *Tidal range* is equivalent to wave height
   b. *Tidal datum* is the reference by which tides are measured
      (1) This level is not always sea level
      (2) Depending on the type of tidal wave and the country measuring it, the
          tidal datum can refer to mean low tide, the lowest tide level recorded
          at that location, or another level
   c. *Tidal bore* is an unusual tidal wave that looks like a breaking wave or small
      wall of water that develops in inlets and rivers
      (1) Tidal bores range in height from centimeters to meters
      (2) Tidal bores develop because of a large tidal range, unique basin geome-
          try (for example, one that tapers upriver), or a gradual upriver de-
          crease in depth
   d. A *tidal seiche* forms in a basin when the period of a tidal wave equals the
      natural period of the basin
4. Tidal waves principally are generated by the gravitational attraction between Earth,
   the moon, and the sun and by centripetal or centrifugal forces (see *Tide-Gener-
   ating Forces,* page 65)

Tide-Generating Forces

The illustrations below show how gravitational attractions between Earth, the moon, and the sun and centripetal force deform Earth's hydrosphere, thereby resulting in tidal bulges. Although the effects of these forces are most notable in the hydrosphere, they also influence the shape of Earth and its layers.

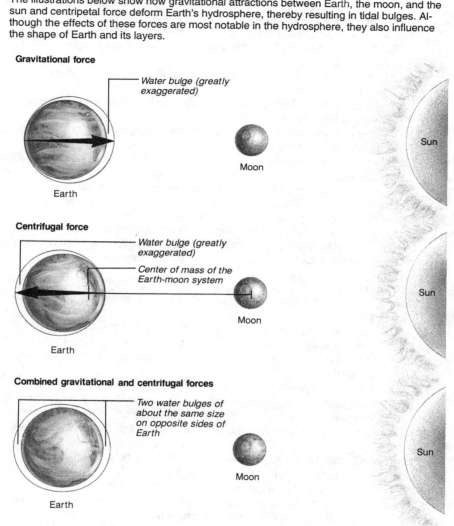

Gravitational force

Water bulge (greatly exaggerated)

Moon

Sun

Earth

Centrifugal force

Water bulge (greatly exaggerated)

Center of mass of the Earth-moon system

Moon

Sun

Earth

Combined gravitational and centrifugal forces

Two water bulges of about the same size on opposite sides of Earth

Moon

Sun

Earth

5. According to Sir Isaac Newton's law of universal gravitation, Earth, the moon, and the sun exert forces on each other based on their masses and the distances between them
   a. This law is written mathematically as $F = Gm_1m_2/r^2$, where F is the force, G is the gravitational constant, m_1 and m_2 are the masses of the two bodies, and r is the distance between them
   b. These gravitational forces deform the hydrosphere and generate bulges

  c. The superimposition of these water bulges forms the tidal bulge

  d. Typically, the tidal bulge extends toward the moon because the gravitational force is greatest between Earth and the moon as a result of the relatively short distance between them

 6. Circular motion generates centripetal and centrifugal forces

  a. *Centripetal force* is the force that causes a moving body to move toward the center of its orbit

  b. *Centrifugal force,* which truly is not considered a force, is equal and opposite to centripetal force

  c. Because Earth is rotating on its axis and spinning about the sun, these forces deform the hydrosphere

 7. Gravity and forces resulting from circular motion also generate tides in the atmosphere and solid earth

 8. Tidal waves lose energy as they propagate around the earth because of the friction that is generated when they move against the earth

 9. Tidal friction slows Earth's rotation; for example, about 350 million years ago, Earth rotated about its axis much faster than it does now — each day was approximately 22 hours long, resulting in about a 400-day year

 10. Because of the effect of tides on navigation and shipping, scientists throughout history have developed models to predict tidal fluctuations; the two principal models are the *equilibrium* theory and the *dynamic* theory

B. Equilibrium theory

 1. Newton first developed the equilibrium theory and made several simplifying assumptions

  a. The earth is completely covered with a film of water, and there are no continents to get in the way of tidal waves generated in this film of water

  b. This film of water is infinitely deep; therefore, tidal waves do not interact with the sea floor

  c. Tidal waves are progressive waves

  d. Tide-generating forces and the hydrosphere are in constant equilibrium

 2. This theory predicts that two tidal bulges are created: one is generated between Earth and the moon, and the other is generated on the side of Earth opposite the moon

 3. According to this theory, Earth rotates beneath these bulges

  a. High tide occurs when a given region is below a bulge

  b. Low tide occurs when a given region is away from a bulge

 4. This theory accounts for some tidal elements, such as spring and neap tides

  a. A *spring tide* is a tide with a greater-than-average tidal range generated by the alignment of Earth, the moon, and the sun; high tides are at their highest and low tides at their lowest because the gravitational attractions among the bodies reinforce the bulge

  b. A *neap tide* is the opposite of a spring tide; tidal ranges are minimized because Earth, the moon, and the sun are not aligned

  c. Spring tides occur during new and full lunar phases (not only in the spring), whereas neap tides occur during first- and third-quarter lunar phases

 5. This theory has significant shortcomings, including the inability to accurately predict the times that tides will occur, tidal phases, or causes of different types of tidal waves

C. Dynamic theory

1. French astronomer and mathematician Pierre-Simon Laplace proposed the dynamic theory to model tides more realistically
   a. He agreed with Newton that the primary tide-generating forces are gravity and forces resulting from circular motions
   b. He went on to propose that many other factors influence tides and that each of these factors could be mathematically predicted
   c. These factors are called *partial tides,* and approximately 400 have been identified
   d. Four partial tides (lunar daily, lunar semidaily, solar daily, and solar semidaily) are responsible for about 70% of all tides
2. The dynamic theory assumes that tidal waves are trapped within an ocean basin
   a. Thus, a tidal wave rotates around the basin, influenced by such factors as basin geometry, depth, and the Coriolis effect
   b. The equilibrium theory fails to take any of these factors into account
3. The dynamic theory regards tidal waves as standing waves rotating about a node, with the tidal range being zero and the edges of the basin the antinodes (for details about standing waves, see section I., part E. in Chapter 6, Waves)
4. This type of tidal motion is called an **amphidromic system**
   a. *Amphidromic points* are nodal points
   b. *Cotidal lines* are lines radiating out from an amphidromic point along which tidal phases occur at the same time (for example, high tide all occurs along the same line)
   c. *Corange lines* encircle the amphidromic point and link points that have equal tidal ranges
5. Within the world's oceans basins, tidal waves rotate around approximately 12 amphidromic points
   a. In the northern hemisphere, rotation is counterclockwise because of the Coriolis effect
   b. In the southern hemisphere, rotation is clockwise

II. Types of Tides

A. General information

1. Three types of tides exist (see *Tidal Waves,* page 68)
   a. *Semidiurnal tides* are semidaily tides with two equal high and low tides per day
   b. *Diurnal tides* are those with one high and low tide per day
   c. *Mixed tides* are those with two unequal high and low tides per day
2. The equilibrium theory predicts that that only one type of tide occurs at a specific latitude; for example, a diurnal tide occurs at the poles
3. Because the types of tides found along coastlines are variable and are not limited to specific latitudes, the dynamic theory is preferred to the equilibrium theory
4. The dynamic theory accounts for the effects of basin shape and depth on tidal wave propagation; thus, tides can be semidiurnal, diurnal, or mixed regardless of latitude

B. Diurnal tides

1. Diurnal tides primarily reflect lunar, solar, and lunar-solar partial tides

Tidal Waves

There are three main types of tidal waves—diurnal, semidiurnal, and mixed. The graphs below show the tidal fluctuations for the different types of tides at representative locations.

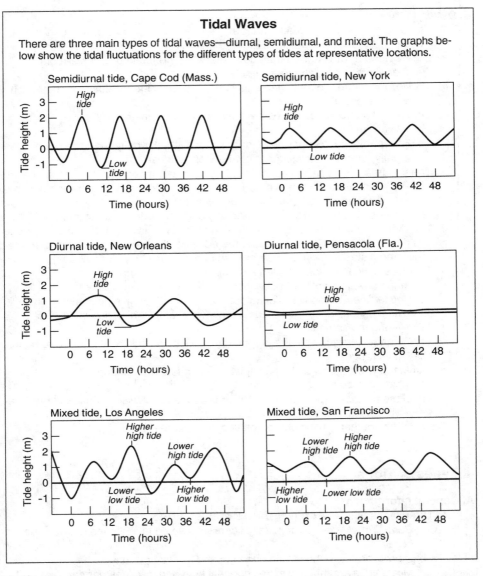

2. Of these gravitational influences, the moon's declination (angle from the celestial equator) is the most important

3. Diurnal tides are found in parts of Australia, the Gulf of Mexico, and Antarctica but are rare elsewhere

4. Generally, these tides have a small tidal range (less than 2 m)

C. Semidiurnal tides

1. Although semidiurnal tides also reflect lunar and solar forces, they primarily are influenced by the relative positions of the moon and the sun

2. Semidiurnal tides are common in the Atlantic and Indian Ocean basins

3. These tides generally have tidal ranges from 2 to 4 m and sometimes as high as 6 m

D. Mixed tides
1. Mixed tides reflect local effects (such as basin geometry) as well as the declination of the moon
2. Mixed tides are common along Pacific coastlines because complex amphidromic systems exist there
3. These tides generally have relatively high tidal ranges of 2 to 6 m

III. Tidal Currents

A. General information
1. Tidal waves transfer water horizontally — forming currents — to create the rise and fall of sea level observed along coastlines
2. Tidal currents have the same diurnal and semidiurnal periods as tidal waves
3. However, other factors can cause currents to fall out of phase with the tidal wave's period
   a. For example, as seawater moves landward into an inlet, the inlet's narrow area can limit the amount of water that flows through that inlet during a given time
   b. Consequently, water can pile up seaward of the inlet, creating an unstable situation
   c. Thus, the water moves horizontally because of the tidal wave and piling-up effect

B. Nearshore tidal currents
1. Three primary tidal currents occur in shallow water and near coastlines
   a. A *flood current* occurs when water moves into an enclosed area, such as bays and estuaries
   b. An *ebb current* occurs when water moves out of an enclosed area
   c. A *slack tide* occurs when current flow is negligible during a transition period between currents
2. The strength of a current is controlled by the volume of moving water and the topography of the basin
3. Wind and river runoff also affect currents
   a. For example, if a steady wind blows in the same direction as a current, the current may be amplified
   b. This phenomenon, called a *storm surge,* is especially catastrophic when hurricanes or gales approach a shoreline

C. Offshore tidal currents
1. Tidal currents in the open ocean are controlled by amphidromic systems and are rotary, meaning that the direction of the current constantly changes
2. Slack tides do not occur in the open ocean
3. In the northern hemisphere, tidal currents rotate clockwise because a tidal wave moves counterclockwise around an amphidromic point
4. The opposite occurs with currents in the southern hemisphere

IV. Tide Effects

A. General information
1. Tides have important effects on human activity; for example, navigation to and from harbors depends on tidal phase
2. Changes in water level and the movement of water via tidal currents have major effects on different marine environments

B. Coastal environments
1. Tidal currents effectively mix waters in coastal environments
2. Bars of sediment can accumulate on both the seaward and landward sides of inlets because of flood and ebb currents
3. Larvae growing in an estuary may be transported oceanward by an ebbing current
4. The periodic and regular oscillations in water level associated with tides affects plant and animal life, such as by exposing intertidal zones

C. Continental margins
1. Rotary tidal currents have a greater effect than reversing (flood-ebb) tidal currents on continental shelves
2. These rotary currents mix shelf waters, thus affecting nutrients, sediments, and organisms

D. Open ocean
1. Of all of the ocean's physiographic regions, tides seem to have the least effect in the open ocean
2. Because ocean basins are so large, tidal currents are relatively slow (cm/second compared with m/second for nearshore tidal currents)

Study Activities

1. Compare the equilibrium and dynamic theories of tide generation.
2. Explain why different types of tides occur.
3. List the controls on tidal currents.
4. Describe the impact of tides on three different oceanographic settings.

8

Wind-Driven Circulation

Objectives

After studying this chapter, the reader should be able to:
- Describe Ekman transport and its role in wind-driven circulation.
- Explain what geostrophic currents are and relate them to ocean basin circulation patterns.
- Describe why geostrophic currents on the western sides of ocean basins are stronger than on eastern sides.
- Explain how wind induces vertical movement of water.

I. Ocean Circulation and Air-Sea Interactions

A. General information
1. Circulation within ocean basins is driven by two processes: wind-driven and thermohaline circulation
   a. *Wind-driven circulation* moves water from the surface to several thousands of meters below the surface
      (1) It has a great influence on marine zoogeography (plant and animal distribution patterns) and shipping because wind-driven currents are the ocean's major surface currents
      (2) These surface currents affect global climate and weather patterns
      (3) Surface currents also transport heat from tropical to polar regions
   b. **Thermohaline circulation** typically moves water deeper than several thousand meters, and is driven by density gradients in water (for more information, see Chapter 9, Thermohaline Circulation)
   c. Both types of circulation interact to move water and energy (heat) around and between ocean basins
2. Solar radiation creates wind-driven circulation
   a. The differential heating of the earth's surface and subsequent development of atmospheric pressure systems cause global winds, which then transfer energy to the ocean's surface layer
   b. As winds move over the sea surface, they create *stress* (that is, force per unit area) on the sea surface
   c. This stress creates waves and other water movement

    d. The direct effects of stress are confined to the layer beneath the surface
        (0 to 100 m), called the ***Ekman layer***
        (1) This layer is named in honor of V. Walfrid Ekman, a meteorologist and
            physicist who explained in 1905 how surface water responds to wind
            stress
        (2) Ekman's work is important because ocean currents do not move directly
            downwind of prevailing wind
        (3) Currents also are controlled by the Coriolis effect, stratification of the
            ocean, and ocean basin boundaries

B. Ekman transport

    1. Ekman developed his model to explain the field observations of another renowned
       oceanographer, Fridtjof Nansen
       a. While exploring the Arctic Ocean, Nansen noticed that icebergs moved at an
          angle of 20° to 40° to the right of the wind
       b. First, Ekman assumed a uniform ocean without any boundaries
       c. Ekman then predicted that the magnitude and direction of motion of a layer
          of the water column is caused by stress from a moving, overlying layer —
          such as the atmosphere or another layer in the ocean — and by the Cori-
          olis effect (see *Ekman Spiral Model,* page 73)
       d. As wind blows across the sea surface, the uppermost layer of water begins
          to move
         (1) Current speed generally is about 2% of wind speed
         (2) The current is deflected by the Coriolis effect
         (3) Thus, in the northern hemisphere, the surface layer moves to the right
            of the wind
       e. The moving surface layer imparts stress to the underlying layer, which in turn
          begins to move and is further deflected by the Coriolis effect
         (1) This cascading effect between layers causes each layer to generate
            motion in the layer beneath it
         (2) This motion is deflected continuously by the Coriolis effect
         (3) These layers are defined by density, which is controlled by temperature
            and salinity
       f. Current velocities diminish with depth because friction between layers causes
          a loss of momentum
       g. Ultimately, an extremely slow current moves in the opposite direction of the
          wind
       h. The Ekman layer extends from the surface to the depth at which this slow
          current occurs in the ocean
       i. The progressive decrease in speed and change in current direction as a func-
          tion of depth is called the ***Ekman spiral***
    2. The overall direction of a surface current, or motion of water within the entire
       Ekman layer, is determined by integrating all individual currents in the Ekman
       spiral
       a. In the northern hemisphere, that direction is approximately 90° to the right of
          the prevailing wind

Ekman Spiral Model

Ekman's theory describes how current velocities and current direction change as a function of depth; velocities decrease with depth. The figure below illustrates currents that have been generated by wind stress, with the arrows indicating current velocity and direction. Ekman's spiral model accounts for the influences that the layering of the ocean's water column, the Coriolis effect, and friction have on current velocity and direction.

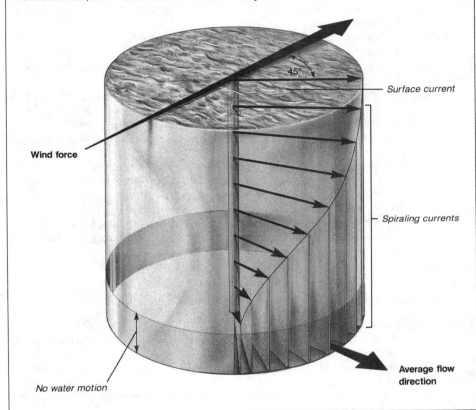

b. In the southern hemisphere, that direction is approximately 90° to the left of the prevailing wind

c. This overall movement is called ***Ekman transport***

3. The complex motions found in the open ocean, such as wave motions and currents, have limited physical oceanographers from directly observing the Ekman spiral; however, Ekman transport has been observed

C. Upwelling

1. Ekman transport causes two principal types of ***upwelling,*** coastal and equatorial

2. Both types of upwelling cause high rates of primary production in these regions

3. Coastal upwelling occurs when surface water moves away from a landmass

  a. For example, in the eastern North Atlantic, Ekman transport moves water away from North Africa as trade winds blow past the continent
  b. Deeper, cooler, nutrient-rich water rises to replace the surface water
  c. The thermocline rises as a result of upwelling
  d. Phytoplankton utilize the nutrients and create a region of high primary production
  e. The high rate of primary production creates a prolific fishery along the north African coast
4. Equatorial upwelling results from northern and southern hemisphere trade winds coming together at approximately 5° N
  a. Ekman transport associated with each of these wind patterns causes surface water to diverge from 5° N
    (1) North of the equator, Ekman transport drives water toward the northwest
    (2) South of the equator, Ekman transport drives water to the southwest
  b. These diverging surface waters create a depression at the sea surface and cause deeper, nutrient-enriched water to rise from 100 to 200 m to the surface
  c. Like coastal upwelling, it generates regions of high production
  d. Equatorial upwelling is especially prominent in the Pacific Ocean basin because of the Pacific's wide expanse along the equator
  e. In the Pacific Ocean basin, the effects of upwelling can be seen in the types of deep-sea sediments that accumulate along the equator (notably radiolarian ooze); these sediments reflect the high rate of biological activity caused by upwelling

II. Geostrophic Currents

A. General information
1. Ekman transport is the first step in the formation of wind-driven currents, such as the Gulf Stream in the North Atlantic
2. Ekman transport causes surface water to *converge* (move toward a zone) or *diverge* (move away from a zone)
  a. In a zone of convergence, surface water comes together, piles up, and forms a hill of water
    (1) Typically, these hills are less than 2 m high
    (2) Physical oceanographers refer to the relief associated with a hill as *dynamic topography*
    (3) Hills generally are located in the middle of ocean basins and have crests that are offset to the west
    (4) Water also is driven down toward the sea floor in addition to piling up at the point of convergence
    (5) This process is called **downwelling**
  b. In a zone of divergence, the lateral movement of surface water creates a depression in sea level generally less than 2 m deep
    (1) Deeper water rises to replace the moving surface water

(2) This process is called upwelling
3. These hills of water are gravitationally unstable
4. The hills also generate horizontal pressure gradients
    a. The pressure at the base of a column of water beneath a hill's crest is greater than the pressure at the base of a water column at the edge of the hill
    b. Therefore, there is more stress beneath the crest than the edge
5. Gravity and the horizontal pressure drive water away from zones of convergence
6. As water moves away from a hill, it is deflected by the Coriolis effect
7. **Geostrophic currents** are currents generated by the balance among the horizontal pressure gradient (gravity) and the Coriolis effect
    a. These currents extend downward several thousands of meters, sometimes as far as the sea floor
    b. The currents flow around the hill of water, not directly downhill, because of the complex interaction of these forces

B. Wind-driven circulation review
1. Wind stress creates a surface current
2. The surface current generates a current in a deeper ocean layer
3. All currents are deflected by the Coriolis effect (Ekman spiral)
4. Net transport of the topmost 100 m is to the right or left of the wind direction, depending on the hemisphere (Ekman transport)
5. Ekman transport results in a zone of convergence near the center of an ocean basin
6. At the zone of convergence, two important events take place
    a. Surface water piles up and creates a hill
    b. Some surface water sinks via downwelling
7. The hill of water generates a geostrophic current that moves water around the hill
8. Geostrophic currents generally extend several thousands of meters downward from the sea surface, even to the sea floor

III. Global Gyre Systems

A. General information
1. Geostrophic flow creates a series of currents called *gyres* that rotate within each major ocean basin
2. Currents that move parallel to a continent within a gyre are called *boundary currents;* generally, such currents run north to south
3. Boundary currents on the western sides of ocean basins flow faster and deeper and are narrower than boundary currents on the eastern sides; this phenomenon is called western boundary intensification
4. An example of gyre formation occurs in the North Atlantic Ocean basin
    a. Ekman transport, generated by the Westerlies (winds blowing from North America toward Europe at approximately 40° N) and the Northeast Trade

Winds (blowing from Europe and North Africa toward the Caribbean at approximately 10° N), move surface water toward the Bermuda Islands
   b. Water converges near Bermuda, forming a hill whose crest lies just south of the islands
   c. The dynamic topography between the hill's crest and its edge (that is, the U.S. east coast) is approximately 1.8 m
   d. Geostrophic currents (the Gulf Stream, Canary Current, and North Equatorial Current) flow clockwise around the hill because of the Coriolis effect, thereby forming the North Atlantic gyre

B. Western boundary intensification
   1. Western boundary intensification is significant in the North Atlantic, South Atlantic, and North Pacific Ocean basins, and less so in the South Pacific and Indian Ocean basins
      a. In the South Pacific Ocean basin, the lack of a continuous landmass along the western boundary prevents western boundary intensification
      b. In the Indian Ocean basin, seasonal changes in currents diminish boundary intensification
   2. Western boundary currents are intensified because of these four factors: latitudinal variability of the Coriolis effect, continental landmasses, basin orientation with respect to the prevailing winds, and vorticity
      a. Because the magnitude of the Coriolis effect is partially controlled by latitude, the effect is greater at higher latitudes; this results in westward drift
      b. Continental landmasses along the western edge of a gyre dam the westward-migrating hill of water
         (1) Consequently, the leading (western) edge of the hill steepens in comparison with the trailing (eastern) edge
         (2) A steeper slope creates a sharper horizontal pressure gradient with stronger currents
      c. Prevailing wind patterns cause Ekman transport to move water toward both landmasses and ocean basins
         (1) For example, in the North Atlantic, Ekman transport caused by the Northeast Trade Winds moves water toward the east coast of North America, where it piles up in response to the damming effect of the continent
         (2) Ekman transport (caused by the Westerlies) moves water toward the open ocean, where it spreads out and does not pile up
      d. The rates at which currents in gyres rotate around an ocean basin must be balanced, or the entire gyre would either accelerate or decelerate
         (1) Two different forces generate **vorticity** (spin) within an entire gyre
            (a) For example, in the North Atlantic, the Westerlies and Northeast Trade Winds create *relative vorticity,* a clockwise spin
            (b) The tendency to spin caused by Earth's rotation increases with higher latitudes (like the Coriolis effect); this spin is called *planetary vorticity*

(2) The addition of relative and planetary vorticities is called *absolute vorticity*
  (a) The direction and magnitude of absolute vorticity must be balanced around a gyre
  (b) The development of western intensification results in an additional component of relative vorticity that compensates for an imbalance in absolute vorticity

Study Activities

1. Outline how geostrophic currents are generated.
2. Describe all of the various types of motion that can affect water in the center of a gyre, along the west coast of Peru, and along the equator in the Atlantic Ocean.
3. List the controls on western boundary intensification.
4. Describe how winds generate horizontal and vertical movements of water.

9

Thermohaline Circulation

Objectives

After studying this chapter, the reader should be able to:
- Define a water mass and explain how it influences physical oceanographic phenomena.
- Describe the effects of temperature, salinity, and density on ocean stratification.
- Explain what thermohaline circulation is and how it works in individual ocean basins as well as in the entire ocean.
- Relate thermohaline circulation to wind-driven circulation patterns.
- Describe the roles that thermohaline and wind-driven circulation play in global heat transport.

I. Relationships Among Temperature, Salinity, and Density

A. General information
1. Thermohaline circulation is controlled by density gradients in ocean basins
   a. The density of seawater is controlled primarily by temperature and salinity
   b. Pressure generally plays a minor role in seawater density, although it is significant at great depths
2. Temperature and salinity are controlled by several phenomena
   a. Changes in temperature can result from heating caused by solar radiation or from cooling caused by the transfer of heat from the ocean to the atmosphere
   b. Changes in salinity result from evaporation or precipitation
3. Temperature and salinity characteristics of seawater are considered conservative
   a. They will not change because of biochemical reactions that take place within seawater
   b. In order for them to change, some physical process must occur; for example, the mixing of two volumes of water with two different temperatures and salinities
4. The world's ocean basins have remarkably uniform temperatures and salinities; approximately 75% of all seawater has a temperature between 0° and 5° C (32° and 41° F) and a salinity between 34 and 35 (for information on measuring salinity, see Chapter 10, Seawater Chemistry)
5. Thermohaline circulation is most significant in deep waters (deeper than 2,000 m)
6. Most thermohaline circulation tends to be relatively slow (in units of m/day for deep thermohaline currents) compared with wind-driven circulation (in units of

m/second in western boundary currents), although some thermohaline currents have velocities equivalent to wind-driven currents

B. Water masses

1. A water mass is a parcel of seawater identifiable by distinctive properties, such as temperature and salinity
2. Water masses tend to retain their unique properties and do not readily mix with each other
3. When physical oceanographers refer to the age of a water mass, they are referring to the time it has taken for a mass to move from its area of origin to its present location
4. Most water masses form as a result of air-sea interactions
5. Water masses are categorized into four groups based on the depth at which they occur
   a. *Central waters* extend from the sea surface to a depth of approximately 1,000 m
   b. *Intermediate waters* occur between approximately 1,000 and 2,000 m
   c. *Deep waters* lie between approximately 2,000 and 5,000 m
   d. *Bottom waters* are found from about 5,000 m to the deepest part of the sea floor (approximately 11,000 m)
6. Water masses also are named according to their place of origin; for example, Antarctic Bottom Water, the densest water mass in the oceans, forms adjacent to Antarctica and flows to the bottom of all ocean basins
7. Approximately 30 water masses have been identified throughout the world's ocean basins (see *Table of Water Masses,* page 80)
8. Other properties can be used to distinguish a water mass
   a. The concentration of radioactive isotopes that enter the ocean via air-sea interactions can help identify a water mass and provide a chronological measurement of its movements
      (1) For example, relatively high concentrations of tritium (an isotope of hydrogen) were released in the atmosphere of the northern hemisphere via atomic bomb testing
      (2) Today, this tritium clearly marks water masses that formed at the air-sea interface in the North Atlantic and that have sunk to deeper depths and moved south
   b. Anthropogenic materials that are associated with little chemical reactivity, such as freon (a chlorofluorocarbon), also can trace water mass movement
   c. Nutrients (such as silica) and dissolved gases (oxygen) that are used to trace water masses must be used cautiously because seawater concentrations of these tracers may change as a result of biogeochemical reactions in the ocean (see Chapter 11, Biogeochemistry)

Table of Water Masses

The chart below lists the name, depth, and characteristic temperature and salinity of the major water masses in ocean basins.

TYPE OF WATER	EXAMPLES	TEMPERATURE (°C)	SALINITY (%)
Central waters (0 to 1 km deep)	South Pacific Central Water	9 to 20	34.3 to 36.2
	North Pacific Central Water	7 to 20	34.1 to 34.8
	North Atlantic Central Water	4 to 20	35.0 to 36.8
	South Atlantic Central Water	5 to 18	34.3 to 35.9
	South Indian Central Water	6 to 16	34.5 to 35.6
Intermediate waters (1 to 2 km deep)	North Pacific Intermediate Water	4 to 10	34.0 to 34.5
	Red Sea Intermediate Water	23	40.0
	Mediterranean Intermediate Water	6 to 11.9	35.3 to 35.9
	Arctic Intermediate Water	0 to 2	34.9
	Antarctic Intermediate Water	2.2 to 5	33.8 to 34.6
Deep and bottom waters (2 km deep)	Common Water	0.6 to 1.3	34.7
	Pacific Subarctic Water	5 to 9	33.5 to 33.8
	North Atlantic Deep Water	3 to 4	34.9 to 35.0
	Antarctic Deep Water	4.0	35.0
	North Atlantic Bottom Water	2.5 to 3.1	34.9
	Antarctic Bottom Water	-0.4	34.6

II. Stratification of the Water Column

A. General information

1. The world's oceans can be viewed as a stable, stratified system consisting of three main layers
   a. The surface layer extends from the sea surface down to approximately 200 m
   b. The base of this layer is delineated by the thermocline, the **halocline,** and the **pycnocline** (collectively referred to as the "clines"); these are zones that indicate major changes in ocean temperature, salinity, and density, respectively
   c. The middle layer extends from approximately 200 to 1,500 m and commonly is referred to as the pycnocline or main thermocline layer
   d. The deep layer extends from the base of the clines to the sea floor; this layer includes most of the ocean's volume
2. Stratification can change seasonally in ocean basins in the middle latitudes

    a. During summer months, high rates of solar radiation and gentle winds cause the sea surface to become very warm
        (1) A sharp temperature gradient develops between the sea surface and cooler, deeper water
        (2) This gradient, called a ***seasonal thermocline,*** generally develops between 50 and 200 m deep
    b. During winter months, less solar radiation and strong winds cool the sea surface and the seasonal thermocline decays, resulting in less stratification than in summer
  3. Stratification also varies with latitude
    a. At high latitudes, year-round cold atmospheric temperatures create cold sea-surface temperatures
        (1) Thermoclines are weak in polar and subpolar ocean basins because this cold surface water overlies cold, deep water
        (2) Consequently, the pycnocline is poorly developed or absent
        (3) As a result, stratification breaks down
    b. Thermoclines and pycnoclines are well developed at middle latitudes; thus, ocean basins in these latitudes are well stratified
    c. At low latitudes, strong solar radiation results in a warm and salty sea surface
        (1) Solar radiation evaporates water, leaving the salts behind
        (2) Extremely sharp thermoclines and haloclines develop, creating distinct pycnoclines
        (3) Tropical ocean basins are thus the most stratified ocean basins in the world
  4. Stratification limits vertical water movement
    a. Circulation largely is horizontal in well-stratified regions
    b. Recycled nutrients generally are trapped in the middle and deep layers
        (1) Sinking organic matter falls through the surface layer too quickly for appreciable amounts of recycling to occur there
        (2) As a result, nutrients are removed from the surface layer, and the nutrient concentrations in the surface layer remain low because of limited vertical water movement

B. Controls on vertical water movements
  1. The vertical movement of water affects oceanic basin circulation in three ways
    a. It diminishes stratification
    b. It transfers nutrients from deeper layers to the surface layer, where phytoplankton use them
    c. It recycles water throughout the world's oceans basins
  2. Vertical movement is controlled by four principal factors: wind-driven upwelling, zones of convergence and divergence, seasonal and latitudinal variations in solar radiation, and the sinking of water masses in polar regions
    a. Wind-driven upwelling generally is confined to the surface layer
        (1) Typically, water rises from the base to the top of the surface layer
        (2) Most wind-driven upwelling does not bring water up from the middle and deep layers of the ocean
    b. Zones of convergence and divergence, generated by Ekman transport, create regions of vertical movement that can extend down to approximately 1,000 m

  c. Seasonal and latitudinal variations in solar radiation, which affect the thermo-
    haline structure of ocean basins, may cause significant vertical mixing
    (1) Vertical mixing may result from the decay of a seasonal thermocline
    (2) If the pycnocline is poorly developed, as in polar latitudes, vertical move-
      ment readily occurs
  d. Vertical movement also occurs in response to the sinking of water masses in
    polar regions
    (1) To compensate for these sinking water masses, water rises elsewhere
    (2) This process is extraordinarily slow and widely diffused throughout the
      world's ocean basins

III. Formation and Movement of Water Masses

A. General information
  1. Most central water masses form in the open ocean as a result of the mixing be-
    tween water masses
  2. Intermediate, deep, and bottom water masses form at only a few locations around
    the world, including polar regions and several small ocean basins, such as the
    Mediterranean Sea
  3. In addition to the air-sea interactions that control temperature and salinity, water
    mass formation also is influenced by ocean basin depth, ocean basin geogra-
    phy, and the formation of sea ice
    a. In shallow basins, winds can vertically mix the water column and prevent
      stratification; thus, the entire water column can be continuously cooled via
      air-sea exchange
    b. In partially enclosed basins, the geometry of the basin can influence rates of
      water exchange between the basin and other oceans
    c. As ice forms from seawater in polar regions, the salinity and density of the re-
      maining water mass increase

B. The North Atlantic Ocean
  1. There are several small basins in the North Atlantic, including the Labrador, Nor-
    wegian, and Denmark basins
  2. Surface water in these basins is cooled by heat exchange from the sea surface to
    the air
  3. Salinities are relatively high because of seasonal ice formation
  4. The cold and relatively salty water sinks and accumulates behind submarine
    ridges at the entrances to these basins
    a. Water spills over these ridges into the North Atlantic
    b. This water mass is called North Atlantic Deep Water (NADW)
  5. NADW moves south and west through the North Atlantic into the South Atlantic
    a. Some NADW rises near Antarctica and contributes to the formation of Ant-
      arctic water masses
    b. Other NADW mixes with Antarctic waters and moves into the Indian Ocean
  6. The flow of NADW is influenced by submarine topography; for example, the mid-
    Atlantic ridge blocks NADW flow where the ridge rises up along the sea floor,
    thereby forcing water through passages in the ridge (such as fracture zones
    and transform faults)

C. Antarctica
1. During the winter, ice forms in the Weddell and Ross seas of Antarctica
   a. The remaining water becomes very cold and salty
   b. This water sinks and combines with other deep water to form Antarctic Bottom Water (AABW), the densest water mass in the world
2. AABW flows into adjacent ocean basins
3. AABW has been traced to northern middle latitudes in the Atlantic and Pacific Oceans
4. Submarine topography also affects the flow of AABW; for example, the mid-Atlantic ridge and Walvis ridge (which extends from the mid-Atlantic ridge to western Africa) block the flow of AABW to the eastern part of the South Atlantic
5. Antarctic Intermediate Water (AAIW) also forms around Antarctica and flows into all adjacent basins at a depth of approximately 1,000 m
   a. At approximately 55° C, cold northward-flowing surface water converges with warmer southward-flowing water
   b. Consequently, downwelling occurs
   c. The colder and denser water continues to flow northward and sinks below the warmer water

IV. Formation of Deep Currents

A. General information
1. The movement of water masses through ocean basins generates deep, relatively slow currents, with velocities typically ranging from 0.1 to 0.01 cm/second (wind-driven current velocities range from 1.0 to 10.0 cm/second)
2. The depths and slow velocities of these currents make them difficult to study
3. Submarine topography can greatly affect the velocities of deep-sea currents; for example, as a water mass moves through a narrow opening, current velocity increases
4. Thermohaline currents, like geostrophic currents, also are affected by the Coriolis effect; for example, as NADW flows southward in the North Atlantic, its trajectory is deflected to the right (westward)
   a. These currents are called western boundary undercurrents
   b. Henry Stommel first suggested the existence of these currents in 1955

B. Western boundary undercurrents
1. Thermohaline currents are intensified along the western sides of ocean basins
2. Since 1955, many studies have confirmed Stommel's model
   a. Many of these studies have been conducted in the North Atlantic, where an undercurrent flows below and in the opposite direction of the Gulf Stream
   b. Current measurements indicate that this undercurrent flows at approximately 1 to 20 cm/second (the Gulf Stream flows at approximately 200 cm/second at the sea surface)
   c. Sedimentary structures, such as ripple marks, along North America's continental margin indicate that the undercurrent erodes and deposits sediment parallel to the margin
      (1) Deposits created by this undercurrent are called *contourites* because the undercurrent follows depth contours

(2) *Turbidites* are deposits formed when turbidity currents flow downslope perpendicular to depth contours

V. Global Circulation

A. General information

1. Global circulation results from the interaction of thermohaline and wind-driven circulation systems
2. Water movement at depths of greater than 2,000 m is controlled primarily by thermohaline processes, whereas shallower water movement is controlled by wind-driven processes
3. In some ocean regions, interaction of the two circulation systems generates vertical water movements, such as zones of convergence and divergence
4. The interaction of these two systems can best be understood as an oceanic conveyor belt

B. Global conveyor belt

1. Developed by Wallace Broecker, the global conveyor belt model demonstrates how geostrophic currents interact with thermohaline processes
2. Starting in the North Atlantic, NADW forms at the surface and sinks, flowing southward along the western side of the Atlantic Ocean basin
3. In the South Atlantic, cold, deep water flows eastward through the Indian Ocean basin into the Pacific Ocean basin
4. Vertical water movement then drives the cold water toward the surface along the eastern sides of the Indian and Pacific Oceans
5. At the surface, water is warmed by solar radiation and transported via gyres
6. The Pacific and Indian Ocean gyres act as opposing gears, driving the warm surface water west toward Africa
7. The Agulhas Current, a major western boundary current off the coast of South Africa, transports the warm Indian Ocean water into the South Atlantic, where it becomes part of that gyre
8. The Atlantic gyres also act like opposing gears to drive warm surface water back to the North Atlantic
9. Scientists postulate that it takes about 1,000 years for a water parcel to travel along the entire belt
10. Although this model demonstrates many of the major elements of global circulation, it oversimplifies the processes
    a. For example, vertical water movements occur in all ocean basins and are pronounced in parts of the Indian and Pacific Oceans
    b. NADW also rises in the South Atlantic as a result of upwelling around Antarctica, contributing to AAIW formation
11. Nevertheless, this model serves to illustrate several important characteristics of global circulation
    a. Deep Pacific water masses are older than Atlantic and Indian water masses
    b. Deep-water circulation is driven by water mass formation in the polar regions
    c. Heat is transported from tropical to polar areas via ocean currents
    d. This heat transfer influences climate; for example, northern Europe is warmer than its latitude would dictate because of the heat contained in the North Atlantic

e. The world's oceans are relatively well mixed, a phenomenon that has important consequences for chemical oceanography (see Chapter 11, Biogeochemistry)

Study Activities

1. List the properties used to identify a water mass.
2. Contrast the different types of vertical water movement.
3. Describe how the world's oceans are stratified.
4. Based on Broecker's conveyor belt model, describe a path that a particle of water could take through the world's oceans.
5. List three ways in which thermohaline and wind-driven circulation processes interact.

10

Seawater Chemistry

Objectives

After studying this chapter, the reader should be able to:
- Explain the origin of seawater.
- Describe the molecular structure and chemical characteristics that make water unique.
- Relate the chemical and physical properties of water to physical, chemical, and biological oceanic phenomena.
- Define salinity and identify the major sea salts.
- Describe the effects of salinity on the chemical and physical properties of water.
- Describe the role that ice formation plays in physical and chemical oceanic phenomena.

I. Origin of Water

A. General information
    1. Water is the most abundant component of seawater (approximately 97%); the origin, chemical and physical characteristics, and global distribution of water are fundamentally important to marine chemistry
    2. Water can occur naturally in any one of three states (gas, liquid, and solid), depending on temperature and pressure
       a. The arrangement of molecules in each phase is distinct
          (1) In the gaseous phase (steam or water vapor), molecules move independently of each other
          (2) In the liquid phase, molecules bond to each other
             (a) However, the bonds that connect water molecules to each other are extremely weak — they constantly are breaking and reforming
             (b) This is why liquid water has the ability to flow
          (3) In the solid phase (ice), molecules are rigidly bonded into a fixed structure
       b. These different arrangements affect the density of water
          (1) Water vapor has the lowest density
          (2) Liquid water that has a temperature of 4° C (39.2° F) has the highest density
          (3) Ice has a density less than that of liquid water at 4° C
       c. The arrangements of molecules also reflect the *kinetic energy* (the energy of molecular motion) of each phase
          (1) Water vapor has the highest and ice the lowest amount of kinetic energy

      (2) Typically, the phase with the lowest amount of kinetic energy is densest because molecules are most tightly packed and motion is minimal

      (3) However, this generalization does not apply to water because of its distinctive molecular structure

B. Origin of the atmosphere and ocean

1. Water on the surface of the earth probably originated from the venting of gases from the planet's interior via volcanism
   a. Water that originated from the mantle is released as vapor during volcanic eruptions
   b. Some scientists believe that an alternative source of water may be comets consisting of ice, which originated from space
2. Based on analyses of volcanic rocks and meteorites, scientists estimate that approximately 0.5% of the mantle is water
   a. *Juvenile water* is water that never has been part of the atmosphere or ocean
   b. Scientists have calculated that only approximately 5% to 7% of the water in the mantle would have had to be released to account for all water in the hydrosphere
3. The sedimentary rock record indicates that oceans have existed for approximately the past 3.8 billion years of Earth's 4.5-billion-year history
   a. When water was released from the mantle during Earth's early history, the planet was probably too warm for it to remain liquid
   b. Thus, water vapor probably was an important component of Earth's early atmosphere
4. As the earth cooled, water condensed and fell from the atmosphere, accumulating in depressions formed by geologic and tectonic processes (for details about plate tectonics, see Chapter 3, Plate Tectonics)
5. These waters became salty as material dissolved in the water
   a. Water is a powerful solvent, or dissolving agent
   b. However, not all sea salts are derived originally from the chemical weathering of surface rocks
6. In 1951, William Rubey estimated the quantity of elements and compounds in the modern hydrosphere and in surface rocks
   a. He discovered that there were excessive amounts of some elements and compounds in the hydrosphere, compared with their presumed source (the earth's crust)
   b. He called these substances — which included carbon, chloride, nitrogen, sulfur, hydrogen, and water itself — *excess volatiles*
   c. For example, he found approximately 3.06×10^{22} g of chloride in the hydrosphere, yet only 5×10^{20} g of chloride in crustal rocks
   d. Rubey concluded that excess volatiles originated from the mantle by volcanism
   e. Geochemical studies done after 1951 support this hypothesis
7. The sedimentary rock record also indicates that seawater chemistry has not changed fundamentally during the last 1 billion years or so
   a. This concept is called the *steady state* or *kinetic principle*
   b. This principle states that elements and compounds dissolved in seawater cycle through the hydrosphere, lithosphere, and atmosphere in equilibrium

II. Distribution of Water

A. General information
1. Water can found in various reservoirs, including the hydrosphere, lithosphere, atmosphere, and organic matter
2. Of these, the hydrosphere is the most significant in oceanography
    a. The world's oceans contain approximately 97% of all water in the hydrosphere
    b. Glaciers contain approximately 2%
    c. Groundwater, lakes, and rivers contain approximately 1%
3. The movement of water among these reservoirs may take days or years
4. The *hydrologic cycle* is the model used by scientists to track water movement among the various reservoirs, and it illustrates that all water reservoirs ultimately are connected

B. Hydrologic cycle
1. Water is transported between the world's oceans and atmosphere by evaporation and precipitation
2. These processes also account for water movement between the atmosphere, lakes, and rivers
3. Water also is transported from land to the atmosphere by *transpiration,* the release of water vapor through the pores of plants
4. Water is transported from ocean to land by two major processes
    a. Water becomes part of marine sedimentary rocks that are uplifted by geologic and tectonic processes
    b. Ocean water evaporates, is transported through the atmosphere, and precipitates over land
5. Water is transported from land to ocean by two principal processes
    a. Rivers carry water to the sea
    b. Water percolates into the ground and then flows through the ground to the sea; this type of water is called *groundwater*
6. The rates of transfer and accumulation within specific reservoirs can change as a result of climatic conditions
    a. For example, approximately 20,000 years ago, Earth's climate was cooler than it is now, and water that evaporated from the ocean became trapped on land as glaciers
    b. Consequently, the volume of water in the ocean decreased and the sea level dropped

III. Molecular Structure of Water

A. General information
1. One water molecule consists of one oxygen and two hydrogen atoms
2. The hydrogen atoms are bound to the oxygen atom by a *covalent bond,* a bond that is formed when atoms share electrons
3. The angle formed by the hydrogen-oxygen-hydrogen atoms is approximately 105°

B. Dipolar characteristics
1. The oxygen atom has eight *electrons* (negatively charged particles)

    a. Two electrons occupy an inner ring and six occupy an outer ring around the oxygen nucleus

    b. Oxygen needs two additional electrons in its outer ring to be electrically stable

    c. Chemists refer to this condition as a *valence* of $^-2$

2. Hydrogen atoms have one electron in one ring around the nucleus; they have a valence of $^+1$

3. When two hydrogen atoms bond with one oxygen atom, the molecule contains 10 electrons

    a. The two electrons in the inner ring of the oxygen nucleus are stable

    b. Of the eight electrons in the outer ring, four are shared between oxygen and hydrogen atoms, while the other four are not shared

4. Electrons in the outer ring orient themselves as far apart as possible because like charges repel each other

    a. The four unshared electrons occupy one side of the oxygen atom

    b. The four shared electrons occupy the other side

5. Consequently, a water molecule has an uneven electron distribution pattern

    a. The oxygen end is negatively charged (as a result of its four unshared electrons)

    b. The hydrogen end is slightly positively charged (as a result of its four shared electrons)

6. The uneven charges cause the water molecule to act like a magnet; chemists call this type of molecule a *dipolar* molecule

7. The dipolar character of water causes the positive hydrogen ends to bond with the negative oxygen ends; this type of bonding is called **hydrogen bonding**

C. Chemical and physical properties of water

1. Although hydrogen bonds are relatively weak and are constantly forming and breaking, these bonds nevertheless are associated with energy

    a. As a result, water has several unique thermal properties

        (1) Because liquid water molecules have hydrogen bonds that must all be broken before the molecules can evaporate, liquid water molecules have higher boiling points than other, chemically similar compounds

        (2) Liquid water also has a higher freezing point than other similar compounds

            (a) Hydrogen bonds help to form a rigid, solid structure

            (b) Less heat needs to be removed from liquid water to make it a solid

        (3) Water has a high heat capacity, that is, the ability to store heat

            (a) Temperature is an indicator of the kinetic energy of molecules

            (b) Because of the hydrogen bonds, water molecules require more energy (heat) to increase the motion of water molecules a given amount

        (4) Water also has high latent heats of fusion and evaporation

            (a) Heat is required to break hydrogen bonds to change water from a solid to a liquid

            (b) Heat also is required to change water from a liquid to a gas

    b. Hydrogen bonds also affect other properties of water

        (1) Water has a high surface tension

            (a) Water molecules cluster together because of hydrogen bonding

(b) Thus, they form a relatively strong surface film; for example, razor blades do not break this film and can float on the water

(2) Water has a relatively high viscosity; the hydrogen bonds linking molecules together do not allow the molecules to flow past each other easily

(3) Water is not readily compressed; the hydrogen bonds support the molecules, and they cannot be pushed together easily

2. The dipolar character of water results in additional properties
   a. Water is an excellent solvent
      (1) The negatively charged oxygen end is attracted to positively charged parts of other molecules
      (2) The positively charged hydrogen end is attracted to negatively charged ends of other molecules
   b. Water also has a high dielectric constant
      (1) In an electrical field, water molecules orient themselves relative to the field
      (2) Hydrogen ends point toward the negative side of the field, while oxygen ends point toward the positive side of the field
      (3) This causes pure water to be a poor conductor of electricity

3. One of the most important consequences of all these properties for oceanography relates to water density
   a. As liquid water cools, molecules move more slowly and hydrogen bonds form
   b. At 4° C, molecules cluster together in closest proximity; thus, density is at a maximum
   c. As the temperature continues to decrease, more bonds form and the molecules form hexagonal clusters
      (1) These clusters are more organized and open than the irregular clusters formed at 4° C
      (2) Therefore, ice is less dense than liquid water at 4° C
   d. Ice's lower density prevents freshwater lakes from completely freezing solid; ice forms a layer at the surface, while denser, 4° C water lies below the ice

4. Water's capacity to store heat affects the weather, climate, and global heat transport
   a. Hurricanes gain energy from warm water
   b. Shore regions have more moderate climates than inland areas at the same latitude
   c. Ocean currents move warm water thousands of kilometers

5. Water's ability to dissolve compounds contributes to the creation of seawater
   a. The resultant dissolved ions, or solutes, are called *sea salts*
   b. Sea salts significantly alter some of the chemical and physical properties of water

IV. Seawater

A. General information
1. Seawater is water that contains four types of substances: solids (substances that can't pass through a 0.45 μm filter), colloids (substances that pass through a 0.45 μm filter but are not dissolved), dissolved solutes (sea salts), and dissolved gases

Major Sea Salts

The chart below lists the major sea salts (the major ions and compounds that are dissolved in seawater), the gram weight of their ions per kilogram of water, and their percentage by weight. The gram weight of ions per 1 kg of seawater, or g/kg, is represented in parts per thousand (ppt).

SALT	IONS IN SEAWATER (ppt)	IONS BY WEIGHT (%)
Chloride (Cl$^-$)	18.980	55.04
Sodium (Na$^+$)	10.556	30.61
Sulfate (SO$_4^{-2}$)	Unknown	Unknown
Magnesium (Mg+2)	1.272	3.69
Calcium (Ca+2)	0.400	1.16
Potassium (K+)	0.380	1.10
Bicarbonate (HCO3$^-$)	0.140	0.41
Bromide (Br$^-$)	0.065	0.19
Boric acid (H$_3$BO$_3$)	0.026	0.07
Strontium (Sr^{+2})	0.013	0.04
Fluoride (F$^-$)	0.001	0.00
Total	34.482	99.99

Adapted with permission from Sverdrup, H.U., Johnson, M.W., and Fleming, R.H. *The Oceans*. Englewood Cliffs, N.J.: Prentice-Hall, 1942 (renewed in 1970).

2. Sea salts can be further categorized according to their chemical reactivity
   a. *Conservative* sea salts are so named because their concentrations in seawater can change as a result of physical processes, such as two water masses mixing
   b. **Nonconservative** sea salts are so named because their concentrations change as a result of processes (such as biogeochemical reactions) occurring within a water mass
3. Several methods can be used to measure salt content
   a. One method is to evaporate seawater and weigh the remaining solids
      (1) This method is extremely inaccurate
      (2) Not all of the water is removed
      (3) Some water is lost because it combines with salts to form compounds
      (4) Some salts become gases and evaporate
   b. Another method is to measure each salt using chemical analyses
      (1) This method is almost impossible to do accurately because seawater contains about 80 elements and hundreds of compounds
      (2) Chemical reactions occur among the elements, compounds, and water, thus making chemical analyses more difficult
   c. A third method measures only the most important sea salts
      (1) Because 11 ions and compounds constitute nearly 100% of sea salts, scientists analyze seawater only for these ions and compounds (see *Major Sea Salts,* page 91)
      (2) Chemical and geological data indicate that the relative proportions of dissolved salts remain constant regardless of total salinity; this is

called ***Forchhammer's principle of constant proportions*** or ***Marcet's principle of constant proportions***

(3) However, this principle does not apply to certain types of water areas, including estuaries, restricted basins, polar regions where sea ice forms, and hydrothermal vents

(4) Because of this principle, only one of the 11 key ions and compounds needs to be measured; the rest can be determined from their relative proportions to the measured salt

(5) Chloride is the most abundant, conservative, and measurable ion, and chemists used chlorinity measurements to determine total salinity during the mid-1800s to the early 1960s

   (a) The method used to measure chlorinity was standardized by an international committee in 1899 and was named after the committee's chairman, Martin Knudsen

   (b) Chlorinity was determined by titrating a sample of seawater with a solution of silver nitrate

   (c) The chlorinity level was then determined using the following equation: Salinity = 1.80655 × chlorinity

d. In the early 1960s, Knudsen's titration method was supplanted by electrical measuring methods

   (1) Pure water is not conductive, but conductivity increases with increased salinity

   (2) An electrical device called a *salinometer* used the conductivity of a seawater sample to measure its salinity

   (3) Although salinometers were first used as laboratory instruments, technological advances during the 1960s led to the development of a device called a *conductivity-temperature-depth (CTD) sensor,* which directly measures conductivity in the ocean

   (4) Today, most salinity measurements are done with CTDs

4. Salinity has historically been measured in parts per thousand

   a. Because the measurement of salinity now is based on electrical conductivity, chemists do not use a unit of measure for conductivity

   b. A sample's conductivity is compared to the known conductivity of a standard and expressed as a ratio

5. Forchhammer's principle is supported by the steady state or kinetic principle

   a. The *steady state principle* states that the rates of input and output of sea salts are in equilibrium

   b. The time that an ion spends in the ocean is referred to as its ***residence time***

   (1) Residence time can be expressed as the equation: residence time = total amount of dissolved ion ÷ the rate of ion input or output

   (2) Residence times of conservative ions are extremely long (for example, sodium has a residence time of 8.3×10^7 years)

   (3) Residence times for nonconservative ions are relatively short (for example, aluminum has a residence time of 6.2×10^2 years)

   (4) The mixing time of the world's oceans is approximately 1,000 years

   (5) Compared with the residence times of major ions (millions of years), seawater is mixed many times over before specific salts react chemically

   (6) Long residence times and the relatively rapid mixing of the world's oceans indicate that the ocean is chemically homogeneous

      (a) Thus, concentrations of ions remain constant relative to each other

      (b) However, the total amount of sea salts can vary, depending on physical processes, such as freshwater input or evaporation

B. Constituents of sea salts

1. The two most abundant sea salts, sodium and chloride, are conservative and, consequently, have long residence times
2. Calcium, potassium, bicarbonate, and some of the other major ions are nonconservative and, consequently, have relatively short residence times
3. Many other ions and compounds are biochemically important even though their concentrations are very low
    a. For example, plants use compounds of nitrogen, phosphorus, and silicon
    b. However, these nutrients are present in seawater in concentrations of parts per million
4. The low concentrations of nutrients in seawater reflect a delicate oceanic chemical balance
    a. For example, if excess nitrates or phosphates are introduced into a small basin by urban or agricultural runoff, marine plants grow and reproduce much more rapidly
    b. Eventually, the plants die and their decomposition consumes oxygen
    c. Fish may die because of the lack of oxygenated water
5. Some dissolved gases, such as oxygen and carbon dioxide, also play an important role in biogeochemical processes
6. Several conservative gases, including argon, neon, and helium, also are found in seawater
7. Nitrogen is the most abundant gas in seawater
    a. Its chemical behavior is not wholly conservative or wholly nonconservative
    b. Most marine plants cannot utilize elemental nitrogen, so it is relatively conservative
    c. Nevertheless, some cyanobacteria can use nitrogen
8. Many elements have concentrations between 1 part per million and 1 part per billion; these elements are called *trace elements*
    a. Although trace elements are present in very small concentrations, some are biogeochemically or economically important
    b. For example, manganese, a mineral required for the commercial production of steel, is the principal component of manganese nodules scattered on the ocean floor

C. Effects of salinity on water

1. Sea salts decrease the freezing point of water; seawater with an average salinity of 35 has a freezing point of approximately 1.91° C (35.4° F)
2. Increasing salinity increases water's boiling point
3. Density increases with increasing salinity
    a. An average parcel of seawater has a density of approximately 1.02412 g/cm^3 at 25° C (77° F)
    b. The average density of pure water is 1.0029 g/cm^3 at 25° C
4. Temperature of maximum density decreases with increasing salinity
    a. At a salinity of 24.7, the temperature of maximum density equals the temperature of freezing
    b. Theoretically, cubes of frozen seawater should sink in the ocean

(1) However, the ice formed from seawater is fresh and does not include salts

(2) Thus, ice is less dense than seawater and floats

5. Vapor pressure decreases as salinity increases

6. Osmotic pressure, viscosity, surface tension, and velocity of sound increase as salinity increases

V. Gases in Seawater

A. General information

1. The concentrations of gases in seawater are controlled by biological (photosynthesis, respiration, and decomposition), physical (temperature and pressure), and chemical (salinity) factors

2. Concentrations of gases dissolved in seawater are different from those in air

3. Generally, gases dissolve more readily in cold water than in warm water and in freshwater than in seawater

B. Oxygen

1. Dissolved oxygen accounts for 36% of the dissolved gas in seawater

2. Oxygen distribution is controlled primarily by biological activity

   a. Surface waters are enriched with oxygen, a byproduct of marine plant photosynthesis

   b. **An oxygen minimum zone** starts at a depth of approximately 500 to 1,000 m, reflecting increased oxygen uptake for respiration and for decomposition of sinking organic matter

   c. Generally, the oxygen minimum zone corresponds in depth to the pycnocline (for details about pycnocline, see Chapter 5, Global Processes)

   d. Oxygen concentration increases with depth because of diminished biological activity and oxygen-rich, deep waters below the oxygen minimum zone

      (1) Deep waters are cold and oxygen is more soluble in colder waters

      (2) Deep waters become saturated with oxygen because of vigorous air-sea interactions at their time of origin in polar seas

3. In some ocean basins, deep-water circulation is restricted and oxygen-rich water cannot flow into the basins

   a. Oxygen that enters the water column at the surface is used in biological activity

   b. Thus, the deep water becomes *anoxic,* or lacking in dissolved oxygen

   c. Anoxic conditions are common in bays and several large marginal seas, such as the Black sea

   d. Anoxic conditions significantly limit marine life

C. Carbon dioxide

1. Although carbon dioxide is not the most abundant gas dissolved in seawater, it strongly affects marine chemistry

2. Carbon dioxide enters the ocean via air-sea interactions

3. Once dissolved in water, carbon dioxide reacts with water and forms a weak acid called carbonic acid

4. Carbonic acid, which is relatively unstable in seawater, reacts with water to form bicarbonate ions

5. Bicarbonate ions, in turn, react with water to form carbonate ions
6. These reactions are controlled by many factors, such as temperature, pressure, and biological activity
7. All of these reactions and factors constitute the carbon-carbonate system, which controls the pH of the oceans
    a. pH measures the amount of hydrogen ions in a given solution; a solution may be acidic (an excess of hydrogen ions represented by a pH less than 7), alkaline (an excess of hydroxide ions represented by a pH greater than 7), or neutral (balance between hydrogen and hydroxide ions represented by pH of 7)
    b. Seawater generally has a pH between 7.5 and 8.5 and therefore is alkaline
    c. The carbon-carbonate system controls the deposition of calcium carbonate sediments by dictating the level of the *carbonate compensation depth (CCD)*

VI. Sea Ice

A. General information
1. Ice forms from seawater when the water temperature goes below the freezing point associated with the specific salinity of the water
2. Sea salts do not physically fit into the hexagonal ice structure
3. When typical seawater (with a salinity of 34) freezes, the ice contains purer water and less salts (salinity is about 5 to 10)
    a. The salts, which are not incorporated into the ice, increase the salinity of the remaining water and generate increasingly salty water
    b. As salinity in the remaining water increases, the water's freezing point lowers, thereby allowing the water to become colder before it freezes
4. Sea ice formation undergoes several distinct stages: first, spicules (ice needles) form, then ice sheets (nilas), and finally pancake ice

B. Effects of sea-ice formation
1. Sea ice consistently forms thick sheets along the continental margin of Antarctica
    a. Water becomes extremely cold beneath these ice sheets
    b. This water is the start of Antarctic Bottom Water
    c. The water sinks to the shelf floor, flows down the continental slope, mixes with other deep water, and then flows seaward into surrounding ocean basins (thermohaline circulation)
2. In the central part of the Arctic Ocean basin, sea ice is permanent and expands seasonally around the basin's margin
    a. High-salinity water accumulates as a result of ice formation
        (1) This water then flows into smaller border basins, such as the Norwegian Sea
        (2) There, it mixes with and increases the salinity of *in situ* water (water that is in the original position); in this case, the in situ water refers to the water in the smaller border basins
    b. The resultant water is North Atlantic Deep Water

Study Activities

1. Describe how the ocean became salty early in the earth's history.
2. List the physical and chemical characteristics that make water unique.
3. Describe three oceanographic phenomena controlled by the chemical and physical properties of seawater.
4. Describe an area of the ocean where conductivity might not accurately reflect its salinity.
5. List four effects that salinity has on the chemical and physical properties of water.
6. Explain how ice formation in Antarctica influences thermohaline circulation.

11

Biogeochemistry

Objectives

After studying this chapter, the reader should be able to:
- Describe nutrient cycles in the ocean.
- Explain how oceanographic processes control the concentrations of nutrients.
- Describe the role of hydrothermal circulation in marine chemistry.
- Explain how chemical processes influence deep-sea sedimentation.

I. Nutrients

A. General information

1. Nutrients can be classified according to plant requirements
   a. Macronutrients, including nitrogen, phosphorus, and silicon compounds, are needed by plants in large quantities
   b. Micronutrients, including iron, cobalt, and zinc, are needed by plants in small amounts but are vital to growth
2. Nutrients enter the ocean through land runoff, wind transportation of particles, rain, recycling within the water column, submarine volcanic activity, and seawater-sediment exchanges
3. Runoff from land and water column recycling are the most significant sources of nutrients
4. Nutrients are recycled by two principal processes: animal excretion and decomposition
5. Nutrients are not distributed evenly throughout the water column
   a. The surface layer has relatively low nutrient concentrations
      (1) Solar radiation promotes **photosynthesis** in this layer
      (2) Photosynthesis utilizes all available nutrients in this layer
   b. The pycnocline generally has the highest nutrient concentration
      (1) This occurs because of the recycling associated with the decomposition of sinking organic matter
      (2) A nutrient maximum generally corresponds with an oxygen minimum zone
   c. Below the pycnocline, nutrient concentrations tend to be vertically uniform, with slightly lower nutrient concentrations than the overlying oxygen minimum zone
      (1) Nutrients are concentrated in the deep ocean because of continuous sinking of organic particles and detritus

(2) This results in a progressive downward movement of nutrients
6. The rapid change in nutrients between the surface layer and the pycnocline is called the **nutricline**
7. Nutrient concentrations also change from ocean basin to ocean basin
   a. Pacific deep waters are older than Atlantic deep waters because of thermohaline circulation
   b. Pacific waters contain more dissolved phosphate and carbon dioxide and less dissolved oxygen than Atlantic waters because biochemical processes have more time to recycle nutrients in Pacific deep waters than in Atlantic waters
8. Nutrient concentrations also change seasonally in middle-latitude ocean basins
   a. During the spring, runoff from land increases as a result of snow melt and increased solar radiation
      (1) Consequently, more nutrients are available in the water column
      (2) Just as on land, primary producers then generate a **spring bloom**
   b. During the summer, nutrient concentrations are lower because of the development of a **seasonal thermocline** that limits vertical mixing, spring productivity has stripped the surface layer of nutrients, and few nutrients are available (although solar radiation is at its peak)
   c. During the fall, nutrients from organic matter are recycled back to the surface because the seasonal thermocline wanes; consequently, another period of relatively high primary production occurs
   d. During the winter, nutrients are distributed more evenly throughout the water column and vertical mixing increases as a result of strong winds and no seasonal thermocline; however, the lack of solar radiation limits primary production
9. Depending on climate, physical oceanographic processes, and biological processes, temporal changes in nutrient concentrations also may occur in other latitudinal zones

B. Macronutrients
1. Chemical analyses of macronutrients in seawater and organic matter indicate that their relative ratios are similar
   a. The carbon-nitrogen-phosphorus ratio is approximately 105:15:1
   b. This ratio is called the *Redfield ratio,* after marine scientist Alfred Redfield, who first described it
2. The Redfield ratio indicates that plants require much more carbon than nitrogen or phosphorus
3. Because seawater is rich in carbon (in the form of bicarbonate ions), nitrogen and phosphorus are the nutrients that limit marine plant growth
4. Silica is the limiting nutrient for some phytoplankton that produce siliceous shells, such as diatoms; the silica-carbon-nitrogen-phosphorus ratio is approximately 40:105:15:1
5. Nitrogen occurs primarily in four forms: molecular nitrogen (N_2) and the three nitrogen compounds (nitrate, nitrite, and ammonia)
   a. Most plants use these nitrogen compounds for growth because they cannot process molecular nitrogen
   b. Bacteria, such as cyanobacteria, use molecular nitrogen; they transform it into compounds that are more readily used by phytoplankton

    c. Nitrogen is essential to flora because it is a primary component of amino acids, the building blocks of proteins

6. Phosphorus occurs in seawater in both dissolved and particulate forms
    a. The principal dissolved phosphorus compound is phosphate, which can be used by phytoplankton
    b. Phosphorus is an essential constituent of some enzymes and adenosine triphosphate (ATP)

7. Silicon also occurs in seawater in both dissolved and particulate forms
    a. The most common dissolved form is the silicate ion
    b. Silicate is essential for the growth of specific groups of marine flora

II. Hydrothermal Circulation

A. General information

1. Seawater circulates through cracks in the sea floor (see *Hydrothermal Vents,* page 100)
    a. Chemical reactions occur as the water passes through sediment and **basalt** in layers of oceanic crust
    b. These reactions affect both local and global geochemistry

2. Hydrothermal circulation was first proposed during the 1960s but was not directly observed until 1977

3. Hydrothermal circulation has been directly observed at only a few sites along divergent plate boundaries, but scientists believe that it is common

4. Seawater with a temperature of approximately 2° C (35.6° F) enters the sea floor and penetrates it to a depth of approximately 1 to 3 km

5. As the seawater is warmed by surrounding hot rocks, its density decreases and the water rises, thereby creating a convection cell

6. The water then exits hydrothermal vents at temperatures of up to 400° C (752° F)

7. Three types of vents have been identified based on their temperature
    a. *Warm-water vents* are vents with water temperatures between 2° C and 25° C (77° F)
    b. *White smokers* are vents with temperatures between 25° C and 270° C (518° F)
    c. *Black smokers* are vents with temperatures between 270° C and 400° C

8. The venting hot water is not converted into steam because the high hydrostatic pressure increases its boiling point

9. Based on isotopic and heat-flow data, scientists estimate that the total volume of the world's oceans circulates through hydrothermal systems every 5 to 11 million years

10. Individual hydrothermal vents probably exist only for tens of years before becoming blocked by minerals precipitated in the cracks

11. Despite their limited life and the extremely limited amount of available data, scientists hypothesize that hydrothermal circulation plays a major role in global fluxes of elements and compounds into and out of the oceans

B. Geochemistry

1. Geochemical reactions take place as seawater percolates down into oceanic crust, rises up through the crust, and vents back into the ocean

Hydrothermal Vents

The diagram below shows how cold seawater seeps through fissures in the sea floor, is heated by deeper rocks, and then rises to the sea floor via hydrothermal vents. Hydrothermal vents also are involved in the precipitation of authigenous sediments.

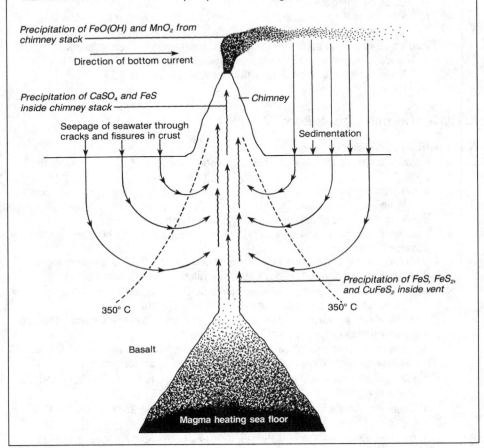

2. Reactions within the crust take place at high temperatures and involve basalt in the crust
   a. Metals are leached from the basalt
   b. Minerals are precipitated from the fractures
3. As water seeps out of vents, several important reactions occur
   a. Sulfur, copper, and zinc compounds are precipitated
   b. Hydrothermal circulation appears to be a major site of sulfur and magnesium formation
   c. Because some metal-rich precipitates are black, black smoke appears to emanate from the vents
   d. Carbon dioxide, silicon, hydrogen, and manganese also are released into the ocean
   e. Trace quantities of calcium, potassium, barium, lithium, and rubidium also are released

4. The presence of some of these elements answers long-term questions about their sources in the ocean
   a. For example, manganese occurs in minute concentrations in seawater
   b. Nevertheless, manganese nodules form on many abyssal plains
   c. Scientists believe that the outflow of manganese from hydrothermal circulation is large enough to account for the nodules

C. Chemosynthesis
1. Hydrothermal circulation also significantly affects deep-sea biology
2. When vents were first discovered near the Galápagos Islands in 1977, their most striking characteristic was the community of clams, mussels, crabs, and worms gathered around the vents
3. These organisms thrived at approximately 2,500 m below sea level, a depth normally too deep for such diverse and prolific communities
4. Studies performed since 1977 have shown that vent communities are based on a form of primary production completely different from that found at the sea surface
   a. Bacteria in the gut of large tube worms and on the gills of some mollusks, including clams and mussels, use sulfur compounds for energy to make organic matter
   b. This process is called *chemosynthesis*
5. Chemosynthesis also occurs in swamps, *anoxic* sediments (those that lack oxygen), and the water column
6. Scientists now speculate that life may have begun at hydrothermal vents

III. Sediment Geochemistry

A. General information
1. Seawater chemistry, which is affected by chemical, biological, and geological phenomena, controls biogenous and authigenous sedimentation
2. Seawater chemistry also influences lithogenous sediments (notably clay minerals)

B. Biogenous and authigenous sedimentation
1. All seawater is undersaturated with silica — it can hold more dissolved silica than the amount that presently is dissolved
2. Siliceous oozes accumulate only on those parts of the sea floor where high rates of biological productivity exist in the overlying water column
3. Surface water is saturated with calcium carbonate
4. Deep waters are undersaturated with calcium carbonate because of the effects of temperature, pressure, dissolved carbon dioxide, pH, and other factors
5. The *carbonate compensation depth (CCD)* reflects the boundary between the saturated and undersaturated waters (see Chapter 4, Marine Sediments)
6. Controls on the CCD are very complex
   a. For example, the amount of carbon dioxide gas dissolved in seawater will influence the acidity of seawater
   b. This affects how much calcium carbonate can then be dissolved (dissolved carbon dioxide makes seawater acidic; calcium carbonate is readily dissolved in acidic conditions)

c. Rates of calcium carbonate sedimentation further influence the amount of dissolved carbonate because sedimentation removes carbonate from seawater
7. Geochemists currently are reevaluating the effects of organic and inorganic chemical processes on authigenous sedimentation
   a. Historically, scientists thought that such sediments form primarily by inorganic chemical processes
   b. Geochemists now think that these sediments form via biological (especially microbial) processes

C. Lithogenous sediments

1. Most deep-sea clays are generated by the chemical and physical weathering processes that break down and alter granite on land
2. Some clays (such as montmorillonite) are produced by the alteration of basalt on land and in water
3. Other clays also may be generated by a theoretical process called reverse weathering
   a. In reverse weathering, seawater reacts with deep-sea clays
   b. Some cations and anions in seawater are then incorporated into new clay minerals
   c. The rates of reverse weathering are so slow that they are difficult to evaluate in laboratory studies
   d. Reverse weathering also can remove hydroxide ions (thus influencing seawater alkalinity), dissolved silicon, and potassium by generating aluminosilicate minerals (for example, glauconite)

Study Activities

1. List the major deposits, sources, and pathways of nitrogen, phosphate, and silica in the ocean.
2. Explain the factors that control nutrient concentrations.
3. Describe a hydrothermal vent and its associated geochemical and biological processes.
4. Explain reverse weathering and its importance in global biogeochemical processes.

12

Primary Production

Objectives

After studying this chapter, the reader should be able to:
- Identify the factors that control primary production in the ocean.
- Describe how the balance of light and nutrients controls primary production.
- Describe how primary production varies with depth, location, and season.
- Explain possible pathways for energy transfer in different regions in the ocean.
- Describe the controls on primary production in different areas of the ocean.

I. Primary Production in the Ocean

A. General information
1. Light energy in the sea is used by photosynthetic organisms to synthesize complex, high-energy organic molecules from carbon dioxide, water, and nutrients
2. Marine *photosynthesis* is the most important type of primary production in the ocean
3. Marine photosynthesis is the same process as photosynthesis found in terrestrial systems
4. Unlike the large plants most commonly seen in terrestrial systems, small planktonic plants and algae carry out most of the primary production in the oceans
5. Other forms of primary production, such as chemosynthesis, are important only in limited areas and contribute relatively little to the oceanic primary production budget
6. Photosynthesis is limited by a number of physical and biological factors, resulting in an uneven distribution of primary productivity, and therefore of life, in the ocean

B. Primary production
1. Primary production is the synthesis of organic matter, such as carbohydrates, from inorganic compounds, carbon dioxide, and water, using energy derived from solar radiation or chemical reactions
2. *Gross primary production* is the amount of carbon fixed into high-energy compounds by *autotrophic organisms*
3. *Net primary production* is what remains after respiration (the basic metabolic needs of the organism) is subtracted from gross primary production
4. The carbon fixed by primary production has five fates

a. It becomes organic matter that is broken down by the respiratory metabolism of the primary producer itself
b. It is incorporated into the tissues of the primary producer; this is the definition of *growth*
c. It is incorporated into the body tissues of primary producers and then eaten by herbivores
d. It is expended by the primary producers as energy on reproduction
e. Some compounds may leak into surrounding water, joining a pool of dissolved organic substances; this leakage accounts for 5% to 15% of gross primary production

C. Photosynthesis
1. Photosynthesis captures most of the energy that is used by life in the oceans
2. Photosynthesis is the synthetic fixation of carbon by autotrophic organisms using light as an energy source, water as a hydrogen donor and liberating oxygen
3. The unbalanced photosynthetic reaction is $CO_2 + 2\ H_2O \leftrightarrow C_6H_{12}O_6 + O_2 + H_2O$ (carbon dioxide plus water with energy from light are combined to produce complex carbohydrates and oxygen)
4. *Respiration,* the combination of fixed carbon and oxygen with water and carbon dioxide as products, is the reverse of photosynthesis
5. Plants undergo photosynthesis and respiration; animals, respiration only
6. Small, freely floating phytoplankton are the most important photosynthesizers in the ocean; large benthic plants, such as benthic seaweeds or kelp, play only a minor role
7. Although oceanic primary producers commonly are microscopic, they are widely scattered throughout a large volume of water and represent the largest biomass in the ocean

II. Factors Controlling Primary Production

A. General information
1. The rate of primary production is very low in much of the ocean, although there are small areas of very high production
2. Four factors control the rate of primary production in the ocean: light, mixing, nutrient availability, and herbivore grazing
3. The balance of these four factors controls the geographic and seasonal distribution of primary productivity

B. Light in the ocean
1. Photosynthesis requires light energy from solar radiation
   a. The quality and quantity of light are controlled by the intensity of solar radiation at the sea surface, which varies with season, latitude, and time of day, and by the amount of suspended particles and dissolved organic matter in the water
   b. Light is absorbed and scattered by water molecules, suspended particles, and organic material dissolved in the water
2. The depth to which light penetrates varies from a few meters in coastal waters to about 100 m in open ocean waters

a. Light penetration is deepest in clear waters found in central gyre areas, where there is little plant life or dissolved and suspended material
b. Only 10% of incident light penetrates to 75 m in the clearest ocean water; only about 1% of light from the surface remains at 150 m
c. In the clearest ocean water, all light from the surface is extinguished by 1,000 m
d. Light penetration is most shallow in coastal waters with high coastal runoff (light is absorbed and scattered by material dissolved and suspended in runoff and river water) and dense populations of phytoplankton
e. Light from the surface may be completely extinguished below a depth of a few meters in coastal waters
3. The absorption of different wavelengths of light, or color, is not uniform in seawater
a. Infrared and red, the longer wavelengths of visible light, are absorbed in the upper few meters of clear open ocean water
b. Blue and blue-green, the shorter wavelengths of visible light, penetrate to the greatest depth in the ocean
4. In general, light limits photosynthesis to a maximum depth of 150 m in the clearest ocean water

C. Light and depth zones
1. The ocean has been divided into biologically significant depth zones based on the amount of light available at those depths
a. The **euphotic zone** is the region in which there is sufficient light for photosynthesis (the depth to which 1% of incident light penetrates)
b. The **dysphotic zone** is the region in which light is insufficient for photosynthesis but is sufficient for animal responses (less than 1% of incident light)
c. The **aphotic zone** is the region in which there is no light of biological significance available from the surface
2. The actual depth ranges for each zone vary with location and time of year

D. General relationship of light and photosynthetic production
1. The rate of photosynthesis varies with the amount of light available; this relationship can be described by the *photosynthetic curve*
2. The rate of photosynthesis is zero when there is no light, although plants and alga continue to use oxygen by respiration to meet metabolic demands
3. The rate of photosynthesis initially increases linearly with increasing light
a. The rate of photosynthesis (P) is proportional to light intensity (I) during this phase
b. The amount of available light limits the rate of photosynthesis during this limiting phase
4. As light continues to increase, the rate of increase of photosynthesis declines and levels off (reaching a maximum), then decreases as light increases further
5. This maximum rate at which a particular plant or alga can photosynthesize, regardless of the amount of available light, is its *photosynthetic maximum* (P_{max}) — the point at which the biochemical mechanisms of photosynthesis are saturated with light
6. *Photoinhibition,* a decline in the rate of photosynthesis at high light levels, results from high ultraviolet light intensity and the overflow of excess light energy into oxidation processes (photo-oxidation)

7. The rate of organic materials leaking from the cell increases during photoinhibition, sometimes reaching 90% of the cell's production
8. The two most important properties of the photosynthetic curve are the slope of the initial linear section of the curve (measured by $\Delta P/\Delta I$), which determines the efficiency of the organism in using low intensity light, and the P_{max}, which indicates the optimum amount of light for photosynthesis by that plant or alga
9. Plants and algae can modify aspects of their biochemical response to light; these modifications are reflected in their slope and P_{max}
   a. Different taxonomic groups of marine algae have different characteristic photosynthetic curves
   b. Dinoflagellates, for example, found in the well-lit open ocean, are better adapted for high levels of light
   c. Brown and red algae that live attached to the bottom in shallow waters are adapted to low light levels
   d. Diatoms, found in coastal waters, are adapted to an intermediate amount of light
10. The rate of respiration, however, is relatively constant in varying amounts of light
    a. When rates of respiration and photosynthesis of an individual phytoplankton cell are plotted on the same graph, there is a point at which photosynthetic production and respiratory dissipation are equal
    b. This point, called the **compensation point,** represents a balance in the cell between the creation of new material via photosynthesis and the expenditure of these resources via respiration
11. A wide range of light-absorbing pigments permits different phytoplankton groups to capture specific wavelengths
    a. *Photosynthetically active radiation (PAR),* light of wavelengths from 400 to 720 nanometers (nm), powers photosynthesis
    b. Light is absorbed by a variety of photosynthetic pigments in plants and algae, each of which is specialized for a narrow range of wavelengths
       (1) These pigments are responsible for the characteristic colors of phytoplankton and other algae
       (2) Chlorophyll *a* is the most important photosynthetic pigment, with peak light absorption at 670 to 695 nm
       (3) Phytoplankton possess many additional photosynthetic pigments that are most active in other regions of the photosynthetically active spectrum, particularly at shorter wavelengths
    c. This allows phytoplankton to adapt to a wide range of light regimes
    d. The photosynthetic capability of a species can be characterized by an *action spectrum,* those wavelengths of light used most efficiently by that species for photosynthesis
12. Photosynthesis varies with ocean depth
    a. Light intensity in the ocean quickly decreases with increasing depth; consequently, the rate of photosynthesis and amount of primary production also decrease with increasing depth
    b. The generalized shape of the photosynthetic curve may be observed in the water column
       (1) A zone of near-surface photoinhibition caused by high light intensity results in decreased photosynthesis in the upper few meters
       (2) Maximum photosynthesis (P_{max}) occurs at a relatively shallow depth
       (3) Below that depth, light becomes limiting and photosynthesis decreases

    c. The depth at which light limits photosynthesis for an individual cell to the rate
       at which that cell respires occurs at the compensation point of that cell
         (1) Individual phytoplankton cells grow and multiply at depths above the com-
             pensation point (the cells create more energy via photosynthesis than
             they spend on respiration)
         (2) At depths below the compensation point, phytoplankton subsist on ac-
             cumulated reserves, form inactive resting bodies, or starve; there is a
             net loss of energy for that cell
         (3) The depth of the compensation point for an individual cell varies with light
             intensity in the water column and the species of phytoplankton
    d. One method for measuring primary production in the water column has been
       through the use of light and dark bottles to incubate phytoplankton cells at
       different depths in the water column
         (1) Seawater is collected from a series of depths, then put in pairs of clear
             (light) and opaque (dark) bottles and returned to the depth from which
             it was obtained and incubated for a few hours
         (2) Changes in these samples' oxygen concentration over time are used to
             calculate rates of photosynthesis and respiration
         (3) An increase in oxygen concentration in the clear bottles above the com-
             pensation point represents net photosynthesis (an excess of gross
             production over respiration)
         (4) A decrease in oxygen in the opaque bottles represents respiration (res-
             piration in the absence of photosynthesis)
         (5) A decrease in oxygen in the clear bottles represents the use of oxygen
             by respiration at a greater rate than it can be replaced by photosynthe-
             sis
         (6) The compensation depth for these cells is the depth at which there is no
             change in oxygen concentration (oxygen is produced by photosynthe-
             sis at the same rate at which it is used in respiration)
    e. The compensation point typically is estimated to be found at the depth to
       which 1% of surface light penetrates
13. The *critical depth* is the water column depth at which the sum of photosynthesis
    equals the sum of respiration for the entire water column
    a. While the compensation point is important for an individual phytoplankton
       cell, the depth at which the critical point occurs controls primary produc-
       tion for all phytoplankton occupying that area
    b. If the critical depth is greater than the depth to which phytoplankton cells are
       mixed by turbulence in the water, the phytoplankton cells will have enough
       light to maintain an excess of photosynthesis over respiration; there is a
       net gain in production for the water column
    c. If the critical depth is less than the depth of mixing, the phytoplankton will be
       pushed below the depth at which there is enough light for net production;
       there is a net loss for the water column
14. Light penetration and the critical depth vary with season and latitude
    a. In temperate and polar latitudes, more light is available in summer, less light
       in winter; the critical point is deeper in summer than in winter
    b. There is more — and more consistent — light in the tropics over 1 year; the
       critical depth varies little with season

E. Mixing
1. Wind-driven turbulence may reach depths of 200 m, resulting in a well-mixed upper layer with consistent temperature, salinity, and density characteristics
2. Phytoplankton cells, which lack the ability to swim, will circulate through the water column to the depth of the wind-mixed layer
3. Wind-driven mixing varies geographically and temporally
   a. Coastal and polar areas have higher mixing
   b. Temperate and polar areas have higher mixing during the winter because of winter storms and a corresponding breakdown of the stratification that exists during the summer
4. Net production is possible only when the depth of the mixed layer is shallower than the critical point, resulting in net production by the phytoplankton throughout the range of mixing
5. If the mixed layer extends below the critical point, as is the case during the winter in temperate zones, average light intensity is not sufficient for net production

F. Nutrient availability
1. Other elements besides carbon, hydrogen, and oxygen are necessary for photosynthesis
2. These elements are the building blocks of proteins, enzymes, and other biologically necessary molecules
   a. *Macronutrients,* such as sulfur, magnesium, potassium, nitrogen, phosphorus, and silicon, are needed in large quantities
   b. *Micronutrients,* which include most other elements, are needed in trace quantities
3. With the general exceptions of nitrogen, phosphorus, silicon, and possibly iron, most of these materials are available in seawater in excess of what is needed for phytoplankton growth
4. Low nutrient concentrations, like low light intensity, can limit photosynthesis
   a. When expressed as a graph, the response curve of phytoplankton cells to increasing nutrient concentrations, as measured by the uptake of that nutrient by the cell, is similar to the relationship of photosynthesis and light
   b. The uptake of nutrients is proportional to the concentration of that nutrient at low nutrient concentrations; the higher the nutrient concentration, the more quickly the phytoplankton cells take it up
   c. A plateau in nutrient uptake is reached at higher nutrient concentrations, as uptake mechanisms reach saturation
   d. Nutrient uptake is an active process that can take place against a concentration gradient but nevertheless requires a sufficient concentration of that nutrient in seawater
5. Nutrient distribution in the ocean is not uniform, and concentrations vary with location and season
6. As with light, various plankton groups have widely differing rates of nutrient uptake; some require high levels of nutrients in water, while others are better adapted to low concentrations
7. Not all forms of these elements are useful to life
   a. For example, elemental nitrogen that occurs in the atmosphere cannot be taken up by most plants, whereas ammonium, nitrate, and nitrite are useful to plants

b. Only certain cyanobacteria and bacteria have the ability to convert *(fix)* elemental nitrogen to the biologically available forms of nitrogen; these organisms are called *nitrogen fixers*
8. Nutrients, particularly the biologically available forms of nitrogen and phosphorus, may limit phytoplankton productivity when in low concentrations in seawater
9. Biologically available nitrogen and phosphorus and possibly iron are rapidly taken up from surface waters by the phytoplankton
10. Surface waters become nutrient depleted in areas without nutrient replenishment
11. Nutrients may be resupplied to surface waters from the bottom (in areas where the mixed layer reaches the bottom) and from nutrient-rich, deeper waters (although, in most areas of the open ocean, surface waters are isolated from deeper waters by the pycnocline)
12. Upwelling causes deep waters to rise to the surface from depths of 50 to 300 m (for a discussion of upwelling, see Chapter 8, Wind-Driven Circulation)
    a. The deep water was formed at the surface in nutrient-rich polar areas and then sank into the deep ocean basins
    b. These deep waters have high nutrient concentrations because light is insufficient for photosynthesis at these depths, with the result that no photosynthetic plants or algae have depleted the nutrients
    c. The replenishment of nutrient-rich waters to well-lit surface waters enhances the conditions for photosynthesis and life
13. Primary production generally follows nutrient availability; for example, primary production is highest in areas of upwelling, where there is an influx of nutrients into well-lit surface waters
14. Although measured nutrient concentrations in seawater may be very low, the individual phytoplankton may not interact with their physical environment in the same way as do scientists' instruments
    a. Zooplankton excretions, which are high in nutrients, may fuel the system
    b. Phytoplankton rapidly take up these nutrients as they become available from the zooplankton, although the measurable concentration of the nutrients in seawater may be very low

G. Herbivore grazing
1. Grazing by zooplankton is a final control on primary production
    a. Phytoplankton biomass may comprise as little as 5% of the potential biomass that can be predicted on the basis of reproduction rates or nutrient availability, with the rest being grazed by herbivorous zooplankton
    b. Herbivores can crop phytoplankton biomass as quickly as it is produced
    c. Herbivores also release nutrients (as excrement) into the environment, fueling phytoplankton production
2. Grazing may increase or decrease primary productivity
    a. Grazing decreases primary production by cropping new production in areas where nutrients are not limiting
    b. Grazing probably has little effect on new production in areas where nutrients are limiting, but it does increase the rate at which nutrients are recycled back into the system

III. Latitudinal and Seasonal Changes

A. General information
1. Solar energy is not distributed evenly around the globe but varies with latitude and season
2. Global input of light is significant because of its direct effect on photosynthesis and because of its effect on the creation and maintenance of stratification in the water column

B. Tropics
1. The tropics have intense solar radiation and relatively uniform periods of about 12 hours of daylight and 12 hours of darkness
2. The constant, high solar input creates strong stratification in the water column, maintained by a relatively shallow permanent thermocline
3. Although the light energy is high, only low levels of nutrients are found in the nutrient-depleted, stratified surface layers
4. The result of this high-light, low-nutrient regime is a low, continuous level of production, approximately 50 to 100 mg carbon (C) fixed/m^2/day

C. Temperate coastal regions
1. Temperate regions have significant seasonal variations in the period of light and darkness
2. During the summer, daylight is longer than 12 hours; during the winter, daylight is shorter than 12 hours
3. Temperate latitudes have lower light intensity and heat input than tropic regions
4. Temperate coastal winters are characterized by a well-mixed water column, high turbulence, low light input, and low production
   a. Low heat input from the sun and high wind mixing from winter storms result in the absence of a thermocline and a well-mixed water column, with the mixed layer often reaching the bottom in areas of continental shelves
   b. High water turbulence replenishes nutrients to surface waters from nutrient-rich deep waters or the bottom
   c. With little light input, the critical depth is shallow, well above the depth of wind mixing
   d. While nutrients are plentiful, there is little production because of low light levels
5. Temperate coastal springs are characterized by a well-mixed water column, high levels of nutrients, increasing light input, and high production
   a. Because wind mixing is still high, the thermocline is not yet established and the water column is not stratified
   b. Nutrient levels remain high in surface waters
   c. Light increases during the spring, thus moving the critical depth deeper in the water
   d. A *bloom* occurs when the critical depth reaches the depth of mixed zone; both light and nutrients are abundant
   e. The *spring bloom* starts in shallow water, where phytoplankton cells cannot be mixed below the critical depth, then progresses into deeper water as the season advances

6. Temperate coastal summers are characterized by a strong thermocline, depleted levels of nutrients in surface waters, high light levels, little wind mixing, and low production
   a. High light input heats the surface waters and establishes a thermocline, resulting in stratification of the water column; there is not enough wind mixing to disrupt its formation
   b. Nutrients are taken up by the phytoplankton and become depleted in surface waters
   c. Phytoplankton production decreases because of decreasing nutrient levels in the stratified euphotic zone and because of grazing by zooplankton
7. Temperate coastal autumns are characterized by reduced light input, higher levels of nutrients, a breakdown of the thermocline and stratification, and increased production
   a. The seasonal thermocline breaks down because of low solar input and increasing winds and storms
   b. Nutrients are recycled from the bottom or deeper waters to the surface waters
   c. A second yearly bloom often occurs while light and mixing conditions remain favorable before the onset of winter

D. Polar regions
1. Light is relatively low throughout the year
2. Although nutrients always are abundant throughout the year because of the well-mixed water column, light is sufficient for photosynthesis only during the short summer
3. A net gain in production is limited to those months of the year when light, nutrients, and depth of mixing all are favorable for photosynthesis
4. Production, particularly in shallow shelf areas, can approach (for brief periods) the highest levels found anywhere

IV. Global Distribution of Primary Production

A. General information
1. The distribution of primary production in the ocean largely is controlled by the availability of nutrients
2. Low nutrient concentrations limit primary production to low levels throughout most of the ocean; only relatively small areas, such as coastal waters or areas of upwelling, are productive enough to support dense populations of marine life or commercial fisheries

B. Global patterns
1. In the primary ocean gyres, very high levels of light are available; however, stratification of the water column, with resulting low nutrient levels, limits production
2. In coastal upwelling systems (such as those found on the west coasts of North America, South America, and Africa), production is high, often supporting commercially important fisheries
3. *Oceanic fronts* are regions of transition where physical properties, such as temperature and salinity, change over a small horizontal distance

a. Large fronts, such as the west wall of the Gulf Stream, may extend for thousands of kilometers
b. These fronts have higher levels of phytoplankton and zooplankton production
c. Physical stress on the water column, such as water moving into shallower depths, results in areas of local upwelling, supplying nutrients to surface waters

4. Island wakes are smaller areas that may have primary production enhanced by turbulence
  a. Turbulence in water flowing past an island, such as the Caribbean Current flowing past many of the islands of the Lesser Antilles, may result in eddies and areas of local upwelling
  b. This may result in temporary or semistable areas of increased production, surrounded by areas of very low production, downstream of islands and shallow banks

V. Oceanic Food Web

A. General information
1. The term *ecosystem* refers to the biotic community, the assemblage of organisms that occupy a definable area and the physical environment with which the organisms interact
2. The concept of *trophic levels,* a hierarchy of production and consumption within an ecosystem, arose in terrestrial ecology and has been used to describe the pathways of energy transfer in the ocean
3. This concept only partially explains the many processes by which oceanic energy transfers occur
4. A description of the many pathways through which energy can be transferred between populations of organisms is called a *food web*

B. Early plankton observations
1. Early work on marine ecosystems was conducted in highly productive, coastal systems and used nets to collect samples
2. This technique catches only organisms that are big enough and rugged enough to remain intact after collection by a towed net
3. This led to a simplified understanding of marine ecology: a short, direct chain in which big phytoplankton were eaten by big zooplankton, which, in turn, were eaten by zooplanktivorous fish, such as herring
4. More recent studies, especially those conducted in open ocean areas, have led to a better understanding of the roles of a greater number of organisms, especially very small organisms

C. Dissolved organic carbon
1. *Dissolved organic carbon (DOC)* is now thought to have a more important role in marine ecosystems than scientists previously believed
2. Almost all organisms in the ocean, including phytoplankton, are leaky to some degree and release DOC into the water
3. This process creates one of the larger active reservoirs of organic carbon in the world

    4. Unlike almost all other marine organisms, bacteria are well equipped to take up
       DOC

D. Marine bacteria
    1. Bacteria have been found to be much more common in open waters than was
       originally thought
    2. Marine bacteria are difficult to study using conventional techniques, so this group
       of oceanic life is not well understood
    3. Marine bacteria were thought to live only on zooplankton fecal pellets and act as
       decomposers
    4. Bacteria commonly are found in association with phytoplankton
    5. These bacteria can live on DOC leaked from the phytoplankton, thus playing an
       important role in nutrient regeneration
    6. Bacteria may process up to 50% of phytoplankton production by taking up DOC
    7. Bacteria are too small to be eaten by large zooplankton, but they are eaten by a
       number of specialized zooplankton and their energy is contributed to the food
       web
    8. This results in a more complex food web, with more steps consisting of very small
       zooplankters that have developed the capacity to ingest food particles as small
       as bacteria, which in turn are eaten by small carnivores

E. Transfer efficiency
    1. *Transfer efficiency* is the ratio of energy passed on to successive trophic levels
       to energy lost between successive trophic levels
    2. Transfer efficiency generally ranges from 6% to 15% in the marine environment,
       while some systems have an efficiency level as high as 20%
    3. Because of this loss, there is a limit to the number of populations that can be sup-
       ported in any system
    4. Each successive population must be smaller than the population that precedes it
    5. It is thus most efficient for a consumer to feed on lower trophic levels in the food
       web
    6. More food is available in lower trophic levels; for example, a baleen whale that
       feeds on plankton (near the base of the food web) has more food than does a
       toothed whale, which feeds on fish (higher up in the food web)

F. Food web variability
    1. Generally, the more productive an area is, the smaller the food web and the larger
       the organisms populating it
    2. Open ocean waters — characteristically nutrient-limited, low-productivity waters —
       are populated by extremely small organisms in a large and complex food web;
       this food web can be summarized as: Nanoplankton → microzooplankton →
       macrozooplankton → megazooplankton → zooplanktivorous nekton → nek-
       tivorous zooplankton
    3. Neritic waters, which have moderate, usually seasonal primary production, are
       populated by intermediate-sized organisms and comprise an intermediate-size
       food chain; this food web can be summarized as: Microphytoplankton → macro-
       zooplankton → zooplanktivorous nekton → nektivorous nekton

4. Upwelling areas, high in nutrients and production, have very small food webs consisting of large-sized organisms; this food web can be summarized as: Macrophytoplankton → planktivorous nekton or megazooplankton → nektivorous nekton or planktivorous whales

---

Study Activities

1. Explain why nutrient concentrations are higher below the thermocline.
2. Describe how the compensation depth and the depth of the mixed layer control primary production.
3. Describe the physical factors controlling primary production over a year in temperate waters.
4. Create a chart comparing primary production in tropical, temperate, and polar regions.
5. Explain the roles of bacteria in the ocean.
6. Compare the food web in a coastal area to that of a central gyre.

13

The Plankton

Objectives

After studying this chapter, the reader should be able to:
- Describe the major groups of phytoplankton and zooplankton.
- Describe the optimal environmental conditions for each of the major phytoplankton groups.
- Describe the feeding methods and preferred prey for the major groups of zooplankton.
- Delineate the relationship between the primary producers and the first level of consumers in the ocean.

I. Plankton Classification Schemes

A. General information
1. The term *plankton* defines all organisms that cannot swim against currents
2. This definition does not rule out all ability to move; plankton may swim weakly in a horizontal or vertical direction
3. Plankton have been further divided into several categories, using different classification schemes
4. These classification schemes may be taxonomic (indicating evolutionary relationships), functional (based on similarities and differences in the life histories of these organisms), or based on size

B. Taxonomic classification
1. Plankton are divided into plant and animal plankton
2. Plant plankton are called *phytoplankton*
3. Animal plankton are called *zooplankton*
4. Bacteria plankton are called *bacterioplankton*

C. Functional classification
1. Functional classifications are based on the portion of the organism's life cycle spent as plankton
2. *Holoplankton* live their entire life cycle as members of the plankton
3. *Meroplankton* spend only part of life, usually a larval stage, as plankton; the adults may be benthic or nektonic

D. Size classification
1. Size classification is a classification of convenience, without any taxonomic or functional intent
2. Size classifications are based on the different mesh sizes of silk used for early plankton nets
3. Net plankton are those plankton that can be caught in nets, the traditional sampling method
4. Not all planktonic organisms can be collected by nets; small or fragile ones may pass through or be damaged by a plankton net and are not represented in towed net collections

II. Phytoplankton

A. General information
1. Plants and algae in the ocean are confined to the upper, well-lit waters, where there is sufficient light for photosynthesis
2. Most marine plants and algae are small, single-celled organisms
3. Because small particles, whether living or inanimate, have a slower sinking rate than larger particles, cell size affects the ability of a phytoplankter to maintain its position in the upper water column
4. A small size also increases surface-area-to-volume ratio for a cell
   a. Because a single-celled plant or alga has no mouth, digestive system, or circulatory system, it depends on diffusion across the cell wall for nutrient uptake and release of wastes
   b. The ratio of the surface area of any three-dimensional shape to its volume increases with decreasing size
      (1) For example, a cube with a 1-cm side has a surface area of 6 cm^2 and a volume of 1 cm^3; its surface-area-to-volume ratio is 6:1
      (2) A cube with a 2-cm side has a surface area of 24 cm^2 and a volume of 8 cm^3; its surface-area-to-volume ratio is 3:1
   c. A high surface-area-to-volume ratio is more efficient for nutrient uptake and release of wastes
5. The phytoplankton are divided into several major taxonomic groups: the diatoms, the dinoflagellates, the coccolithophores, the phytoflagellates, the silicoflagellates, the bacteria, and the cyanobacteria (see *Representative Phytoplankton,* page 117)

B. Diatoms
1. Diatoms are medium-sized phytoplankton classified as Phylum Chrysophyta, Class Bacillariophyceae
2. Diatoms are unicellular algae with diameters of 10 to 100 μm, varying greatly both between and within species
3. Currently, 100,000 species of diatoms have been identified
4. Most diatoms have a two-part, pillbox-like silica skeleton called a *frustule*
5. The transparent frustule is made of silica, and diatoms have a correspondingly high requirement for the nutrient silicon
6. The principal photosynthetic pigments are chlorophyll *a* and fucoxanthin
7. Most diatoms are solitary, but they may aggregate into loose groups

Representative Phytoplankton

The illustrations below depict four of the most common phytoplankton found in marine ecosystems. Plants inhabit the upper depths of the ocean, which has sufficient light for photosynthesis.

Diatom
(Planktonella)

Dinoflagellate
(Gonyaulax)

Coccolithophore
(Coccosphaera)

Silicoflagellate
(Dictyocha)

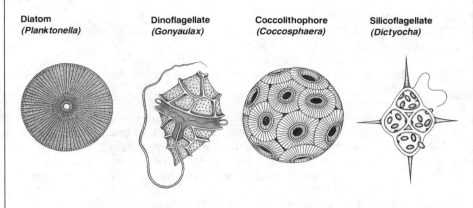

8. Although planktonic diatoms have no ability to swim, spikes, spines, and other structures on the frustule of some species slow their rate of sinking, thereby helping them to stay in surface waters

9. These spikes and spines also make them more difficult for many small grazers to ingest by increasing the total diameter of the diatom without decreasing its surface-area-to-volume ratio

10. In addition, many diatoms group together into chains to slow sinking rates and to limit predation

11. Some species of diatoms, especially those found in shallow coastal waters, can form resting spores that are able to survive the winter or other unfavorable conditions

12. Diatoms most often are found in areas of high nutrient concentrations or high water turbulence, such as coastal and polar regions; they rarely are found in nutrient-poor, stratified, open ocean areas

13. Some species of diatoms are benthic (that is, living on the bottom); these usually are found in shallow water areas
    a. These benthic diatoms form mats on rocks and other submerged surfaces
    b. Benthic diatoms provide a food source for many grazers
    c. Some benthic diatoms are motile; they are able to glide on the bottom of the ocean

14. Diatoms have an unusual method of reproduction
    a. The two halves of the frustule, the top (epitheca) and the bottom (hypotheca), split apart
    b. Each half then acts as a new epitheca, which forms a new hypotheca
    c. Each generation becomes smaller than the previous generation
    d. When the diatom becomes very small, it no longer divides but undergoes *auxospore formation*
    e. During auxospore formation, the frustule is abandoned and cytoplasm escapes from its frustule

f. The cytoplasm then forms a new frustule of the original size, and the cycle begins again

g. Any sample of diatoms of the same species will contain individuals of many different sizes

C. Dinoflagellates

1. Dinoflagellates (Phylum Pyrrophyta, Class Pyrrophyceae) are one of the more abundant groups of phytoplankton
2. They are relatively large, ranging from 25 to 500 μm in length
3. Dinoflagellates are more diverse than diatoms, with more than 100,000 species identified
4. Two orders of dinoflagellates exist
   a. The Peridiniales have an armored, rigid cell wall composed of cellulose
   b. The Gymnodiniales are naked or unarmored, with no cellulose cell wall
5. Many dinoflagellates have a body surface with two grooves, each with a *flagellum,* a whiplike structure that is used to scull through the water
   a. Dinoflagellates are capable of limited swimming, at speeds ranging from 0.05 to 3 cm/minute
   b. Flagella give dinoflagellates their characteristic spinning motion as they swim through water
   c. Dinoflagellates can move short distances into areas favorable for plant productivity
   d. Some dinoflagellates can move vertically through the water column, thus allowing them to select favorable light and nutrient conditions
6. Most dinoflagellates are photosynthetic
   a. They have small, numerous chromatophores located peripherally in their bodies
   b. The principal photosynthetic pigments are chlorophyll *a,* chlorophyll *c,* and some xanthophylls
7. Other dinoflagellates are *heterotrophic* (meaning that their energy is derived from the production of other organisms), some are parasitic, and some live symbiotically with a variety of animals
8. Dinoflagellates reproduce asexually by longitudinal cell division
   a. Unlike diatoms, there is no reduction in cell size during each division
   b. Dinoflagellates reproduce rapidly; rates of cell division may exceed once per day in favorable conditions
9. Many species of dinoflagellates are *bioluminescent,* having the ability to convert chemical energy to light
10. Many dinoflagellates produce toxins that are passed through trophic levels
    a. Shellfish can filter toxic dinoflagellates from the water while feeding
       (1) The shellfish can concentrate toxins in their tissues
       (2) The toxins can accumulate to levels toxic to humans eating the shellfish
    b. *Red tides* are a bloom of dinoflagellates that can reach extremely high population densities
       (1) **Blooms** may reach concentrations of 200,000 to 1,000,000 cells/liter, imparting a red or brown tinge to the water
       (2) Some red-tide species, such as *Alexandrium,* may produce powerful poisons that may affect marine mammals and humans
       (3) The blooms of dinoflagellates eventually die and decompose in the water column

(4) This decomposition can use all the available oxygen (O_2) that is dissolved in the water, killing other organisms through anoxia

c. ***Ciguatera*** is a third type of poisoning caused by dinoflagellates

    (1) Ciguatera toxins accumulate in a food web of a coral reef, sometimes reaching levels toxic to humans in the larger predatory reef fish, such as barracuda and jacks

    (2) Many methods to detect and avoid ciguatera have developed in the folklore of Caribbean and Bahamian Islands, although none are effective

11. Dinoflagellates may live in a symbiotic partnership with other organisms

  a. These symbiotic dinoflagellates are called ***zooxanthellae***

  b. Zooxanthellae are found in the tissues of a variety of animals, including radiolaria, tube worms, many cnidarians (especially corals), and the giant clam *Tridacna*

  c. The zooxanthellae assist the animal by taking up carbon dioxide (CO_2) and nitrogenous wastes from the animal and by providing O_2 and food, which are used by the host

  d. Zooxanthellae have an additional role in corals by helping secrete calcium carbonate ($CaCO_3$), which forms the limestone structure of the coral animal

D. Coccolithophores

1. Coccolithophores (Phylum Chrysophyta, Class Haptophyceae) are small, single-celled flagellates and are members of family Coccolithophoraceae
2. The word coccolithophore means "round stone bearer"
3. There are approximately 300 species of coccolithophores, ranging from 50 to 200 μm in diameter
4. Coccolithophores are flagellated organisms covered with calcium carbonate plates called coccoliths
5. *Coccoliths* are calcium carbonate structures shaped like disks or plates and 1 to 35 m in diameter; the smaller individual plates are about the size of a bacterium
6. Coccoliths were first discovered in deep-ocean sediments, then later found to be a part of living coccolithophores in the water column
7. Coccolithophores are most abundant in tropical and subtropical areas; populations may reach densities as high as 1×10^8 cells/liter during blooms
8. Coccolithophores reproduce by binary fission, a simple, asexual division
9. Coccolithophores have a low nutrient requirement and sink slowly through the water column, allowing them to live successfully in the oligotrophic open ocean
10. One species, *Coccolithus huxleyi,* may be responsible for most primary production in the Sargasso and Mediterranean Seas

E. Phytoflagellates

1. Phytoflagellates are small organisms (less than 10 μm in diameter) that consist of a single cell with two flagella
2. Phytoflagellates reproduce by binary fission and have low nutrient requirements and low sinking rates
3. Phytoflagellates are not sampled well by traditional methods, such as towed nets, and were not thought to be an important group until recently
4. New methods of sampling are showing that phytoflagellates are numerous and significant, particularly in the subtropics and open ocean systems

F. Silicoflagellates

1. Silicoflagellates (Class Chrysophyceae) are small flagellates with an internal structure consisting of silica (SiO_2) and a single, long flagellum used for propulsion
2. The skeletons of silicoflagellates were found first in deep-ocean sediments
3. Silicoflagellates are a less abundant group than the other groups of phytoplankton; not much is known about the ecology of silicoflagellates

G. Bacteria

1. Bacteria are very small single-celled organisms with an extremely simple structure; they range in size from 0.2 to 2 μm
2. Bacteria are too small to be collected by traditional sampling methods and were missed in early marine studies
3. Most bacteria are heterotrophic, although some are photosynthetic
4. Bacteria commonly are motile and reproduce by binary fission
5. Bacteria grow rapidly in the euphotic zone in upper layers of the ocean
6. Recently, bacterial production has been estimated to rival that of phytoplankton in some areas of the ocean; extremely high numbers of bacteria have been found in the open ocean, with concentrations reaching 1×10^6 per milliliter
7. Our understanding of the role of bacteria in the ocean has been revised recently (see Chapter 12, Primary Production, for more information)
   a. Traditionally, the role of bacteria in the ocean was thought to be solely that of decomposers, recycling phosphate (PO_4^{3-}) and nitrate (NO_3^-)
   b. Newer ideas of the role of bacteria are based on better methods of counting and determining bacterial growth rates
   c. Bacteria also can attach to particles of dead material, excreting enzymes to break down and dissolve this detritus, providing a food source
   d. Bacteria add the nutrients ammonium (NH_3), NO_3^-, and PO_4^{3-} to water via leakage across their cell wall
   e. Bacteria also may attach to detrital particles in the water column, such as tests of dead organisms, thereby enriching these relatively large particles as a food source
   f. Phytoplankton excrete dissolved organic matter (DOM), which is then taken up rapidly by bacteria
   g. Bacteria consume **dissolved organic carbon (DOC),** then are eaten, having now transformed DOC to particulate organic carbon (POC), which can be transported in the food web
   h. Bacteria are an important food source for zooplankton that have developed methods to harvest food particles of this very small size

H. Cyanobacteria

1. Cyanobacteria (Class Cyanophyceae) formerly were called blue-green algae; they are small, with a length of 1 to 2 μm
2. Cyanobacteria are a poorly studied group with an unknown number of species
3. Cyanobacteria probably have no motility and reproduce by binary fission
4. Cyanobacteria are important as *nitrogen fixers;* that is, they possess the ability to convert elemental nitrogen (N_2) to biologically useful NH_3, which usually is the limiting nutrient in marine systems
5. Until recently, cyanobacteria were not thought to be as important in oceans as in freshwater systems, where they are most noticeable as freshwater blooms in areas or times of high phosphorus input

6. *Trichodesium* is the best-known oceanic cyanobacterium, commonly seen as tufts of cells in the surface waters of warm, nitrogen-limited oceans
7. Recently, large numbers of another cyanobacterium, *Synechococcus,* have been found in tropical and subtropical oceanic waters, where they may comprise a large proportion of primary production
8. The cyanobacteria probably are very important in low-nutrient areas, where they may replace other phytoplankton

III. Zooplankton

A. General information
1. Zooplankton are a diverse group that includes members of all animal phyla
2. Zooplankton may be herbivores, carnivores, parasites, or **symbionts**
3. Zooplankton play an important role in the ocean by transferring energy from primary producers to fish and other nekton

B. Protozoa
1. The Kingdom Protista consists of protozoa — small, single-celled animals that comprise several phyla; some of the more common marine types are foraminifera, radiolaria, zooflagellates, and ciliates (for illustrations of some common species, see *Representative Protozoa,* page 122)
2. Foraminifera are protozoans of Class Sarcodina
   a. They are small amoebae, usually less than 1 mm in diameter, although some grow to several millimeters
   b. Foraminifera secrete calcium carbonate shells in various shapes, adding additional chambers as they grow
   c. The calcium carbonate shells of foraminifera may be abundant in sediments and have been used as indicators of past climatic conditions
   d. Cytoplasm streams out through apertures in the shell, forming netlike pseudopodia to feed on phytoplankton, bacteria, and microzooplankton
   e. Some foraminifera carry symbiotic algae that photosynthesize, supplying the foraminifera with nutrients from the algae's waste products
   f. The foraminifera move slowly (less than 1 cm/hour)
   g. Foraminifera are most abundant in upper layers of the water column, in the photic zone
3. Radiolaria (Class Sarcodina) also are protozoans and are somewhat similar in appearance to the foraminifera
   a. Radiolaria are larger, found either as spherical single cells about 50 µm in diameter or in colonies reaching several millimeters
   b. Radiolaria have intricate internal silicate or strontium sulfate skeletons
   c. Radiolaria also extend cytoplasm, which is external to the shell (unlike foraminifera), to feed on small phytoplankton
   d. Radiolaria are another important component of marine sediments
4. Zooflagellates are very small, with a length of less than 10 µm; they have one or two flagella
   a. Zooflagellates are poorly understood, because they are very delicate and poorly sampled by conventional collecting techniques; their role in the food web has been discovered only in the past 5 years

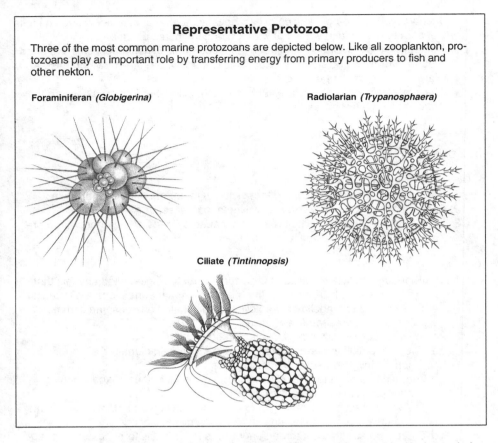

Representative Protozoa

Three of the most common marine protozoans are depicted below. Like all zooplankton, protozoans play an important role by transferring energy from primary producers to fish and other nekton.

Foraminiferan *(Globigerina)*

Radiolarian *(Trypanosphaera)*

Ciliate *(Tintinnopsis)*

       b. Zooflagellates feed on bacteria, small phytoplankton, cyanobacteria, and phytoflagellates

       c. These protozoans provide a pathway for introducing bacteria, which are too small for most zooplankton to eat, into the oceanic food web

  5. Ciliates are small, cilia-covered single cells, less than 50 μm in length, that use cilia for locomotion

       a. Most have no shell or skeleton, although one group — the tintinnids — does excrete a chitinous shell

       b. Ciliates feed mainly on bacteria, phytoplankton, and zooflagellates

       c. Although scientists are just beginning to understand their role, ciliates may be important in such areas as Long Island Sound, where tintinnids are thought to process 25% of the primary production

IV. Gelatinous Zooplankton

A. General information

  1. The gelatinous zooplankton are a diverse group of about 9,000 species that includes hydrozoans, jellyfish, and ctenophores

  2. Gelatinous zooplankton display **radial symmetry**

3. Gelatinous zooplankton may consist of more than 95% water
4. Gelatinous zooplankton's soft, gelatinous body may seem disadvantageous, but it does have several advantages over a hard body plan
   a. They typically are transparent, making them more difficult for visual predators to see
   b. They have low nutrient requirements
   c. Because their density is similar to that of water, they do not need to expend much energy to maintain their depth in the water column
   d. They are able to engulf large food particles, sometimes even larger than themselves
   e. A notable disadvantage of their fragile body structure is that they cannot tolerate turbulent water conditions
5. Gelatinous zooplankton have not been studied extensively, despite their numbers and wide distribution, because of the difficulty of capturing them intact and undamaged with nets
6. Recent methods of studying these organisms, including the use of divers and submarines, has led to a better understanding of their importance in the oceanic food web

B. Phylum Cnidaria
1. Planktonic Cnidaria have two forms, the medusa and the polyp
   a. The medusa, the more familiar form, resembles a free-swimming umbrella
   b. The polyp is a *sessile* (unmoving) bottom-dwelling form
2. Many cnidarians have life cycles that display alternation of generations, alternating between the medusa form and polyp form after each reproduction
3. The free-swimming medusa have a downward-directed mouth surrounded by feeding tentacles; they move by rhythmic pulses of their swimming bell, which resembles an umbrella
4. Cnidarians feed by extending their tentacles
   a. These tentacles are armed with stinging cells called *nematocysts*, which are similar to harpoons, with a barb and elastic tether
   b. The nematocyst injects toxin into the prey (commonly macrozooplankton or smaller fish) on contact
   c. The cnidarian then pulls its tentacle into its mouth and eats the prey
5. Three major groups of cnidarians exist
   a. Chondrophores (Suborder Chondrophora) are *pelagic* (live in the open ocean), *polymorphic* (take several forms even within a single species), and *polyzooid* (reproduce asexually) communities
      (1) *Velella* and *Porpita* are common examples of chondrophores
      (2) The body of the chondrophore is a modified polyp, not a medusa
      (3) Generally, chondrophores resemble a disk with hanging tentacles and float on the surface
      (4) Chondrophores are relatively common in warm-water oceans, such as the Caribbean Sea, and the tropical and subtropical Atlantic, Pacific, and Indian Oceans
   b. Siphonophores (Order Siphonophora) also are colonial organisms, combining both polyp and medusa stages into one colony
      (1) Siphonophores are large, gas-filled floats or bells that have long, trailing tentacles

(2) The bell or float is a modified medusa stage, while the long hanging tentacles consist of colonies of polyps

(3) This group also is found largely in warm seas

(4) *Physalia physalis,* the Portuguese man-of-war, is a common example of a siphonophore

(5) Siphonophores paralyze their prey (often fish) with nematocysts

(6) Colonies of siphonophores develop through budding

(7) The larval polyp forms the float that gives rise to budding zones, at which various members of the community develop

c. Scyphozoans (Class Schyphozoa), or true jellyfish, have the medusa as the dominant form

(1) The medusa's bell ranges from 2 to 40 cm in diameter

(2) Scyphozoans feed on all types of small animals, particularly crustaceans and small fish

(3) Scyphozoans may undergo alternation of generations during reproduction

(4) Some produce polyps that attach to the bottom of the ocean

(5) These polyps may undergo asexual reproduction while on the bottom, thus releasing medusae into the water column

(6) Oceanic scyphozoans generally do not produce polyps because the bottom is too far from the surface waters where the medusae live

C. Ctenophores

1. Ctenophores (Phylum Ctenophora), or comb jellies, are a small group consisting of approximately 50 species

2. Transparent, golf-ball-sized ctenophores are abundant in coastal and open ocean waters

3. Ctenophores are biradially symmetrical, with eight equally spaced rows of cilia and, typically, two tentacles

a. The cilia bands are called comb cells or ctenes

b. The rows of cilia become iridescent in sunlight when they beat the water to propel the ctenophore

4. Ctenophores have *colloblasts,* sticky cells that trap particles on their trailing tentacles

5. Ctenophores can be voracious predators, feeding mainly on copepods and other macrozooplankton

6. Ctenophores range from 1 to 10 cm in diameter, large enough to be sampled by nets; however, they generally are reduced to an unidentifiable mass of jelly when collected by this technique

7. Ctenophores are noted for bioluminescence; light production takes place in the meridional canals, appearing to radiate from the comb rows

V. Crustaceans

A. General information

1. Crustaceans (Subphylum of Phylum Arthropoda) are the most important and numerous group of zooplankton and the only major group of aquatic arthropods

2. There are 31,312 known species of crustaceans (see *Representative Crustaceans,* page 125)

Representative Crustaceans

Crustaceans constitute the most numerous group of zooplankton, comprising more than 31,000 species. The illustrations below depict three of the more common crustaceans, which have segmented bodies and appendages covered by a rigid exoskeleton.

Copepod *(Copepoda)*

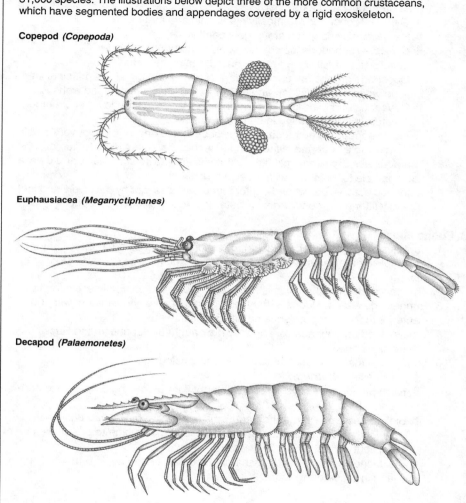

Euphausiacea *(Meganyctiphanes)*

Decapod *(Palaemonetes)*

3. Crustaceans have segmented bodies and appendages covered by a rigid exo-skeleton composed of chitin
4. Crustaceans have five pairs of head appendages: two pairs of antennae, one pair of mandibles, and two pairs of maxillae

B. Copepods

1. Copepods (Subclass Copepoda) are the most abundant group of planktonic crustaceans, comprising the bulk of net plankton in most areas
2. More than 7,500 species have been identified; about 90% of this species live in the ocean

3. The name copepod means "oar foot"
4. Copepods are small — 100 μm to 1 cm in length — with a short, cylindrical body
5. Copepods generally are pelagic, but parasitic and benthic forms also exist
6. Three orders of copepods exist
   a. *Calanoid* copepods are mostly planktonic and marine
   b. *Harpacticoid* copepods are largely benthic
   c. *Cyclopoid* copepods include planktonic and benthic species
7. The mechanics of copepod feeding have been closely studied
   a. Copepods are the major consumers of phytoplankton and a principal link between phytoplankton and higher trophic levels in the food web
   b. Copepods and their food are small in size, and thus live in an environment different from anything in human experience
   c. Water appears to be much more viscous in this environment of very small sizes; to a copepod, water seems as thick as honey does to humans
8. Copepods use the seemingly high water viscosity to select, rotate, and draw a food particle to its mouth without ever touching it
9. Copepods actively detect and capture food particles, not by passively and inefficiently filtering large volumes of water (as was previously thought)

C. Euphausids

1. Euphausids (Order Euphausiacea), commonly known as "krill," are marine, shrimplike organisms; they are abundant and fairly large (usually 1 to 6 cm long)
2. The **carapace** of euphausids is loose and does not completely enclose the gills
3. Euphausids are filter feeders; they feed primarily on phytoplankton, with their anterior thoracic appendages modified to filter water
4. Whales feed on euphausids, and they are caught by Japanese and Russian commercial fisheries
5. Many euphausids produce bioluminescence, using specialized light-producing organs called **photophores**
   a. Each photophore consists of a cluster of light-producing cells, a reflector, and a lens
   b. Bioluminescence in marine organisms is a simple biological reaction in which two chemicals, luciferin and luciferase, combine to produce a chemical light
   c. Bioluminescence is used as an adaptation for swarming, in reproduction, and in predator avoidance

D. Decapods

1. The true shrimp and benthic lobsters and crabs are decapods (Order Decapoda)
2. Order Decapoda is the largest order of crustaceans, with 8,500 known species
3. Planktonic decapods are well adapted for swimming; they have cylindrical bodies that may be laterally compressed and five pairs of slender legs
4. Adult planktonic decapods range in size from millimeters to centimeters
5. Decapods are distinguished from euphausids by a carapace that encloses the gills tightly; compound eyes that are set on stalks (that is, they are not part of the carapace); and appendages that are adapted for grasping, not filtering
6. Most shrimps are found in the upper 1,000 m of the water column, in the epipelagic and mesopelagic zones

7. Decapods may be transparent in upper waters or red in deep waters; many deep-water forms are bioluminescent
8. Decapods include herbivores, carnivores, and scavengers
9. Decapod development includes diverse larval stages
10. The larvae of benthic decapods may be meroplankton, prominent in the plankton during some period of their development

E. Ostracods
1. Ostracods (Class Ostracoda) are small crustaceans, typically less than 5 mm in length, that are widely distributed in freshwater and marine environments
2. More than 2,000 living species of ostracods exist
3. Ostracods have an external bivalve shell that looks somewhat like a tiny clam shell and is composed of chitin
4. The organism lives inside the shell, filter-feeding on phytoplankton and small zooplankton
5. Like many euphausids and decapods, ostracods are bioluminescent; unlike euphausids and decapods, which produce light by photophores, ostracods produce an external cloud of light that lasts for 1 to 2 seconds

F. Amphipods
1. There are more than 5,500 species of amphipods (Order Amphipoda), most of which are marine
2. Amphipods are relatively large plankters, ranging in length from millimeters to centimeters
3. Amphipods are somewhat shrimplike in appearance but display extreme morphological adaptations for some roles
   a. They are laterally compressed and have large sessile compound eyes and no carapace
   b. The eyes of some bathypelagic amphipods are divided into upper and lower portions
   c. Although most amphipods have robust bodies, some (especially the caprellids) have a reduced, almost skeletal, body structure that helps them climb on and over other benthic organisms
4. Amphipods are mostly detritus feeders and scavengers that supplement their diet by feeding on smaller zooplankton; some are filter-feeders, and a few are parasites
5. Recently, scuba-diving and submarine observations have shown that amphipods commonly live in or on gelatinous zooplankton, such as jellyfish, ctenophores, and salps
   a. One example is the *Phronimid* amphipod, which kills a salp, eats its internal organs, and then lays her eggs inside the salp
   b. The *Phronimid* also uses the salp body as a home and a nursery

VI. Insects

A. General information
1. The *Halobates,* or water striders, comprise the only species of marine insects (Phylum Arthropoda, Class Insecta)
2. *Halobates* live in tropical and subtropical areas

B. *Halobates* motility and feeding patterns
1. *Halobates* use surface tension to remain on the water surface
2. They also can dive under the surface and remain there for several hours during rough sea conditions
3. *Halobates* have excellent eyesight and can jump vertically from the water surface to avoid predators and sampling nets
4. They eat small zooplankton and gelatinous zooplankton, such as *Porpita* and *Velella*, found at the surface

VII. Mollusks

A. General information
1. Mollusks (Phylum Mollusca) are a diverse group of more than 100,000 living species
2. Most mollusks have a soft body that normally is covered with a hard shell; some species, however, do not have shells
3. Most are benthic, with the exception of the Heteropods and Pteropods

B. Heteropods
1. Heteropods (Suborder Heteropoda), which live planktonically in the water column, have reduced shells and a finlike foot that acts as a swimming fin
2. They are most closely related to snails (gastropods)
3. Heteropods are large (ranging from 1 to 4 cm in length) and wormlike in appearance
4. Heteropods are carnivorous, eating other zooplankton

C. Pteropods
1. Pteropods (Suborder Pteropoda), sometimes known as sea butterflies, can be abundant
2. Pteropods are smaller than heteropods, with lengths ranging from 1 to 2 cm
3. The word *pteropod* means "winged foot," a reference to the modification of the foot into a swimming appendage
4. There are two forms of pteropods: shelled (Order Thecosomata) and naked (Order Gymnosomata)
5. Shelled pteropods have an external shell composed of aragonite, a type of calcium carbonate that may be an important component of sediments
6. Each pteropod form has a different feeding method
    a. Shelled pteropods feed on small food particles — such as phytoplankton, some bacteria, and small zooplankton — by producing a mucus net
    b. Food particles stick to the net, which is then retracted into the pteropod's mouth
    c. Naked pteropods are exclusively carnivorous, eating other zooplankton
7. Naked pteropods are an important source of food for whales

VIII. Chaetognaths

A. General information

1. Chaetognaths (Phylum Chaetognatha) are the sole members of a small phylum comprising about 50 species
2. Chaetognaths, which sometimes are called arrow worms although they are not worms, are small, arrow-shaped, transparent organisms that are 1 to 3 cm in length
3. Chaetognaths are second in abundance to copepods among the zooplankton

B. Feeding habits

1. Chaetognaths are carnivorous, feeding particularly on copepods
2. Chaetognaths detect their prey by means of the tufts of sensory hairs, which sense the slight water currents created by their swimming prey; they cannot sense nonmoving prey
3. The prey then are grasped with large spines on the chaetognath's head; this gives chaetognaths their nickname, "bristle mouth"

IX. Chordates

A. General information

1. All Chordates (Phylum Chordata) have a notochord (a rodlike structure that takes the place of a backbone in primitive animals) and gill slits at some stage in their development
2. There are two subphylums of Chordata: the Vertebrata, which have a true backbone as adults, and the Urochordata, which do not

B. Urochordates

1. The subphylum Urochordata includes the Larvaceans, also called Appendicularians, and the Thalaceans, or salps
2. There are about 70 species in Class Larvacea
   a. Larvaceans are small, ranging from a few millimeters to about 1 cm in size; they look somewhat like a comma
   b. Larvaceans create a 2- to 4-cm-diameter mucus structure, called a house, in which it lives and feeds
   c. The larvacean uses its tail to move and to produce a water current that draws small phytoplankton and bacteria into the sticky house, thus capturing the prey
   d. The mucus house is used like a fishing net for 2 to 4 hours, then cleaned of food particles and abandoned; a new house is built later
   e. The abandoned house may be an important attachment site for bacteria and is a source of *marine snow,* particles of living and detrital material that look like snowfall when seen underwater
   f. Larvaceans were used in early research as a method of catching bacterioplankton, which were too small to be collected by other means; the bacteria-filled house was dissected from the remainder of the animal
3. Salps (Class Thaliacea) are transparent, barrel-shaped organisms with circular muscle bands that expand and contract to pump water through the body for propulsion

a. Salps, which are 1 to 5 cm in length, may occur as solitary individuals or as colonies
b. Some colonial salps, such as *Pyrosoma,* may grow to a length of several meters
c. Salps also produce a mucus net with which they capture their prey, mostly phytoplankton
d. Salps may have complicated life cycles, displaying an alternation of generations, with asexual budding and sexual reproduction
e. Many salps are bioluminescent, producing light when touched or disturbed

Study Activities

1. Explain how the ability to move affects the distribution of diatoms and dinoflagellates.
2. Describe several methods used by phytoplankton to maintain their position in the water column.
3. Describe how copepods use their small size to select and capture food particles.
4. Summarize the differences in appearance between euphausids and decapods. Relate your answer to their preferred food.
5. Explain how recent advances in sampling methods has improved our understanding of the diversity of life in the ocean.
6. Describe the advantages and disadvantages of having a soft body in the ocean.
7. Describe which groups of phytoplankton and zooplankton might be found in coastal and oceanic systems, and explain why.

14

The Nekton

Objectives

After studying this chapter, the reader should be able to:
- List the major groups of nekton.
- Describe the adaptations that squid have made to find and capture food.
- Identify and distinguish the major groups of fish.
- Discuss the modifications that fish have made to flourish in different marine environments.
- Summarize some of the issues faced by contemporary commercial fisheries.

I. The Pelagic Environment

A. General information

1. *Nekton* are organisms capable of independent movement within the oceans; they swim against currents, control their position, and, in many instances, undertake long migrations
2. Nekton normally comprise the larger organisms in the ocean, with a length of more than 5 cm; this category includes most fish and squid
3. Most nekton are vertebrates; however, two major groups — large decapod shrimp and the cephalopods — are invertebrates

B. Oceanic depth zones

1. The nekton occupy an oceanic environment that usually is classified into a three-layer scheme
2. The *epipelagic zone* extends from the surface to 200 m in the water column
   a. This zone has sufficient light for photosynthesis and primary production
   b. Most food is produced in the epipelagic zone
3. The *mesopelagic zone* extends from 200 to 1,000 m, the limit of significant light penetration from the surface in the deep ocean
   a. This is a twilight zone, with only a small amount of light from the surface available
   b. No photosynthesis occurs in the mesopelagic zone; some inhabitants of this region migrate to the epipelagic zone to feed
4. The *bathypelagic zone* extends below 1,000 m
   a. No light of biological significance from the surface is available in this zone

b. Little food is available; with the exception of hydrothermal vent communities, all food enters the bathypelagic zone from the upper layers of the water column

II. Crustaceans

A. General information
1. Some of the larger decapod shrimp, which range from 5 to 10 cm in length, are members of the nekton
2. These decapod shrimp eat macrozooplankton, copepods, chaetognaths, and euphausids

B. Mesopelagic shrimp
1. The larger decapod shrimp may be abundant in the mesopelagic zone
2. Many are bioluminescent
3. Many shrimp that inhabit the mesopelagic zone are red; a wavelength of light that is quickly absorbed in surface waters, red is as difficult as black to see in the poorly lit mesopelagic zone
4. Many decapod shrimp migrate from the mesopelagic zone to surface waters and back again, a distance of hundreds of meters, in 1 day; this is called *diel vertical migration (DVM)*

III. Cephalopods

A. General information
1. This class includes the most highly specialized and highly adapted mollusks
2. Nektonic cephalopods (Class Cephalopoda) include the squid, nautiluses, cuttlefish, and octopuses
3. These organisms are members of Phylum Mollusca, which also includes clams and snails
4. While some are adapted for benthic life, most species are adapted for swimming

B. Basic squid body plan
1. Most adult squid are between 20 cm and 1 m in length, the largest size of any invertebrate; some species, including the giant squid, can grow to extremely large sizes (one example is the genus *Architeuthis*)
   a. These squid are found at depths of 300 to 600 m over continental slopes
   b. Specimens up to 17 m in length have been found
   c. These squid may have mantles 7 m long and tentacles up to 15 m long
   d. Such squid have never been caught alive; their bodies occasionally wash up on beaches, usually in Scotland or Newfoundland, or are found in the stomachs of sperm whales
2. Squid have remarkable mobility, with the ability to hover, cruise slowly, or dart in any direction
3. Squid also have the fastest swimming speed of any invertebrate
   a. One species of flying squid can reach heights of 4 m above the water's surface and speeds of 16 miles/hour
   b. Squid swim by rapidly expelling water from their mantle cavity

c. Most species control motion by aiming their *siphon* (a pipelike structure in mollusks used for water intake or output) in any direction

4. Squid are carnivorous, feeding on fish and shrimp
5. Squid display complex behavior; individuals have shown evidence of learning, memory, and tactile and visual discrimination

C. Depth range

1. Squid inhabit various levels of the water column
2. Most are found in the upper 100 m, but many are adapted for far greater depths
3. Squid that inhabit depths below the epipelagic zone display many modifications to the physical conditions of these depths
4. Many squid exhibit DVM, traveling from the deeper waters where they live during the day to shallow waters at night, and returning at dawn

D. Buoyancy adaptations

1. Squid, particularly those living in the mesopelagic and bathypelagic zones, display modifications — including reduction of the denser organs and musculature — that decrease density and reduce the energy required to maintain their position in the water column
2. The cranchiid squid, a mesopelagic species, provides a good example of a common adaptation found in many groups of organisms to increase their buoyancy
   a. The cranchiids are small and much more bulbous and less firm than the familiar shallow-water squid
   b. This group has a fluid-filled *coelom,* a cavity between the body wall and the digestive tract, that contains a fluid high in ammonium ions derived from metabolic wastes
   c. The relatively light ammonium ions replace the heavier ions found in seawater, making the fluid contained in the coelom *isotonic* (having the same osmotic pressure as seawater) but less dense
   d. The squid, much like a helium blimp in the air, is thus filled with a lighter-than-seawater fluid, reducing its density and lessening the energy required for the animal to maintain its position in the water column

E. Nervous system

1. The squid's well-developed nervous system is used for locomotion and prey sensing, helping it to feed
2. The animal locates prey with highly developed eyes that are similar to human eyes
   a. The pupil is slit shaped and horizontal
   b. Behavioral experiments suggest that squid can detect color
3. Members of the family Histioteuthidae, which occupy the mesopelagic zone, have unusual asymmetrical eyes, an adaptation to the light field in this zone
   a. One eye is large, and the other is small
   b. The large eye is directed up toward faint light from the surface, and the small eye is directed down, to detect light from other bioluminescent organisms
4. The squid's arms have tactile and chemical receptors; this well-developed sense of touch may be more important than vision in poor-visibility water

F. Chromatophores and photophores

1. *Chromatophores,* color-producing cells in the skin, control the squid's unusual coloration
   a. Chromatophores are controlled by the nervous system
   b. A squid's color is related to background environment, camouflage, or behavioral needs
   c. These cells expand and contract under muscular control
      (1) When the chromatophore muscle contracts, the chromatophore is drawn out into a flat plate, allowing the pigment of that chromatophore to be visible
      (2) When the muscle relaxes, the pigment is compressed and becomes less visible
   d. Most species have chromatophores of several colors, including yellow, orange, red, blue, and black
   e. Chromatophores may occur in groups or layers
   f. Skin coloration results from light passing through the chromatophores
2. *Photophores,* light-producing organs, are arranged in patterns on the bodies of most squid
   a. Squid may emit either brief flashes of light or a sustained glow
   b. This biologically produced light may provide camouflage from visual predators by counterillumination, acting like a flashbulb to startle predators

G. Ink sac

1. Squid release ink into the water to protect themselves from predators
2. This brown or black fluid, which is secreted near the intestines, has a high concentration of melanin
3. Ink is released into the water to hide the squid or to confuse a predator and allow the squid to escape

IV. Fish

A. General information

1. Fish are members of Phylum Chordata and Classes Agnatha, Chondrichthyes, and Osteichthyes
2. They generally are cold-blooded vertebrates that possess gills and fins and are adapted to life in an aquatic environment; there are, however, many exceptions to this definition
   a. Not all fish are cold-blooded
   b. Not all fish are completely aquatic
   c. Some fish have lungs
   d. Some fish have modified or absent fins or may have fins that are more limblike than finlike
3. The many adaptations to the basic fish body plan allow fish to occupy a wide range of habitats
4. Fish are not uniformly distributed throughout the ocean; most are found near continents and islands, usually in colder waters
5. There are 25,000 species of fish, composing one-half of all vertebrate species
   a. Of these, about 700 species are members of Class Chondrichthyes
   b. Approximately 20,000 species are members of Class Osteichthyes

c. Approximately 2,500 of all fish species are pelagic

B. Agnathids
1. Agnathids — fish without jaws — are the most primitive fish still living
2. All other living vertebrates have jaws
3. Agnathids, such as lampreys and hagfish, live in freshwater and most are parasites or scavengers
4. The lamprey feeds parasitically on other fish; the hagfish is a scavenger

C. Chondrichthyes
1. The Chondrichthyes, which include skates, rays, and sharks, consist of about 700 species, most of which are predators
2. Members of this group have a skeleton composed of cartilage; some areas of the skeleton may be calcified to strengthen the cartilage
3. Skates and rays are specialized for life on the bottom of the ocean (most skates and rays are marine; some live in freshwater in India, China, and rivers entering the Gulf of Mexico)
   a. Their pectoral fins have developed into winglike forms, and their eyes are located on the dorsal side of the fish — these are adaptations to benthic life
   b. Most skates and rays use blunt teeth to feed on benthic invertebrates
   c. Some rays have venomous spines for protection
   d. Some rays have electric organs in the head and tail for prey sensing and capture and for defense against predators
4. Sharks are well-developed marine organisms with good sense organs and brain, powerful jaws, and the ability to swim swiftly
   a. Sharks are covered with placoid scales
      (1) The scales form a layer of toothlike structures called *dermal denticles* that are covered with enamel
      (2) This denticle layer is modified in the mouth to form teeth
   b. Most sharks are carnivores
      (1) Many have a protrusible hinged jaw connected to the body by muscles; the shark can throw out both the top and bottom of the jaw for an extremely wide gape
      (2) Most predatory sharks have several rows of sharp teeth for tearing and shredding food; these nonpermanent teeth are replaced as they break or wear down
   c. Some sharks, such as whale and basking sharks, are filter feeders
      (1) Although these are the largest sharks, they feed on smaller organisms than do other sharks
      (2) These sharks feed by creating a vortex to suck in plankton and smaller fish
      (3) More food is available to the large sharks because they feed closer to the primary producers in the food web, before energy is lost through consumption at higher trophic levels in the food web
   d. Sharks have internal fertilization; the eggs of some sharks are carried in the female until they hatch
   e. Sharks use several techniques to maintain their position in the water column with little expenditure of energy
      (1) Sharks can maintain buoyancy and reduce density because their huge livers have a high concentration of oil that is lighter than seawater

      (2) Sharks also use fins to help regulate position
         (a) Most sharks are large but not very maneuverable
         (b) The pectoral fins of most pelagic sharks are larger and stiffer than those of bony fish, providing the shark with lift (like a wing) at the expense of greater maneuverability

D. Teleosts

1. The teleosts, or true bony fish (Class Osteichthyes), are an immensely varied group
2. These active, swift swimmers display advanced behavior
3. The teleosts have lighter bodies than the more primitive armored fish, thus enabling them to colonize new areas of the oceans and freshwater systems

E. Fish anatomy

1. Fish have several fins that aid locomotion and maneuverability; the position and shape of the fins vary among species
   a. The pelvic and pectoral fins are paired fins most commonly used for maneuvering
      (1) The pectoral fins are located near the head of a fish
      (2) The pelvic fins usually are soft and lobelike; pelvic fins may be modified for walking on the bottom, or greatly reduced, as in the threadlike pelvic fins of a swordfish
      (3) In primitive fish, the pectoral fins are on the lower part of the body and the pelvic fins are set further toward the back end, reflecting a bottom orientation
      (4) In advanced fish, the pectoral fins are moved up, and the pelvic fins are positioned below the pectoral fins; this provides better mobility
   b. The dorsal fin is located on the back of a fish
      (1) A fish may have one, two, or three dorsal fins
      (2) Some dorsal fins are soft and consist only of rays (rodlike but soft supporting material), whereas other dorsal fins are firm and have bony spines
      (3) Elaborate musculature is associated with fins and fin rays
   c. The caudal fin is used for swimming power and maneuverability
      (1) The attachment point for the caudal fin is the caudal peduncle; a narrow caudal peduncle, as seen in tunas, provides strong propulsion
      (2) Caudal fins are not always symmetrical; they are classified according to relative size and shape
         (a) In *homocercal* fins, both lobes are the same size
         (b) In *heterocercal* fins, the top lobe is larger
         (c) In *hypocercal* fins, the bottom lobe is larger
         (d) In *lunate* fins, the lobes are narrow and moon shaped
2. The mouth position of a fish suggests its feeding strategy
   a. A bottom mouth is characteristic of bottom feeders; these fish may have barbels, feelers, or other chemical sensors to assist them in finding food
   b. A terminal mouth is characteristic of zooplankton feeders, piscivorous fish, and coral reef fish
      (1) Zooplankton feeders have small mouths and fine gill rakers
      (2) Piscivorous fish have larger mouths and coarse gill rakers
      (3) Coral reef fish have strong, heavy jaws that can crush coral rock

c. A top mouth is characteristic of surface-oriented fish
  (1) A top-oriented mouth commonly is associated with large, upward-facing eyes
  (2) Fish with top-facing mouths look for the silhouette of their prey, usually plankton and small fish, in the light from the surface
  (3) This arrangement is common in estuarine and mesopelagic fish
3. With the exception of benthic species, fish try to attain neutral buoyancy so that the total weight of the fish equals the weight of the water its body displaces
  a. In their evolution, some fish have reduced their heavy body structures, some have developed buoyancy to counteract the heaviness, and some have combined the two strategies
  b. Many fish have a gas-filled swim bladder that allows the fish to maintain neutral buoyancy over a wide range of depths
  c. A swim bladder may constitute between 5% and 10% of a fish's volume
  d. A swim bladder can be open or closed
    (1) An open swim bladder provides a direct connection to the atmosphere through the esophagus; primitive fish, such as the bowfin, gulp air into the swim bladder
    (2) A closed swim bladder is filled internally by gases secreted through the swim bladder wall
      (a) The *rete mirabile* is the site of gas exchange between the blood and the swim bladder
      (b) This is a countercurrent exchange system that concentrates gas in the swim bladder
      (c) A countercurrent exchange system brings the blood entering the rete in close contact with the blood exiting the rete; gases in the gas-saturated blood leaving the rete diffuse into the undersaturated blood entering the rete, allowing the fish to maintain high gas pressures in the rete with little expenditure of energy
4. Several groups of fish are *endothermic* (able to maintain body temperature above ambient water temperature)
  a. Most fish are cold-blooded, their body temperature fluctuating with water temperature
  b. This strategy is more difficult for fish than for terrestrial animals because the surrounding water cools the fish, and water circulation through the gills during breathing causes additional heat loss
  c. Tunas, swordfish, many sharks, and several dozen other species are endothermic
    (1) The goal of endothermy is to allow the fish to be active in areas of varying water temperature
    (2) Endothermy expands the potential range of the fish in the ocean
  d. Some fish keep parts of their body warm instead of the entire body; billfish, for example, heat their brains and eyes only
    (1) Blood is passed through a special eye muscle, which acts as a furnace to heat the blood
    (2) This does not increase the fish's aerobic capacity, allowing it to swim farther or faster, but does allow the fish to function better as a predator by improving its visual acuity

e. Tunas warm their brains with a special vascular plumbing system that captures and recycles the heat created in their muscles before it is lost to the water via its gills

5. Because there are no structural hiding places in the open ocean, other strategies, such as protective coloration, must be developed for avoiding predators

   a. Juvenile fish, such as leptocephali (eel larvae), have become transparent to avoid visual predators; the eyes, brain, and, sometimes, the gut are opaque

   b. Cryptic coloration is the most common coloration strategy

      (1) *Countershading* is a bicolored pattern, with the top of the fish a dark green or blue; the bottom, white or silver

      (2) This camouflage provides the fish with a dark surface that matches the dark bottom or deep water when seen from above, and a light surface that matches the sunlit surface waters when seen from below

      (3) Silvery dorsal surfaces are common in schooling shallow-water fish; light reflecting from these fish makes them almost invisible when in a group

   c. *Disruptive coloration* eliminates the natural outline or body features of the fish

      (1) Some fish use a mask to disrupt the outline of the eye area because many predators home in on the eye of their prey

      (2) Other fish use multiple false eye spots called *ocelli;* these help deceive the predator about the true direction in which the prey fish is swimming

   d. *Warning coloration* is a bright coloring that warns predators away from poisonous prey fish; this pattern also may provide a means of intraspecific recognition

   e. *Deceptive coloration* is a method of camouflage by which the fish mimics its surroundings

      (1) Examples include Sargassum fish and pipe fish, which live in mats of *Sargassum,* an algae commonly found floating at the surface of many warm areas of the western Atlantic Ocean

      (2) These fish may have adapted their fins, body shape, and coloration to mimic the *Sargassum* fronds and float bladders

F. Reproduction and life history

1. Most marine fish are fecund, producing a large number of eggs

   a. A single adult salmon may produce 5,000 eggs; a large cod, 1 million eggs

   b. These eggs usually are small, with a diameter of about 1 mm

2. Fish eggs usually are laid in midwater and drift with plankton

   a. Water depth is too great in pelagic systems for attached benthic eggs

   b. However, nearshore fish can lay their eggs on the bottom in shallow areas

3. Eggs develop and hatch into larvae in about 3 weeks

4. All larvae that live in the plankton are classified as meroplankton

   a. Most larvae are small (3 to 10 mm long) and translucent

   b. The larvae subsist on the yolk of their egg for 2 weeks after hatching

   c. The larvae will starve and die if they fail to find food within 2 weeks after the yolk is exhausted

   d. This period, between yolk and feeding, is called the critical period

   e. Successful larvae feed on copepods or mollusk larvae and, possibly, algae (such as diatoms)

   f. Larvae grow in nursery grounds until they become adults

            (1) Nursery grounds generally are shallow and protected areas, such as bays or grass beds

            (2) Most larvae move into deeper water as they become adults

  5. Larvae metamorphose into juvenile fish at the end of the larval period, developing fins and scales

  6. Fish continue to grow throughout their adult life

  7. Most fish do not die of old age; rather, they are eaten by other predators, including humans

G. Swimming adaptations

  1. Epipelagic fish are fast swimmers, commonly undertaking ocean-basin-wide migrations

    a. Most have a long, stiff caudal peduncle and lunate fins for strong propulsion

    b. This swimming form — using a strong caudal fin — is called *tunniform swimming* because it is characteristic of tuna fish

    c. The optimum hydrodynamic body shape resembles a teardrop; very streamlined, it has the least amount of drag during swimming

    d. Modifications, such as fins that can retract into grooves, eyes with no lids, and eyes that do not bulge, decrease water resistance

  2. Coral reef fish do not swim long distances but need to hover and duck in and out of crevices

    a. Many coral reef fish exhibit *ostracaform swimming;* they do not use the powerful caudal fin for propulsion, but paddle using the pectoral fins

    b. Coral reef fish need precise maneuvering, not speed, and may use their tail as a rudder

V. Fish Ecology

A. General information

  1. Fish are at or near the top of the pyramid of food consumption and production in the ocean

  2. Humans are the final predators, consuming or otherwise utilizing fish, turtles, and whales

B. Population dynamics

  1. The population dynamics of commercially important species is better known than that of other marine organisms

  2. Most species use their ability to move horizontally to maintain themselves in a food-rich environment and to select habitats that are best suited for different stages in their life history

    a. The littoral zone often supports high densities of larval and young nekton feeding on abundant plankton and benthos

    b. However, the littoral zone may not provide food suitable for adult nekton, which then migrate offshore

  3. Fish have an extremely high mortality rate

    a. A female fish may produce 5 million eggs during its lifetime

    b. A mortality rate of 99.99996% between egg and mature adult is common

    c. The youngest and smallest stages of most organisms, usually planktonic, suffer the highest mortality; one example is the mortality rate for the plaice,

Mortality Rate of *Pleuronectes platessa*

Plaice (*Pleuronectes platessa*) have an extremely high mortality rate, primarily because of intensive predation. As this chart shows, if an individual survives 1 month, its mortality rate drops to 80%; 4 months, 40%; 1 year, 10%. The chances of a plaice reaching 15 years is statistically remote, however; only extremely high fertility rates keep fish like plaice viable as a species.

AGE-GROUP	MORTALITY
0 to 3 weeks	96%
1 to 2 months	80%
4 to 8 months	40%
9 to 12 months	10%
5 to 15 years	1%

        Pleuronectes platessa (see *Mortality Rate of* Pleuronectes platessa, page 140)
    d. High mortality rates are mainly due to small size
        (1) Small organisms can be consumed by a greater number of predatory organisms, both small and large
        (2) Larval nekton must grow quickly through the smaller life stages to avoid numerous, small predators
        (3) A high growth rate can be achieved only in areas of relative food abundance, such as those found in the littoral zone
    e. Surface currents control the distribution of larval nekton
        (1) The currents can pose a hazard to larvae attempting to reach nursery grounds
        (2) If the adults cannot spawn directly over the nursery grounds, currents may sweep the larvae out of high-productivity areas and into unsuitable areas
    f. Even if the adult fish population is halved, by fishing or some other means, a mortality reduction from 99.99996% to 99.99992% would allow the adult population to be replenished
    g. This may be a reasonable reduction in mortality because the reduction in the adult population would result in greater food availability
    h. Increasingly large adult populations do not always result in the maximum numbers of juvenile fish being *recruited* (entering the adult group)

C. Fisheries management
    1. Commercial fisheries are a relatively inefficient method of energy transfer
    2. Humans harvest primarily carnivores from the upper end of the oceanic food web; much more energy is available lower in the food web
    3. Many, if not all, major fishery areas and desirable fish species are now overfished and in danger of collapse
    4. The goal of fisheries management is to maintain or increase yields of desirable fish species caught in the wild
    5. Fisheries management relies on fisheries' catch statistics and research cruises to provide data for sophisticated models of how fish species react to changes in fishing

6. There is an increasing trend toward aquaculture — fish grown in commercial quantities in managed farms — although practical methods have been worked out for only a few species
7. There also is a shift toward the use of underutilized species, such as skates and dogfish; many of the underutilized species are now discarded because they are either not desirable as food or too fragile to reach markets in usable condition
8. Currently, there is little prospect for significantly increasing fisheries' yields
   a. Predictions for such increases usually include the harvest of small, midwater fish at extremely low population densities, thus making them impractical to harvest economically
   b. Additional gains from species not currently harvested, such as squid or krill, are entirely speculative
   c. New production will most likely occur only if new fishing grounds, such as the Indian Ocean, are exploited; few gains are possible from existing fisheries
   d. Modern fishing techniques, which enable humans to catch a very large percentage of a fish population and temporarily increase yields, are driving fish stocks below the levels needed for the fisheries to survive

Study Activities

1. Describe the different depth zones in the ocean.
2. Explain the importance of the swim bladder in fishes.
3. Describe how and why squid control their skin color.
4. Explain how some fish maintain their body temperature above seawater temperature.
5. Describe how sharks maintain their position in the water column.
6. Define some of the techniques used by fish to avoid visual predators.
7. Explain why female fish produce so many eggs.

15

The Benthos

Objectives

After studying this chapter, the reader should be able to:
• Describe the major categories of the benthos.
• Describe the general nature of interactions between organisms in benthic communities.
• Identify how food reaches benthic communities.
• Describe coral reef systems and explain their diversity and productivity.
• Explain the energy source of hydrothermal vent communities.

I. The Benthic Environment

A. General information
1. **Benthos,** or benthic organisms, are those that live on, in, or in contact with the bottom of the ocean
2. The benthic environment is almost two-dimensional
   a. It is superficially similar to the terrestrial environment
   b. Life inhabits only a very thin layer on the bottom, a vertical scale of centimeters, instead of kilometers as found in the pelagic environment
3. Almost all large marine plants and more than 90% of all marine animal species live on or in the bottom
4. Large plants are found only in shallow areas where sufficient light is available for photosynthesis
5. Animals, which do not require light, are found at all depths in the ocean, from areas only splashed by waves to deep-sea trenches
6. Because buoyancy is unnecessary for benthic organisms, they can have heavy external shells for protection from predators
7. The large number of species reflects the large degree of variability found in benthic environments
8. The benthos *biomass* (the amount of living matter present) also varies greatly, ranging from densely populated coral reef systems and hydrothermal vent communities to the vast, lightly populated abyssal and trench regions
9. Except in the cases of shallow-water communities and hydrothermal vent systems, food is supplied by particles that fall from above

B. Physical environment
1. Sediments may accumulate to depths of several kilometers on the continental shelf

2. Most marine sediments, excluding those in the deep ocean, do not contain oxygen except for a thin surface film; they are, therefore, uninhabitable except by bacteria
3. The thickness of the oxygenated zone can reach 10 cm in coastal areas and several meters in the deep ocean
4. The thickness of this aerobic layer depends on the amount of productivity in the overlying surface waters and on the sediment type
5. Benthic sediments underlying productive coastal areas are rich in hydrogen sulfide and ferrous ions formed as a result of biological activity
    a. Organic materials from the water column settle out into sediments
    b. They are decomposed by bacterial activity and then buried by the deposition of later sediments
    c. Sediments release NH_4^+, NO_3^-, PO_4^{3-}, and Si, recycling nutrients that fuel primary production in the water column
6. The type of sediments present in an area is controlled by near-bottom water velocity
    a. Sand, a coarse sediment, occurs in areas of high water movement
    b. Muds and particles with smaller grain sizes are found in areas of lower water movement
    c. The surface layers of sediments may be temporarily suspended by currents, allowing oxygenation of deeper sediments

II. Classification Schemes

A. General information
1. Several schemes are used to classify benthic organisms into functional groups
2. These are based on the benthic organism's sedimentary habit, size, and feeding strategy

B. Sedimentary habit
1. *Epifauna* are organisms found on top of the substrate (the ocean floor)
2. *Infauna* are organisms that live buried in the bottom
3. Epifauna include sea stars, crabs, lobsters, and sponges; examples of infauna include worms and clams

C. Size classifications
1. *Macrobenthos* are the most familiar organisms, such as clams, lobsters, and crabs; they are greater than 1 mm in diameter
2. The *meiobenthos* (meiofauna) include benthic foraminifera, nematode worms, small benthic copepods, and rotifers; these organisms range from 100 μm to 1 mm in diameter
3. The *microbenthos* protozoa, bacteria, and diatoms (where light is sufficient for photosynthesis) are organisms less than 100 μm in diameter

D. Location
1. The **supralittoral zone** is the spray zone, which is covered with water only during extremely high storm tides
2. The **intertidal zone** is the range that is alternately covered and exposed during normal tides

3. The *littoral benthic zone* is found from the low tide line to the shelf break, about 200 m
   a. Several types of littoral benthic communities exist, including rocky substrate, sand substrate, and mud substrate
   b. Coral reef systems also are included in this classification
4. The *suboceanic zone* is the benthic environment at depths of more than 200 m
   a. The suboceanic zone contains more than 60% of the benthic surface area
   b. No attached plants grow in the suboceanic zone because light is insufficient for photosynthesis
   c. The suboceanic zone is covered primarily by soft oceanic sediments
   d. The suboceanic zone also includes hydrothermal vent environments

E. Feeding processes
1. Most benthic primary producers photosynthesize, although chemosynthesis is important in some areas
   a. Benthic primary producers include benthic diatoms, cyanobacteria, and some photosynthetic bacteria that are important in coastal wetlands and salt marshes
   b. Nonphotosynthetic, chemosynthetic bacteria are important in hydrothermal vent systems and coastal wetlands
2. Relatively few higher plants inhabit the benthos; they include eel grass, *Zostera,* found in shallow waters of northern areas; turtle grass, *Thalassia,* in tropical areas; and *Spartina,* salt marsh grass, in coastal wetlands and mangroves in tropical and subtropical coastal areas
3. Benthic animals are classified according to their feeding method
   a. *Plant grazers* feed on attached plants
      (1) Snails crawl along the bottom and scrape algae off plants
      (2) Sea urchins are specialized to eat encrusting algae
      (3) Green turtles feed on turtle grass
   b. *Suspension feeders* filter food particles out of the water
      (1) These food particles include zooplankton, phytoplankton, and detritus
      (2) Suspension feeders include barnacles, clams, and sponges
   c. *Deposit feeders* ingest sediments so that they can digest the organic detritus contained in the sediments
      (1) They then defecate the depleted sediment
      (2) Deposit feeders rarely are seen because, for the most part, they live buried in the sediments
      (3) Deposit feeders include some clams, snails, most polychaete worms, and sea cucumbers
   d. *Carnivores* kill and eat other animals, and *scavengers* eat dead plants and animals
      (1) This category includes a wide variety of taxonomic groups
      (2) Common carnivores and scavengers include lobsters, crabs, some carnivorous snails, many worms, and most starfish
   e. *Symbionts* are two dissimilar organisms — often one plant, one animal — that live together symbiotically (in a mutually beneficial relationship)
      (1) Some benthic animals have symbiotic algae or bacteria
      (2) These symbionts supply nutrition derived from photosynthesis or chemosynthesis to the animal

Structure of a Coral and a Tube Worm

The illustrations below show the anatomical structures of a coral and a tube worm. Corals and hydrothermal vent tube worms are symbiotic organisms.

Coral

Tube worm

Tentacles

Mouth

Mesentery

Gastric filament

Coenosarc

Limestone calyx

Pharynx

Coelenteron

Tentacles

Vestimentum

Trophosome

Coelom

(3) Corals and hydrothermal vent tube worms also are symbiotic organisms (see *Structure of a Coral and a Tube Worm,* page 145)

F. Distribution of biomass
1. Benthic biomass is highest in areas where primary production occurs on the sea bottom; this occurs in coastal and other shallow areas and at hydrothermal vents
2. No primary production occurs on the sea bottom in many regions
   a. The benthic community must depend on the productivity of the overlying water column in these areas
   b. Higher productivity in the overlying water column results in higher benthic biomass

III. Benthic Organisms

A. General information
1. The benthic environment, particularly the suboceanic zone, is characteristically cold, still, and dark; life moves at a slow pace
2. Benthic organisms must either rely on food falling from well-lit upper water layers or feed on each other
3. Deep-sea benthic organisms commonly have a wide geographic range
   a. Physical conditions can be similar over a wide area and stable for long periods

b. These large, stable areas allow characteristic assemblages of organisms to develop

B. Intraspecific and interspecific interactions
1. Benthic habitats can be limited by space, food, or both, leading to competition between individuals and species for limited resources
2. Although competition in the benthos does not necessarily result in the elimination of competing species, it may result in lower growth, higher emigration, and a smaller expenditure of energy on reproduction
3. Four types of benthic organisms have lifestyles that cause them to interact with other organisms
   a. Some feed by collecting material as it settles onto the surface of sediment
   b. Some construct tubes or mucus-lined burrows or otherwise preempt and stabilize the sediment
   c. Some actively move through the substratum
   d. Some produce large quantities of fecal materials
4. *Interference competition,* the best-known type of benthic competition, is an interaction in which one organism renders the habitat unsuitable for other organisms
   a. Conditioning the environment to make it unusable by other species may be the accidental result of *pelletization* (ingestion and subsequent excretion of sediment in the form of compact pellets), **bioturbation,** or some other physical alteration of the sediment
   b. This also may be achieved by releasing noxious chemicals into the environment, essentially making it toxic for organisms of other species
   c. One example of interference competition is demonstrated by the gastrotrich *Turbanella,* which releases a substance into surrounding sediments that causes the competing polychaete worm *Protodriloides* to avoid the area
   d. Another example of interference competition is the monospecific aggregation of brittle stars that is common on many areas of the continental shelf
      (1) Dense aggregations of omnivorous brittle stars seem to be able to consume anything that descends onto them from the plankton, including the metamorphosing larval stages of other organisms, such as worms or mollusks
      (2) Brittle stars stop feeding during the brief period during which they brood their young
      (3) This period provides a short opportunity for other species to invade the area and grow too large to be eaten by the brittle stars when they resume feeding
      (4) In this case, competition is indiscriminate in excluding all organisms that colonize from above
   e. Other species can coexist with the dominant organism if they develop other strategies to colonize an area; for example, polychaete worms can spend their larval stages in a burrow system in an area dominated by brittle stars
   f. Other forms of interference competition include the disruption of burrowing organisms by tube-dwelling organisms and the aggregation of sediments into pellets by deposit feeders; many types of competitive interactions take place, making few generalizations possible
5. Predation keeps one or a few species from dominating an environment, maintaining higher species diversity by lowering the population levels of superior competitors

a. Without predation, the number of species in a given area decreases

b. Predation helps keep organism density and species richness below the carrying capacity of the environment

c. A secondary effect of predation is that it channels energy from reproduction to regeneration in the prey species

d. Predators may not ingest an entire animal but only a portion of it

    (1) For example, predators bite off only the siphons of mollusks or the tentacular crowns of tube worms

    (2) Although these insults do not kill the animal, they force it to regenerate biomass instead of allocating its supply of energy for general growth or reproduction

6. Resource competition, competition for food, is often the controlling factor in situations in which predation does not determine benthic population densities

a. In general, deposit feeders compete most aggressively for food; suspension feeders, for space

b. As a result of the competitive process, the superior competitor restricts other species to areas of lower productivity or to areas that it finds inaccessible or unattractive

C. Stability

1. The physical conditions of the benthic environment — temperature, salinity, and light — are highly stable over long periods, especially in the deep ocean

2. Because of this, deep-water benthic communities seem to be stable over long periods of time, although those in shallow waters may fluctuate in the short term because of seasonal cycles

3. Shallow-water areas may have high mortality rates in the winter, causing seasonal variation in abundance

4. Large physical instabilities, such as those caused by storm damage or tidal action, also may result in the mass mortality of benthic organisms in shallow-water areas

a. The rate of recolonization of a disturbed area is proportional to the dispersal faculties of the fauna

b. The time required for a benthic community to return to its original state after a major disturbance ranges from 1 to more than 20 years

D. Diversity

1. In general, the shallow tropical benthos has the greatest species richness

2. The diversity of benthic organisms decreases toward the poles in coastal and shallow waters

a. Food is available only during certain months of the year in temperate areas

    (1) Animals must subsist on food reserves for the rest of the year

    (2) Most organisms produce a few well-provisioned young; population growth rates are low

    (3) The low rates of speciation and population growth result in species poverty in latitudes nearer the poles

b. Food is available throughout the year in the tropics

    (1) High population densities increase competition for available food, resulting in high growth rates

    (2) Predation is probably highest in the tropics

(3) A moderate population increase in the tropics leads to a species-rich epifauna

(4) The dominant epifaunal organisms, such as corals, provide complex structures of great spatial heterogeneity; this encourages diversity by allowing microhabitat specialization

IV. Food Sources for Benthic Communities

A. General information

1. With the exception of very shallow water areas and hot vents, food must enter benthic systems from above
2. Complex food webs have developed in benthic communities to process and transfer food that enters the system
3. The highest benthic biomasses have been recorded in inshore waters, which are areas of high water column productivity
4. Production in the benthic fauna rarely is greater than 5% of that in the overlying waters

B. Trophic relationships

1. Food can enter benthic communities by two main avenues: through production within the benthic community or from overlying waters
2. Food is derived from living and nonliving organic matter associated with the sediment in shallow water areas
   a. Photosynthetic plants contribute to the food supply in areas with enough light for photosynthesis
   b. Unicellular and filamentous algae live in areas of the littoral zone where the photic zone extends to the bottom of the ocean
   c. Some microbenthos (bacteria) also contribute to the food supply by recycling dissolved organic compounds to the primary producers
3. The benthos of the shelf and deeper areas of the ocean are supported entirely by pelagic production and detrital materials washed in from coastal areas; these enter the benthic system in the form of detritus and living plankton that settle from the water above
   a. The rate of food input depends on the depth of the water through which the particles travel and on the magnitude of pelagic production
   b. These are not linear relationships; a higher percentage of falling material will reach the bottom in areas of high productivity
4. Some material that reaches the bottom consists of the fecal pellets of herbivorous zooplankton
   a. Most material in a fecal pellet remains undigested after passing through the short and inefficient digestive tract of most herbivorous zooplankton
   b. Fecal pellets package detrital particles in a form that sinks more quickly than smaller, unpackaged particles
5. Suspension feeders play an important role by removing material from the water column and transferring it to the sediment
   a. Not all of the material filtered by suspension feeders is suitable for food
   b. Unsuitable materials that are not ingested are rejected as pseudofecal pellets, which often are bound in mucus
   c. Both fecal and pseudofecal pellets are then available for deposit feeders

C. Utilization of food sources
1. The nutritive value of detritus particles decreases as they fall through the water column
   a. These particles lose soluble organic compounds through leaching
   b. More losses occur as the detrital particles pass through several guts, as they are ingested and excreted several times before arriving at the sea bed
   c. By the time a detrital particle arrives at the bottom, it probably contains only skeletal or other refractory substances
   d. The detrital particles are colonized by various bacteria when they eat the sediments and support colonies of metazoans that feed on bacteria
   e. A particle of detritus ingested by a polychaete worm is a microcosm in its own right; bacteria, ciliates, amoebas, flatworms, and nematodes probably will become associated with original detrital material
2. Deposit feeders ingest sediment and its associated detrital component
   a. Deposit feeders have a low assimilation efficiency — only about 1%
   b. Deposit feeders digest the living component of the detrital aggregate; the inert components are returned to the environment, where they are recolonized
3. The supply of suspended food determines the productivity of suspension feeders
4. Suspension feeders can obtain high-quality food somewhat more easily than deposit feeders because they consume and digest microbenthic algae, living plankton, and dead phytoplankton cells in a feeding process similar to that of planktonic herbivores
5. The rate of fall of potential food particles determines the productivity of deposit feeders
6. The production of deposit and suspension feeders is available to benthic carnivores and to benthic feeding members of the nekton

V. Coral Reef Ecology

A. General information
1. Coral reefs are extremely productive and diverse benthic communities in an otherwise nutrient-poor area
2. Corals rival humans' ability to alter Earth's surface
3. Corals change the ocean bottom's form and structure
4. Corals are important land builders, creating banks, islands, and chains of islands
5. True coral reefs are limited to warm, clear waters in equatorial and subtropical waters

B. Biology
1. A coral consists of a thin, almost two-dimensional film of living material covering a block of limestone that it has deposited
2. Corals are members of Phylum Cnidaria, which also includes jellyfish and sea anemones
3. Unlike sea anemones, corals continually build hard skeletons of calcium carbonate, which is deposited beneath the living tissue
4. Some corals are solitary, existing as single *polyps;* however, most corals are members of colonies of small polyps that range from 1 to 3 mm in diameter

5. Each polyp is connected to its neighbor by a thin sheet of tissue called the *coenosarc,* which extends over the limestone between the polyps
6. The stony corals are members of Order Scleractinia
7. Hermatypic (true) corals are called *hexacorallia* because they have six (or multiples of six) tentacles
8. Soft corals (such as the fire coral, *Millepora*) and the gorgonians are called *octocorallia* because they have eight tentacles
9. Each coral polyp sits in the *calyx,* a cuplike depression in the limestone rock secreted by the coral
   a. The calyx has radiating fins that project from its base
   b. During the day or in times of danger, the polyp retracts into the calyx for protection

C. Feeding

1. The polyp extends its tentacles to feed on zooplankton, usually at night
   a. The mouth is centered within a crown of tentacles
   b. The stomach of a coral is a simple sac that encloses numerous longitudinal folds called *mesenteries*
   c. Corals can be very efficient feeders, removing 60% to 90% of diatoms and small zooplankton from the water passing over a reef
2. Corals also can extrude a mucus net to trap and filter extremely fine particles
3. The growth rate of corals depends on the species and on the physical conditions in which it lives
   a. Massive corals, such as the brain corals and starlet corals, grow slowly (0.5 to 2.0 cm/year); faster growing corals, such as elk and staghorn corals, grow at rates of 10 to 20 cm/year
   b. The growth rate of corals also depends on temperature, cloud cover, and water depth
4. Most corals contain a symbiotic dinoflagellate called **zooxanthellae**
   a. All species of coral that have zooxanthellae contain a single species of dinoflagellate, *Symbiodinium microadriaticum*
   b. Zooxanthellae may account for 50% of the biomass of rapid-growing corals; the amount is slightly less in the slower-growing, more heterotrophic corals
   c. The coral's nutritive needs are supplied partly by the zooxanthellae
   d. This symbiosis also assists in the deposition of the coral skeleton by changing the internal chemistry of the coral to make it easier to secrete calcium carbonate
   e. The coral's growth will stop if the zooxanthellae somehow are removed
   f. In recent years, large areas of coral have temporarily lost their zooxanthellae
      (1) This is known as *coral bleaching* because the normally olive-colored coral tissue turns white without the zooxanthellae
      (2) Bleached corals can survive only for a relatively short time
      (3) High water temperatures are suspected to be the cause of the coral bleaching episodes, although several other mechanisms also have been suggested
5. Most corals also use cilia to feed
   a. Cilia, which cover much of the coral tissue, move small food particles to the mouth
   b. Edible particles are consumed and inedible particles released back into the water currents

6. Some corals are able to trap extremely fine particles, such as bacteria, in mucus nets
7. The size of the polyp is related to the feeding method
   a. Corals with small polyps generally depend on photosynthesis
   b. Corals with large polyps usually are carnivorous
   c. Corals with large polyps commonly live in shaded areas because they do not need as much light as those with small polyps
8. The shape of the colony suggests the predominant type of feeding
   a. Autotrophic colonies, which depend on photosynthesis, usually develop branching forms to maximize light collection in relatively shallow water
   b. Heterotrophs, which are usually more rounded, are very efficient at filtering particles from the water

D. Reproduction
1. Corals release larvae, called planulae, into the water as a method for dispersal
2. Planulae are tiny, and several thousand are released into the water column at the same time
3. Planulae respond to light, switching from photopositive to photonegative
   a. They are photopositive, swimming toward light and into currents at the water's surface, for about 2 days
   b. The planulae then become photonegative after 2 days and settle out onto a hard, unoccupied surface
4. If the larvae settle onto a favorable site, they then develop into polyps
5. Polyps reproduce by budding; an entire colony is a clone of the original polyp

E. Distribution
1. The physical characteristics of an area determine its suitability for coral growth
2. Corals require warm water; year-round water temperature must exceed 20° C
3. Corals require bright light and clear water to enable the zooxanthellae to photosynthesize
4. Corals are usually restricted to depths shallower than 60 m because of light limitations at increasing depths
5. Corals are restricted to areas of low turbidity because particles in the water smother their ciliary feeding system
6. These requirements rule out areas like the coast of South America, which has high river water input, and Africa, where the water is cool because of local currents
7. Corals can be killed as result of any physical movements that increase sedimentation, such as dredging or industrial activity; this has become a serious problem in many areas in recent years

F. Reef structure
1. Coral reefs are classified as one of three general types: fringing reefs, barrier reefs, and atolls
2. *Fringing reefs* project seaward directly from the shore
   a. Fringing reefs surround islands and border continents
   b. Fringing reefs are the most common reef type in the world
3. *Barrier reefs* are separated from land masses by a lagoon
   a. Barrier reefs can be very extensive
   b. The Great Barrier Reef is more than 1,000 miles (1,609 km) long

4. *Atolls* rest above the flanks of a submerged volcano
   a. The volcano slowly sinks because of isostasy (for details about isostasy, see Chapter 2, Geologic Structure of the Oceans)
   b. The coral grows, maintaining itself in the well-lit waters, developing a circular or oval shape above the perimeter of the volcano; this idea was first developed by Charles Darwin on the HMS *Beagle*
   c. The reef surrounds a central lagoon after the volcano is submerged completely
   d. Over 300 atolls exist in the Pacific and only 10 in the Atlantic Ocean because of the much greater volcanic activity in the Pacific
5. All reef types show a similar profile, the result of physical factors acting on the corals
   a. The reef front does not present a solid wall to waves
      (1) It consists of a series of fingerlike projections called *spurs* and sand-filled valleys between the spurs called *grooves*
      (2) This structure helps dissipate the force of waves breaking on the reef front
   b. Coral morphology has adapted to different wave-energy conditions
      (1) Branching corals, which do not present a barrier to incoming waves, are dominant in shallow, high-energy zones
      (2) Branching corals orient their arms into the predominant current to aid in capturing prey
      (3) Rounded forms, typical of brain corals, are found in lower-energy, deeper waters
      (4) Many corals become bigger in deeper waters to resist rolling by waves
   c. The same species of coral may have different morphologies in different light conditions
      (1) Corals growing in deeper waters tend to be more platelike to provide greater surface area for capturing light
      (2) The Caribbean reef-building coral, *Montastrea annularis,* typifies this scheme
         (a) *Montastrea* is rounded or pagoda-like in shallow waters
         (b) It becomes platelike or shingled in deeper waters because this improves light collection and because calcium carbonate is deposited more slowly at greater depths

G. Coral hierarchy

1. The corals' need for space and light leads to competition between species
2. Some coral species, particularly branching corals, grow faster than others, but do not overgrow slower-growing corals to become a single, dominant species in a reef
3. Corals that are overgrown and shaded do not get enough light and eventually die; a reef would then be dominated by fast-growing corals
4. Studies have shown a hierarchy of aggressiveness among different species of corals
   a. The most aggressive species are slow-growing and massive; the least aggressive are the fastest-growing species
   b. Aggressive corals can modify and extend their tentacles to kill adjacent corals

      c. A buffer zone of dead coral is eventually established between two different species

      d. This hierarchy of aggression allows slow- and fast-growing corals to coexist on the same reef

H. Production

1. Coral reefs are extremely productive, producing up to 1,000 g carbon $(C)/m^2/year$, while surrounded by areas of extremely low productivity (40 g $C/m^2/year$)
2. Coral reef systems combine energy from three sources
      a. Corals obtain energy from photosynthesis via zooxanthellae, which leads to efficient nutrient recycling within the coral organism itself
      b. Corals feed as predators and herbivores through tentacular feeding
      c. Corals feed on bacteria and other small particles by ciliary feeding or mucus nets
3. Coral reefs attract other organisms, such as predatory fish, to the reef; they then contribute to the system through excretion
4. Reef platforms support many other organisms, both plant and animal, in addition to the corals themselves
      a. Red and green algae, which incorporate calcium carbonate as a structural material, contribute to calcareous reef sands
      b. Other benthic organisms, such as sponges, tube worms, anemones, and sea urchins, all help to create and shape a coral reef ecosystem
5. These additional food sources contribute to the entire reef ecosystem; reefs act as a nutrient trap, capturing energy from the outside and recycling all energy within the reef

VI. Hydrothermal Vent Communities

A. General information

1. Diverse and productive communities were discovered in 1977 at hydrothermal vents located on midocean ridges, first in the Pacific Ocean and then later in the Atlantic Ocean
2. New vent systems are discovered as more of the midocean ridges are explored
3. These communities do not derive their energy from sunlight through photosynthesis, but from the chemical energy of sulfide compounds through ***chemosynthesis***
4. The temperature of water exiting a vent may exceed 300° C

B. Hydrothermal vent community ecosystem

1. Over 300 new species have been discovered in these communities
2. Organisms found in these systems include large tube worms, giant clams, anemones, crabs, shrimp, mussels, and pink sea urchins
3. Different populations of organisms have been found at Pacific and Atlantic vents; it is not known why these communities differ
4. It also is not known how organisms colonize newly formed vents, which may be tens to hundreds of kilometers away from an older vent
5. Sulfur-oxidizing bacteria provide food in these communities
      a. These bacteria oxidize the sulfide compounds that are discharged in the water from the vents

b. These bacteria live symbiotically with tube worms, clams, mussels, and
   some other organisms, providing the organisms with nutrition
6. Other animals at the vents may feed on free-living bacteria or act as predators on
   other animals
7. Such communities contain 10,000 to 100,000 times more living matter than other
   deep-sea benthic communities, and they rival coral reefs in productivity

Study Activities

1. Describe the differences between suspension feeders and deposit feeders.
2. Explain how filter feeders can prevent larvae of other organisms from becoming
   established.
3. Describe how physical conditions change as depth and distance from shore increase.
4. Explain how coral reefs can be highly productive when surrounded by waters of low
   productivity.
5. Describe the source of energy for organisms living in hydrothermal vent communities.

16

Mesopelagic and Bathypelagic Life

Objectives

After studying this chapter, the reader should be able to:
- Compare the epipelagic, mesopelagic, and bathypelagic zones.
- Describe the various uses of biologically produced light in the deep ocean.
- Describe how organisms have adapted to an environment with very little food and light.
- Explain why some organisms migrate hundreds of meters vertically each day.

I. The Deep-Ocean Environment

A. General information
1. The mesopelagic and bathypelagic zones are the largest volumes available for life on Earth; by volume, the epipelagic zone contains 5% of the ocean; the mesopelagic, 21%; and the bathypelagic, 74% (see *Ocean Zones,* page 156)
   a. The epipelagic zone encompasses depths from 0 to 200 m
   b. The mesopelagic zone encompasses depths from 200 to 1,000 m
   c. The bathypelagic zone encompasses depths greater than 1,000 m
2. The deep ocean is still the great unknown area of the ocean; only a small percentage of it has been studied by any means
   a. Scuba diving is limited to the upper 30 m of the ocean
   b. Deep-diving submarine exploration is very limited
      (1) Dives are very expensive
      (2) Dives are very brief and can study only a small area
   c. Recently, remotely operated vehicles have been used to study areas that humans cannot thoroughly or safely investigate

B. Physical environment
1. The main thermocline occurs in the mesopelagic zone; temperature may change from above 20° C near the top of the mesopelagic zone to 2° to 4° C at the bottom
2. Changes in salinity and density coincide with the thermocline (for more information, see Chapter 9, Thermohaline Circulation)
3. The intensity and quality of light change quickly with increasing depth
   a. Light is absorbed and scattered by seawater
   b. Light intensity decreases exponentially with increasing depth
   c. Only about 1% of the light that hits the ocean surface penetrates to 150 m, even in the clearest ocean water

Ocean Zones

The illustration below depicts the three primary ocean zones. The epipelagic zone contains 5% of Earth's ocean volume; the mesopelagic zone, 21%; and the bathypelagic zone, 74%. Organisms living in the deep-ocean environment of the mesopelagic and bathypelagic zones have become adapted to extremely low levels of food, light, and temperature.

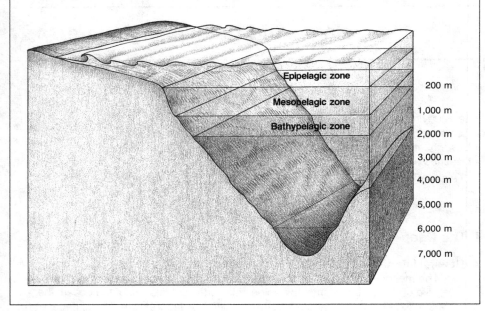

d. No light of biological significance from the surface penetrates below 1,000 m
4. Different wavelengths of visible light penetrate to various depths
   a. Red light is absorbed most quickly, in shallow water
   b. Blue-green light can penetrate to the greatest depth in clear ocean water
5. Pressure increases with increasing depth: 1 atmosphere (or atm, the pressure of air at sea level, approximately 14.7 psi) for each additional 10 m of depth

II. Mesopelagic Life

A. General information

1. Scientists have found it extremely difficult to learn about the organisms of the deep ocean
   a. Most knowledge of deep-sea organisms is derived from the study of the contents of nets towed behind research vessels
   b. Only organisms that are slow to avoid nets are captured
   c. Of those organisms captured, only those with robust bodies, such as crustaceans and most fish, are identifiable when the net returns to the deck of the research vessel

    d. Almost no information is collected about those organisms swift enough to avoid nets or so fragile that they disintegrate while in the net

    e. Much of our knowledge of the organisms of the deep ocean is derived from the study of their dead bodies, which are collected in nets or washed up on beaches, not from observing them in life

    f. Only recently have observations of living organisms been made by scuba diving scientists in the upper 30 m of the ocean or by scientists in small research submersibles at deeper depths

  2. The deep ocean is a vast area without internal boundaries

    a. There are no structures to hide the inhabitants of the mesopelagic and bathypelagic zones

    b. These vast areas are characterized by uniform physical conditions; temperature, salinity, light, and pressure change very little over great distances at a given depth

  3. The organisms inhabiting the mesopelagic and bathypelagic zones are not inherently different from those living in surface waters

  4. They have, however, become adapted to the extremely low levels of food and light, high pressure, and low temperatures found in the ocean at depths below 200 m

B. Visual adaptations to low light

  1. Visual predators use sunlight for hunting prey over great distances

  2. The organisms that live at great depths cannot use this tactic because there is less light and very little food; they must try to expend as little energy as possible when searching for food

  3. Ambient light in the mesopelagic zone has specific characteristics

    a. Light is almost completely restricted to the blue-green wavelengths, with the other wavelengths having been absorbed at shallower depths

    b. Light at these depths comes down from the surface; very little scattered or reflected light travels upward or horizontally

    c. Light in the mesopelagic zone is best described as downwelling; it has one wavelength and is unidirectional

  4. The eyes of mesopelagic organisms have adapted to these low light levels at great depths by becoming 15 to 30 times more sensitive to low light than human eyes

    a. In general, the eyes of mesopelagic organisms are proportionally bigger, with greater enervation and more visual pigments

    b. The eyes have a *tapetum,* a shiny surface in the back of the eye that acts like a reflector

    c. Mesopelagic fish eyes have rods but no cones

      (1) Human eyes have rods (which are sensitive to low light levels but do not perceive color) and cones (which provide color vision at higher light levels)

      (2) Because only one limited band of wavelengths is available to them, mesopelagic fish cannot use color vision

      (3) Their rods may be stacked, or arranged sequentially, to amplify the available dim light

    d. Although mesopelagic organisms have eyes specialized to see in the blue-green region of the spectrum, some have eyes with photopigments that make it possible to receive any red light produced by bioluminescence

e. Mesopelagic organisms watch for pattern changes in the uniform down-welling light field; they look for any disruption, such as a silhouette or flashes from other organisms

f. The eyes of mesopelagic organisms are commonly pointed upward to see more easily the silhouettes of prey above them

5. Some organisms — primarily zooplankton, squid, and gelatinous organisms — reduce their visibility by becoming small or transparent

   a. The stomach is usually opaque to trap light from still-glowing luminescent prey

   b. Eyes are opaque to increase visual efficiency

6. Color may be used as camouflage

   a. Many upper mesopelagic organisms are silver; the color helps the fish re-flect light back at the predator, making the prey fish difficult to see

   b. Deep mesopelagic and bathypelagic organisms are usually black or red

C. Bioluminescence

1. **Bioluminescence** seems to be an essential part of mesopelagic life

2. Bioluminescence has evolved independently in several groups of marine organ-isms at all ocean depths

   a. Almost all mesopelagic and bathypelagic organisms produce light

   b. About 90% of all fish species living at 500 m are bioluminescent

3. **Photophores,** the light-producing organs of fish, range from simple to complex in structure

   a. The simplest type of photophores are gardens of symbiotic, luminescent bac-teria cultured in chambers in the skin of some mesopelagic fish and squid

      (1) This chamber is usually connected to the outside skin through an open-ing

      (2) The bacteria produce light continuously, but the fish or squid can control its light output with shutters or a skin flap of black-pigmented cells

      (3) Some squid combine *chromatophores* (color-producing cells) with these bacterial photophores, allowing them to produce light of different color and intensity

   b. Most bioluminescence in mesopelagic organisms is produced by a simple biochemical reaction controlled by the nervous system

      (1) This is the same process that occurs in fireflies

      (2) A substrate called luciferin is oxidized in the presence of the enzyme luciferase, producing energy in the form of light

      (3) While the amounts of luciferin and luciferase may vary from organism to organism, the reaction is similar

   c. The photophore may be complex, with systems of lenses and reflectors to amplify, regulate, and direct light output

4. Probable reasons for bioluminescence include camouflage, predator distraction, species recognition, and mate attraction

   a. Bioluminescence is used as camouflage in the mesopelagic zone

      (1) Many predators find their prey by looking up for a silhouette

      (2) *Counterillumination* is a technique in which light produced by an organ-ism is used to minimize its silhouette

      (3) Counterilluminating mesopelagic organisms have photophores on their ventral side; the photophores produce light that precisely matches the intensity and wavelength of the ambient downwelling light field

(4) This light eliminates the silhouette of the organism
(5) The eyes or a dorsal photosensor is used to sense ambient light and bioluminescence, so that bioluminescent output can be matched to ambient light
(6) This complex but efficient method of bioluminescent camouflage is seen in almost all mesopelagic organisms, including crustaceans, squid, and fish
(7) Some organisms have the ability to produce two wavelengths of light, to match downwelling moonlight as well as sunlight
  b. Bioluminescence may be used to startle or distract predators
(1) Dinoflagellates, which are found at the surface, use bioluminescence when disturbed
(2) This may startle predators, especially when the dinoflagellates are found in dense aggregations; these flashes of light also may attract predators of the grazers feeding on the dinoflagellates
(3) Some deep-sea squid have large photophores that resemble flashbulbs; these are used to startle or blind predators
(4) Other deep-sea squid can release a cloud of luminescent ink that serves as a decoy to distract predators
  c. Some deep-sea organisms use bioluminescent feeding lures to attract prey
(1) This prey-capture strategy saves energy because prey swim directly to the predator
(2) For example, the angler fish has a lure at the end of a short pole that resembles a glowing copepod fecal pellet, one of the most important food items transported from the epipelagic zone to the deep ocean
  d. The patterns of photophores on a bioluminescent organism are species specific and may be used for identification
(1) The patterns on male and female fish of the same species may differ, thus serving as attractants for mating
(2) Bioluminescence may also be useful for species recognition during schooling behavior in fishes
  e. Some fish use photophores for illumination
(1) Certain species of fish emit light from large patch photophores located beneath the eyes
(2) Red, instead of blue-green, light is produced in these unusual photophores
(3) Because most other mesopelagic organisms cannot see red light, the red-light-producing fish may use this light to search for prey
(4) In a further escalation of this strategy, predators of this fish have developed the ability to see red light and thus can capture these red-light-producers

D. Adaptations to scarce food

1. Food is relatively abundant in the epipelagic zone, a region where light is sufficient for photosynthesis
2. There is less food in the mesopelagic zone and even less in the bathypelagic zone
3. Organisms living at these depths may eat only a few meals per year
4. With the exception of hydrothermal vent systems, where the food web is based on bacterial chemosynthesis, all food in the mesopelagic and bathypelagic zones must come from the overlying waters of the epipelagic zone

5. Food-hunting methods must change in the deep ocean
   a. Without abundant energy at these depths, the organisms cannot swim long distances in search of food
   b. Most predators of the deep ocean have adopted a sit-and-wait strategy for capturing prey
      (1) Mesopelagic fish that use this feeding strategy have a long, slender, pike-like body plan
      (2) They are able to dart forward quickly for a few body lengths to capture prey within a small radius
      (3) A slender body also helps minimize the fish's silhouette
6. These deep-sea organisms must be able to capture any available prey, almost regardless of size; as a result, the organisms have developed several adaptations for capturing prey as large as or larger than the predator
   a. Deep-sea predators usually have large, sharp teeth to ensure the successful capture of available prey
   b. Many mesopelagic predators have large jaws with a wide gape
   c. Other deep-sea predators have extensible jaws and stomachs
7. In this food-poor environment, deep-sea organisms cannot spend much energy on maintaining their depth by swimming
   a. Instead, energy is devoted to hydrostatic methods of buoyancy
   b. Reduction in the total size of the organism is a common strategy
   c. Most mesopelagic organisms are less than 15 cm long; the fierce-looking fish that appear in most texts actually measure just a few inches
   d. Heavy bone and muscle mass are reduced, thus reducing density and the tendency to sink
   e. The heart and gills also are reduced; the hunting strategy adopted at this depth requires less swimming
8. Other adaptations attempt to increase buoyancy directly
   a. Some fish have a fat-filled swim bladder
   b. Some deep-sea squid have a bladder filled with a fluid less dense than seawater or store lightweight fluids in their tissues, particularly in the arms

E. Low-temperature adaptations
1. Because most mesopelagic organisms are *poikilothermic,* temperature affects their metabolism, growth, and reproduction
2. Biological reactions have a preferred range of temperatures but are generally faster at warmer temperatures
3. Muscles are less efficient at cold temperatures, so more energy is needed to swim at the same speed at low temperatures
4. Except in polar regions, the epipelagic zone is relatively warm, generally from 18° to 30° C
5. The mesopelagic zone is colder, approximately 4° to 18° C, with some seasonal variation in the upper depths
6. The bathypelagic zone is uniformly cold, between 0° and 4° C, with no seasonal variation
7. No single organism has adapted to the full range of temperatures found in the ocean, but some species have adapted to more than one temperature range

F. High-pressure adaptations
1. Pressure is directly proportional to ocean depth; pressure increases 1 atm for every 10 m of depth
2. Ocean pressure ranges from 1 atm at the surface to more than 1,000 atm at the greatest depths
3. Pressure affects organisms with swim bladders and influences the rate of some biochemical reactions
4. High pressures are not necessarily bad for life; the organisms found at great depths have adapted to that condition
5. A famous example of the effect of pressure on life in the deep ocean resulted from an unplanned experiment aboard the deep-ocean research submarine *Alvin*
   a. The *Alvin* accidentally flooded at the surface, before the scientists could board the submarine, and sank to the ocean floor in 1,540 m of water, with the passenger sphere flooded
   b. When the *Alvin* was recovered 1 year later, an examination of the submarine revealed that the lunches packed for the scientists — sandwiches and fruit wrapped in waxed paper — had not decomposed
   c. This observation led to a thorough investigation of life processes in high-pressure environments
6. Bacteria adapted to extremely high pressures have metabolic rates 100 times slower than those of surface bacteria maintained under the same light and temperature conditions

G. Reproductive adaptations
1. Little is known about methods of reproduction in the deep ocean
2. The organisms that inhabit these depths must have remarkable methods of finding mates in the extremely low population densities of the mesopelagic and bathypelagic zones
3. One unusual adaptation to low population density is seen in the angler fish
   a. The male becomes permanently attached to the female as a parasitic dwarf, deriving nourishment from her
   b. The male does little more than produce sperm
   c. The rate of contact between individuals is so low that it is advantageous to maintain constant contact

III. The Bathypelagic Zone

A. General information
1. The bathypelagic zone is a large environment with virtually constant conditions
   a. No light penetrates from the surface
   b. There is little variation in temperature or salinity
2. Organisms of the bathypelagic zone display an exaggeration of the trends seen in organisms of the mesopelagic zone

B. Adaptations
1. Because even less food is available in the bathypelagic zone, the inhabitants swim even less than those of the mesopelagic zone
2. Bathypelagic organisms are found in extremely low densities
3. They are small in size, grow slowly, and have great longevity

4. Bathypelagic organisms have an extremely low rate of activity and metabolism
5. Because they do not need to reduce their silhouettes or move to capture prey, there is no need for a thin body form; thus, most bathypelagic organisms are spherical or bulbous
6. Bathypelagic organisms have reduced hearts, muscles, and nervous systems; weakly ossified skeletons; and weak gills
7. Bathypelagic organisms have a low protein content and a high water content
8. These fish are black (or red in the case of crustaceans); they have small photophores that are not used for counterillumination and small or reduced eyes
   a. In the absence of any color but blue in the deep ocean, red is as effective as black for camouflage
   b. Fish produce the pigment melanin, which is black
   c. Crustaceans produce a red pigment, astaxanthin, which is derived from carotene

IV. Transport of Food to the Deep Ocean

A. General information
1. All food entering the mesopelagic and bathypelagic zones must come from overlying waters
2. Only a fraction of the food in surface waters is available to the waters below
   a. Copepod fecal pellets and marine snow are important food sources in the mesopelagic and bathypelagic zones
   b. Food falls, while infrequent, are another food source

B. Particle aggregations
1. Copepods are the major herbivores in surface waters, as they feed on larger phytoplankton
   a. The copepod digestive system is short and inefficient
   b. Copepods package phytoplankton into relatively large fecal pellets that sink quickly in the water column
   c. The pellets can sink to the ocean bottom in a period of days, compared to months or years for unpackaged detritus
   d. This rain of copepod fecal pellets is a food source for organisms inhabiting the mesopelagic and bathypelagic zones
2. Other aggregations of small particles, called marine snow, sink through the water column relatively quickly because of their increased size
3. Nutrient-poor particles may be enriched by bacterial colonization as they sink through the water column
4. Thus, bacterial food is made available to larger organisms that would otherwise not be able to handle particles as small as individual bacteria

C. Food falls
1. A large organism, such as a fish or whale, occasionally dies and sinks quickly into the deep ocean before epipelagic scavengers can consume all of the flesh
2. Many benthic organisms, such as amphipods and brittle stars, have the ability to sense a food fall from a great distance and aggregate on it to feed

3. Studies have shown both benthic and pelagic organisms dwelling near the bottom, rapidly clustering from great distances on major food objects that reach the bottom, and dispersing after the food is consumed, usually within 24 hours

V. Diel Vertical Migration (DVM)

A. General information
1. More than 1 billion tons of pelagic organisms exhibit *diel vertical migration* (*DVM*), a daily migration from near the ocean surface to the upper mesopelagic zone and back
2. This process is the largest migration of any kind
3. In the course of 1 day, organisms travel distances of 10,000 to 50,000 body lengths each way, somewhat similar to a 6′ human walking 50 miles for breakfast
4. Most migrating organisms display a similar pattern of migration
5. Zooplankton remain relatively deep in the water column during the day, ascend to the surface at dusk, disperse somewhat through the night, reaggregate at dawn, and descend to the day depth again

B. Discovery of DVM
1. A deep scattering layer was first observed during World War II, with the advent of acoustic depth recorders, and it was interpreted as a false bottom
2. The deep scattering layer is the depth region in which zooplankton congregate
3. This acoustic reflection occurred at 300 to 500 m during the day but near the surface at night

C. DVM in pelagic organisms
1. From 10% to 30% of pelagic organisms migrate vertically; however, many species, representing all taxonomic groups, do not migrate
2. Representatives of most groups of pelagic organisms, including crustaceans, chaetognaths, fish, and squid, do migrate
3. Not all migrating organisms migrate through the same depth ranges; some move from relatively shallow depths to the surface, whereas others move from deeper depths to within several hundred meters of the surface

D. Body plan of epimesopelagic migrators
1. Organisms that migrate between the epipelagic and mesopelagic zones characteristically have a small body and a large number of counterilluminating photophores
2. They also have an active, warm-water metabolism during the night and an inactive, cold-water metabolism during the day
3. The depth to which they descend during the day may depend on the amount of energy available for counterillumination; the less food available to fuel the production of counterilluminating light, the deeper these organisms must go during the day

E. Light-intensity cues
1. Migrating organisms seem to follow an *isolume,* a constant light intensity, from their daytime depth to the surface or near the surface at night

a. The absence of an isolume during the middle of the night causes the organisms to disperse somewhat without a light cue to follow
b. The extent of migration is affected by cloud cover and moonlight
c. Organisms have been observed to begin upward migrations during total solar eclipses as isolumes move toward the surface
2. Physical and biological aspects of the water column also may modify the pattern of migration
a. Some migrating species will not cross a strong thermocline
b. Zooplankton may remain in the surface waters during a polar phytoplankton *bloom* and remain at a depth during polar winter, when no food is available in surface waters
c. DVM is suppressed when food is abundant and increased during periods of poor food availability

F. Reasons for DVM
1. The environment changes more quickly in the vertical plane than in the horizontal plane
a. Significant changes in temperature, the light field, and food availability occur over relatively short distances
b. Within the same geographic area, surface depths are well lit and warm, whereas mesopelagic waters are poorly lit and cold
2. Many ideas have been advanced to explain DVM
a. Organisms may leave well-lit surface waters during the day for poorly lit deep waters to avoid visual predators
(1) This theory is supported by the observation that most migrators use light as a cue
(2) One shortcoming of this theory is that many organisms do not migrate deep enough to hide from visual predators, while others go deeper than is necessary
(3) In addition, many migrating organisms are transparent, making them difficult for visual predators to locate
b. Herbivores may migrate to surface waters to feed on abundant phytoplankton
(1) Nighttime aggregations of zooplankton occur at the same depth as high concentrations of phytoplankton
(2) A migration of herbivores to surface waters to feed only at night — a time during which the phytoplankton are not growing and reproducing — would allow the maximum production by the primary producers and, thus, the maximum harvest by herbivores
(3) This theory has two shortcomings: predators also migrate, and it is extremely unlikely that herbivorous zooplankton cooperate to maximize phytoplankton production
c. DVM may aid the horizontal transport of organisms
(1) Migrating organisms may take advantage of opposing surface and deep-water currents to maintain or change their position by selecting their depth in the water column
(2) These organisms may go in one direction in the surface current during the night and in another direction in a deep current during the day
(3) Little evidence exists to support this theory
d. There may be an energetic advantage to migration

(1) DVM may increase phytoplankton production by allowing them to grow rather than being grazed during the day
(2) It may be an energetic advantage to herbivores to feed in warm water at the surface at night, then sink into colder waters during the day
(3) Cold waters reduce metabolism and respiration during the day, conserving energy for reproduction and growth
(4) This theory is based on the assumption that DVM uses less energy than what would be expended for remaining at one depth
3. Although DVM has been studied for almost 100 years, scientists have not established a definitive reason for it; DVM probably results from a combination of several factors

Study Activities

1. Explain how mesopelagic organisms use the light field of that depth range to hide from predators.
2. Relate how the availability of food influences the characteristic body shapes of fish in each depth zone.
3. Explain why counterilluminating organisms closely match their light output to the ambient light.
4. Describe how mesopelagic and bathypelagic organisms differ.
5. Describe how food reaches the deep ocean.
6. Explain why so many different organisms participate in diel vertical migration.
7. Design a fish that might live in the bathypelagic zone. Consider the physical conditions of this zone in your design.

17

Pelagic Biogeography

Objectives

After studying this chapter, the reader should be able to:
- Describe the most important relationships that exist between the physical environment of the ocean and the organisms that live there.
- Explain why the scope and duration of a physical event may or may not have an effect on organisms.
- Compare divergent and convergent systems.
- Describe the major biogeographic provinces of the open ocean.

I. Distribution of Ocean Life

A. General information
1. Life in the open ocean is concentrated in the upper 500 m
2. Life in the ocean is not uniformly distributed over distance or time
3. Biologically distinct regions in the ocean, called *biogeographic provinces,* are closely related to patterns of surface circulation
4. Biogeographic provinces are inhabited by stable groups of organisms that have adapted to the characteristics of the physical environment

B. Physical environments
1. The differential heating of Earth's surface by the sun and Earth's rotation establish large *gyres* in the major ocean basins
   a. The western sides of these gyres have strong warm-water currents that meander and break off into *eddies*
   b. The eastern sides of the ocean basins generally have weak currents
   c. The various gyres have different nutrient and temperature characteristics because of their different patterns of weather and vertical circulation
   d. These physical differences result in biologically distinct oceanic habitats
   e. Coastal and upwelling systems provide additional areas of variability in the world ocean
2. Biogeographic provinces differ in the abundance and diversity of organisms found in them

C. Physical controls of primary production
1. The amount of primary production depends on the amount of light and nutrients available for photosynthesis

2. Total ocean production is estimated to be 20 to 25 billion tons of carbon (C) per year
    a. This amount is equivalent to an annual production of 200 to 250 billion tons of plant material
    b. By comparison, humans collectively eat about 3 billion tons of food annually
3. The physical characteristics of the open ocean and of coastal and upwelling systems create regional differences in primary production
4. Tropical waters and subtropical gyre centers have sufficient light for photosynthesis
    a. The open ocean comprises about 90% of the surface area of the world ocean
    b. It is characterized by very low production, only about 50 g $C/m^2/year$
    c. Although the productivity level is low in the open ocean, this region is so large that it is responsible for 50% to 80% of the ocean's total primary production
    d. The light available in the open ocean is usually strong enough to establish a permanent thermocline that isolates nutrients from the well-lit surface waters
5. Coastal waters have sufficient light for photosynthesis and higher nutrients
    a. These conditions result in moderate to high production
    b. Coastal zones comprise about 10% of the surface area of the world ocean and have an average productivity of 100 g $C/m^2/year$
    c. Some areas, such as coral reefs and estuaries, have an annual productivity of as much as 1,000 g $C/m^2/year$
    d. Favorable light and nutrient conditions are closely related to latitude, both north and south of the equator
6. Upwelling systems, which are areas of divergence, have a small total area, comprising less than 0.1% of the surface area of the world ocean
    a. Upwelling systems are areas of high production, averaging nearly 10 g $C/m^2/day$ (about 300 g $C/m^2/year$)
    b. Upwellings commonly occur on the eastern side of ocean basins, such as the coasts of Oregon and Peru and the western coast of Africa, in areas that experience seasonal along-shore winds
    c. During the warmer seasons of the year, areas of coastal upwelling have sufficient light and a plentiful supply of nutrients from deep waters, resulting in seasonally high primary production
7. A pattern in the distribution of primary production emerges when the factors of continents, latitude, upwellings, and gyres are combined
8. The numbers and proportions of organisms present — including primary producers, grazers, and carnivores — vary among regions
9. Distinct regions of the ocean can be identified according to the complement of organisms present

II. Oceanic Biogeographic Provinces

A. General information
    1. Biogeographic provinces consist of large ocean regions with distinctive environmental conditions
    2. These provinces have measurable differences in physical parameters, such as temperature, salinity, nutrient concentrations, light, and turbulence

3. Such physical differences are reflected in the number and type of organisms present in each province
4. Oceanic biogeographic provinces are different from those found in terrestrial ecosystems

B. Comparison of pelagic and terrestrial biogeographic provinces

1. Nutrients are more dilute in oceanic ecosystems than in terrestrial ecosystems
2. Plants and primary consumers, the phytoplankton, are smaller than those found in terrestrial ecosystems
3. The pelagic ecosystem provides no protective cover
4. Pelagic organisms are dispersed throughout three dimensions and are in almost constant movement, whereas the terrestrial system essentially is two-dimensional (few organisms move vertically) and has lower overall movement
5. The pelagic environment has no direct oceanic analog for humus, peat, or forest litter; particulate organic detritus in the ocean is derived primarily from animals, not plants
6. In the ocean, the residence time for detritus is short
   a. Recycling of essential plant nutrients, including nitrogen and phosphorus, tends to come from animal excrement as well as from the bacterial decay of plant materials
   b. Marine algae have little or no material that is difficult to recycle, unlike lignins or xylans found in terrestrial plants
   c. Nutrient recycling is thus a much more rapid process than is found in terrestrial systems
7. Fewer species are found in a typical oceanic ecosystem when compared to a typical terrestrial ecosystem
8. The high heat capacity of water limits climatic variation in the ocean
9. Plants do not create microclimates in the ocean; for example, there are no shaded forest floors in oceanic systems
10. Primary productivity in the ocean is generally lower per unit area than that found on land
11. A food web, composed of primary producers, herbivores, and carnivores, exists in all ecosystems, whether oceanic or terrestrial
12. The organisms of oceanic ecosystems can be grouped into tropic levels in the same manner as terrestrial or coastal ecosystems

C. Oceanic provinces

1. Oceanic provinces are huge but few in number when compared to terrestrial provinces
   a. For example, the North Pacific has only 5 open ocean provinces
   b. The continent of North America, a much smaller area, has 24 biogeographic provinces
2. Oceanic biogeographic provinces have fewer and less dramatic boundaries than those found on land
3. The boundaries of oceanic provinces, such as strong currents or large stretches of unfavorable water, are much less impenetrable to oceanic organisms than are terrestrial physical barriers, which include mountain ranges and deserts
4. Oceanic biogeographic provinces are semienclosed systems in which a great deal of mixing takes place across physical boundaries
5. Gulf Stream cold core eddies constitute one example of mixing across boundaries

a. These eddies transport organisms as well as the water transported by the eddy from nutrient-rich coastal areas to the nutrient-depleted Sargasso Sea

b. As the eddy decays over a period of months, the transported organisms die in the unfavorable conditions of the Sargasso Sea

6. The boundaries of oceanic biogeographic provinces have been established by the characteristic communities inhabiting each province

7. Because they are poorly defined, the exact boundaries of any oceanic province may be difficult to identify

D. Age

1. Oceanic provinces may be up to 15 million years old, whereas the oldest terrestrial ecosystems are only about 10,000 years old

2. Oceanic provinces result from the shape of the ocean basin, the direction of Earth's rotation, the wind system of the atmosphere, and variations in water density caused by differences in precipitation, evaporation, and runoff; all of these are extremely stable characteristics

3. Many aspects of the circulation pattern of an ocean basin have been established for tens of millions of years

4. This period has been sufficiently long for evolution to attune marine organisms to their environment and to each other

E. Climate

1. The characteristics of oceanic ecosystems are influenced by long-term changes in climate rather than by short-term changes introduced by individual storms

2. Various species of organisms evolve at the rate of climatic change within a region, which is much longer than the duration of an individual storm or season

3. Within the ocean's upper hundreds of meters, temperature and salinity show gentle or no gradients

4. During the same seasons of different years, an oceanic province will have an almost uniform number and proportion of different types of organisms

5. Within the range of an ecosystem, the proportions of zooplankton and small nekton are similar from sample to sample

F. Differences between ecosystems

1. *Divergent systems,* such as areas of upwelling, are characterized by high nutrient concentrations, while *convergent systems,* such as the central areas of gyres, are characterized by very low nutrient concentrations

2. Provinces with divergent circulation may have abundant nutrients but limited light

3. Provinces with convergent circulation may have abundant light but limited nutrients

4. Rates of primary production in brightly lit equatorial systems will differ from those found in sporadically or poorly lit coastal or polar regions

G. Human influence

1. While extreme changes have been noted in some coastal areas in the past 50 years, smaller changes have occurred in open oceans

2. Changes in open ocean systems are generally smaller and slower than those observed in coastal systems

3. Relatively little exploitation and pollution of open ocean systems have occurred

4. Fishery activity in open ocean systems has been limited, involving such species as yellowfin tuna in the east tropical Pacific and salmon in subarctic waters
5. Habitat destruction and pollutant levels are not at the same levels as those found on land or in coastal oceans
6. However, plastic and tar pollution can be observed at the water's surface in all areas, irrespective of distance from shore or shipping lanes
7. Although evidence of human activity is increasing, open ocean systems remain the most undisturbed

III. Pelagic Biogeographic Provinces

A. General information
1. Oceanic provinces can be classified into five types: subpolar, central, equatorial, eastern tropical, and transition (for details about the major characteristics of these provinces, see *Comparing Oceanic Provinces,* page 171)
2. Oceanic ecosystems have been defined on the basis of organism distribution pattern, the result of many studies of the biota of these regions, particularly of euphausids (krill) in the Pacific and myctophids (lanternfish) in the Atlantic

B. Subpolar provinces
1. The North Atlantic and North Pacific oceans and the Antarctic Circumpolar current comprise the subpolar provinces
2. Although additional subpolar provinces probably exist, scientists do not yet have enough information to define them
3. Salinity is low in subpolar provinces because of low evaporation and high precipitation rates
4. Surface circulation in these areas is divergent, resulting in high nutrient levels
5. Light is low and seasonal at these high latitudes, yielding only moderate levels of production despite high nutrient concentrations; primary production is therefore highly seasonal in the subpolar provinces

C. Central provinces
1. The large subtropical gyres make up the central provinces
2. These large areas are found in the North and South Atlantic, the North and South Pacific, and the Indian oceans
3. The best-known example of a central province is the Sargasso Sea
4. Central provinces are areas of convergence
5. Surface water temperatures become very high in these provinces because this water has been isolated at the surface for a relatively long time without being renewed with cold water from deeper regions
6. Characteristically, the central provinces have very limited production
7. Although light levels are high and relatively constant, strong, permanent thermoclines preclude the resupply of nutrients to surface waters
8. Salinity is high in these areas because there is a great deal of evaporation from the surface and little precipitation

D. Equatorial provinces
1. The narrow regions of the equatorial countercurrents comprise the equatorial provinces

Comparing Oceanic Provinces

The five biogeopelagic provinces are characterized by distinctive differences in temperature, seasonality of light, primary production, and other factors. Use this chart for a quick analysis of these major differences.

CHARACTERISTIC	SUBPOLAR	CENTRAL	EQUATORIAL	EAST TROPICAL	TRANSITION
Circulation	Divergent	Convergent	Divergent	Divergent	Divergent
Temperature	Low	High	High	Moderate	Moderate
Salinity	Low	High	Moderate	Moderate	Moderate
Light	Low	High	High	High	Moderate
Seasonality of light	Large	Low	Low	Low	Moderate
Nutrients	High	Low	Moderate	Very high	Moderate
Primary production	Moderate	Low	Moderate	Very high	Moderate
Primary production values	80	40	80	120	70
Zooplankton size (related to temperature and primary productivity)	High	Low	Moderate	Moderate	Moderate
Plankton size (related to season)	Large	Low	Low	Low	Moderate
Primary producer size (affects length of food chain)	Large	Small	Moderate	Moderate	Moderate
Length of food chain	Short	Long	Moderate	Moderate	Moderate
Diversity (number of species related to length of food chain)	Low	High	High	High	Moderate

2. Equatorial provinces primarily are confined to the western sides of ocean basins
3. Salinity is moderate because of high evaporation and high precipitation
4. Light is bright and seasonally constant at low latitudes
5. Nutrients, which are returned to surface waters in equatorial upwellings, are found at moderate levels
6. Because of the abundant light and moderate nutrients, primary production is moderate and continuous throughout the year

E. Eastern tropical provinces
1. The eastern sides of ocean basins comprise the eastern tropical provinces
2. These provinces are associated with areas of the strongest upwelling of any type of oceanic province
3. Although small in area, eastern tropical provinces have developed their own unique ecosystems
4. Salinity is moderate because of high evaporation and precipitation
5. Light is abundant and constant throughout the year
6. Nutrient levels are seasonally very high because upwelling returns nutrients into surface waters from nutrient-rich deep water
7. Because they have plentiful light and nutrients, eastern tropical provinces are extremely productive areas

F. Transition provinces
1. Areas between the central and subpolar provinces, characterized by a high degree of mixing, comprise the transition provinces
2. Transition provinces are areas of divergence at the boundaries of convergent provinces
3. Transitional provinces have moderate surface water temperatures because their waters — which come from cooler sources, including high latitudes and oceanic front upwellings — are warmed quickly by sunlight
4. Light is moderate in intensity and seasonality in these middle latitudes
5. Nutrient levels are moderate in these areas because much of the water comes from higher latitudes and not from deep upwellings
6. Because light and nutrient levels are moderate, primary production also is moderate

G. Patchiness
1. Within an oceanic province, organisms occur in aggregations of differing sizes that can persist for longer or shorter periods
2. For example, plankton is not evenly distributed within an oceanic province but is aggregated into patches that exist for varying amounts of time
3. Nonrandom aggregations range in scale from those that span the width of an ocean basin to those no larger than a square millimeter
4. Aggregations are tied to changes in the physical environment and to the behavior and biological characteristics of the organisms that comprise the patches
5. The size of these aggregations, or patches, affects our methods of sampling the ocean
6. Understanding the concept of **patchiness** is necessary to appreciate the impact that different physical or biological factors may have on organisms within an oceanic province

Study Activities
1. Explain why biogeographic boundaries in oceanic systems are more permeable than those of terrestrial ecosystems.
2. Explain why surface waters in a convergent system, such as the Sargasso Sea, are warmer than the surface waters of a divergent tropical system.
3. Describe how large eddies transport organisms across biogeographic boundaries.

Appendix
Selected References
Index

Appendix: Glossary

Active margin—tectonic plate boundary characterized by seismicity

Amphidromic system—system that rotates about a fixed point, or node; it describes the rotation of tides in ocean basins

Aphotic zone—region in which there is no light of biological significance available from the surface; lies beneath the euphotic zone

Asthenosphere—layer of earth that forms part of the upper mantle, extends from approximately 100 to 400 km, and is described as plastic

Authigenous sediments—sediments, or solids, that result from chemical reactions involving the substances dissolved in seawater

Autotrophic organisms—organisms that synthesize food from simple chemical substances

Bacterioplankton—members of the plankton that are bacteria

Basalt—type of igneous rock that forms the major component of oceanic crust

Benioff zone—dipping zone of seismicity associated with a subduction zone

Benthos—organisms that live on or within the sea floor

Biogenous sediments—sediments derived from the remains of plants and animals

Biogeographic provinces—large regions that are characterized by the presence of distinctive species of both plants and animals

Bioluminescence—light produced by living organisms

Bioturbation—homogenization of the upper layers of sediments by the activities of animals living on or above the ocean floor

Bloom—excess growth of phytoplankton

Capillary wave—type of progressive wave that is restored by surface tension

Carapace—shieldlike hard cover composed of chitin on the back of marine organisms, such as crustaceans

Carbonate compensation depth (CCD)—depth in the ocean below which material consisting of calcium carbonate ($CaCO_3$) is dissolved and does not accumulate on the sea bottom; less than 20% of tests found in surface water are preserved below this depth

Chemosynthesis—form of primary production that uses chemical energy to produce organic matter

Chromatophore—color-producing cell that commonly is found in an organism's skin

Ciguatera—poisoning of humans caused by ingestion of marine organisms whose flesh contain toxic substances

Compensation point—point at which photosynthesis is equal to respiration for an individual phytoplankton cell

Convergent plate boundary—boundary at which two plates come together

Coriolis effect—apparent deflection of any moving particle as a result of Earth's rotation; in the northern hemisphere, particle deflection is to the right of the particle's trajectory, while in the southern hemisphere, particle deflection is to the left

Cosmogenous sediments—sediments originating from outer space

Critical depth—depth in the water column at which the sum of photosynthesis is equal to the sum of respiration for an entire water column

Deep-water wave—progressive (gravity) wave that has a water depth-to-wavelength ratio greater than 0.5

Diel vertical migration (DVM)—mass vertical movement of plankton and nekton from a deep location during the day to the surface or near the surface at night

Dissolved organic carbon (DOC)—carbon dissolved in water that may have leaked from cells or may have been released as a waste product

Divergent plate boundary—boundary at which two plates are moving away from each other

Downwelling—water at the surface of the ocean forced to sink to deeper depths, perhaps the result of convergence (coming together) of surface waters; also refers to the movement of light in the ocean

Dysphotic zone—region in which light is insufficient for photosynthesis because it receives no more than 1% of incident light that strikes surface water; however, animals can inhabit this zone

Ecosystem— a biotic community; the assemblage of organisms that occupy a definable area and the physical environment with which the organisms interact

Eddy—parcel of water that circulates in a rotary motion

Ekman layer—surface layer of the ocean in which water movement generated by wind stress is controlled by Ekman transport

Ekman spiral—screwlike pattern of wind-driven currents that extend from the sea surface to a depth of approximately 100 to 200 m; in this spiral, current velocities diminish as depth increases

Ekman transport—net movement of water at approximately right angles to the prevailing wind direction; in the northern hemisphere, movement is to the right of wind direction; in the southern hemisphere, movement is to the left; it also is a consequence of the Coriolis effect

Epifauna—benthic organisms that live on top of sea-floor sediments

Euphotic zone—region in which there is sufficient light for photosynthesis, defined as the depth to which 1% of incident light penetrates

Food web—structure describing the pathways of energy transfer between populations of organisms

Forchhammer's principle of constant proportions—principle stating that the relative ratios of sea salts remain constant, although the total volume of salt in the ocean may change

Geostrophic current—current that results from a balance among the Coriolis effect, a horizontal pressure gradient, and gravity

Gyre—circular series of ocean currents that rotate around the center of the circle

Halocline—zone in the water column indicating where a major change in salinity occurs

Hot spot—point on the earth's surface at which there is steady volcanism, presumably caused by action of a mantle plume beneath the lithosphere; as the lithosphere moves (as a result of plate tectonic activity), a chain of volcanoes is created

Hydrogen bond—relatively weak bond that forms between a hydrogen atom in one molecule and another atom in an adjacent molecule because the positively charged hydrogen atom is attracted to the negatively charged end of the other molecule

Hydrogenous sediments—see *Authigenous sediments*

Hydrothermal circulation—circulation of heated seawater through fractures in oceanic crust

Igneous rocks—rocks formed from molten material originating from the mantle

Infauna—benthic organisms that live in sea-floor sediments

Intermediate wave—progressive (gravity) wave that has a water depth-to-wavelength ratio between 0.5 and 0.05

Internal waves—waves that propagate along boundaries within the water column

Intertidal zone—area of the shoreline between the highest normal high tide and the lowest normal low tide

Island arc—curved series of volcanic islands commonly associated with a subduction zone

Isolume—light of equal intensity

Isostasy—theory stating that different masses of the earth's crust stand in gravitational balance with each other and within the earth

Lithogenous sediments—sediments derived from the erosion of rocks

Lithosphere—outermost, rigid layer of the earth

Littoral benthic zones—area comprising the low tide line to the shelf break where benthic organisms reside

Magnetic anomaly—deviation from the average strength of Earth's magnetic field that is recorded in the magnetic characteristics of rocks in the lithosphere

Marcet's principle of constant proportions—see *Forchhammer's principle of constant proportions*

Metamorphic rocks—rocks formed by extreme temperature and pressure changes of existing rocks

Mohorovicic discontinuity (Moho)—boundary in the earth that separates the crust from the mantle; it occurs approximately 5 to 10 km below ocean basins and approximately 50 km below continents, and is marked by increased seismic wave velocity

Nekton—those animals that are able to swim against currents

Nonconservative—element or compound whose concentration changes because of biogeochemical processes occurring within a water mass

Nutricline—depth zone in which nutrient concentration dramatically changes

Ophiolite—piece of oceanic crust that has been extruded and subsequently made into land

Oxygen minimum zone—depth zone (between 500 and 1,000 m) in which the dissolved oxygen concentration is at a minimum because of oxygen utilization by such biochemical processes as decomposition

Passive margin—type of tectonic margin that has little or no seismicity associated with it

Patchiness—nonrandom aggregation of individuals or species for a particular area or period of time

Photoinhibition—decline in photosynthesis at high levels of light in the water

Photophores—light-producing organs of many fish, crustaceans, and squid

Photosynthesis—production of complex organic molecules from carbon dioxide and water using energy from light

Phytoplankton—plant members of the plankton

Pillow basalt—type of rock, formed by overlapping lava flows resulting from submarine volcanism, that resembles a pillow in a cross-sectional view; it comprises part of the second layer of oceanic crust

Plankton—organisms, both plant and animal, that cannot swim against currents

Plate tectonic paradigm—concept that the earth's outer rigid layer (the lithosphere) is broken up into a series of plates that move across the surface of the earth and float on the more plastic asthenosphere

Poikilothermic—referring to organisms that cannot maintain their body temperatures at a constant temperature above ambient temperature

Polyp—hollow tubular body that has one end closed and the other end functioning as a mouth

Primary wave—type of seismic wave to first reach a recording station after a disturbance; particle motion is due to compression parallel to wave propagation

Progressive wave—wave that transmits energy away from a disturbance

P wave—see *Primary wave*

Pycnocline—zone in the water column indicating where a major change in density occurs

Radial symmetry—form that can be divided into two like and equal halves along any line drawn through its midpoint

Residence time—time an element or compound remains in solution in seawater; residence time is calculated according to the equation: residence time = total amount of ion in ocean ÷ rate of ion input or output

Respiration—chemical process whereby organic matter (combination of fixed carbon and oxygen) is oxidized, thus releasing energy, carbon dioxide, and water

Sea-floor spreading—idea that new oceanic crust continuously is being formed at midocean ridges by submarine volcanism

Seasonal thermocline—thermocline that forms as a result of summer heating of the sea surface

Secondary wave—type of seismic wave that arrives at a recording station after the primary wave; particle motion results from shear perpendicular to wave propagation

Sedimentary rocks—rocks formed from the accumulation or precipitation of material

Shallow-water wave—progressive (gravity) wave that is characterized by a water depth-to-wavelength ratio less than 0.05

Spring bloom—bloom of phytoplankton in the middle latitudes that occurs during the spring; it is associated with an increase in available solar radiation, water mixing and stratification, and nutrient availability

Standing wave—wave that oscillates about a fixed point (called a node)

Subduction—descent of a plate margin toward the earth's interior underneath an overriding tectonic plate

Suboceanic zone—benthic environment that exists below a depth of 200 m

Subsidence—sinking of a mass because of its density

Supralittoral zone—the spray zone of the shoreline that is above the highest normal high tide

S wave—see *Secondary wave*

Symbionts—two different plants or animals living together for mutual benefit

Terrigenous sediments—sediments derived from the erosion of continents

Thermocline—area in which a rapid change in water temperature occurs in a short vertical distance; this typically results when two water masses having markedly different temperatures come into contact with each other

Thermohaline circulation—circulation driven by density gradients, which are controlled by temperature and salinity

Tides—regular rise and fall of the sea or other body of water during the period of one day

Transfer efficiency—ratio of energy passed onto successive trophic levels to the energy lost between successive trophic levels

Transform fault—fault that has shear or lateral motion

Transform plate boundary—boundary at which two plates slide past each other

Transitional crust—continental crust that has been modified as a result of plate tectonic processes (for example, rifting and ocean basin formation)

Trophic level—functional classification of organisms in a community based on feeding relationships

Tsunami—shallow-water wave generated by a geologic phenomenon (such as an earthquake) that becomes a large wave when it reaches shore; also called seismic sea wave

Turbidity current—submarine gravity-directed water flow in which solid particles are held in suspension by water turbulence

Upwelling—transport of deeper water to the surface, usually caused by horizontal movements of surface water

Vorticity—circular motion of water around a vertical axis

Zooplankton—animal members of the plankton

Zooxanthellae—dinoflagellate that lives symbiotically with other organisms, such as corals and radiolaria

178

Selected References

Bearman, G. (ed.). *Open University Oceanography Series.* Oxford, England: Permagon Press, 1989.

Duxbury, A.C., and Duxbury, A.B. *An Introduction to the World's Oceans* (4th ed.). Dubuque, Iowa: Wm. C. Brown Publishers, 1994.

Garrison, T. *Oceanography.* Belmont, Calif.: Wadsworth Publishing Co., 1993.

Gross, M.G. *Oceanography* (6th ed.). Englewood Cliffs, N.J.: Prentice-Hall, 1993.

Pinet, P.R. *Oceanography: An Introduction to the Planet Oceanus.* St. Paul, Minn.: West Publishing Co, 1992.

Pipkin, B.W., et al. *Laboratory Exercises in Oceanography* (2nd ed.). New York: W.H. Freeman, 1987.

Thurman, H.V. *Introductory Oceanography* (6th ed.). New York: Macmillan Publishing Co, 1990.

Index

i refers to an illustration; t, to a table

i refers to an illustration; t, to a table

i refers to an illustration; t, to a table

Notes

Notes